Andy Johnson

Nov. 9, 1993

Jane —

GUIDING GIFTED READERS

From Preschool through High School

A Handbook for Parents, Teachers, Counselors and Librarians

JUDITH WYNN HALSTED

Ohio Psychology Publishing Company
131 North High Street, Suite 300
Columbus, Ohio 43215

Published by Ohio Psychology Publishing Company
131 North High Street, Suite 300, Columbus, Ohio 43215

Printed and bound in the United States of America.

Library of Congress Cataloguing in Publication Data

Halsted, Judith Wynn
Guiding Gifted Readers

Bibliography: p 296
Includes index.
1. Gifted children — Books and reading. 2. Gifted children — Education. 3. Youth — Books and reading.

ISBN 0-910707-11-1
Library of Congress Catalogue Card Number 87-29655
First Printing, 1988

TABLE OF CONTENTS

To my father, George H. Wynn,
who models for his children and grandchildren a dedicated,
contributing life lightened by laughter

and

to the memory of my mother, Ruth S. Wynn,
who never once thought her children
were reading too much.

Be equal to your talent, not your age.
At times let the gap between them be embarrassing.
Fear not
to be young, precocious.

— Yevgeny Yevtushenko
"Others May Judge You"

PREFACE

In *Guiding Gifted Readers*, I have tried to weave together two threads I have followed for more than 20 years: the librarian's art of bringing children and books together, and the concern of parents and teachers to meet the needs of gifted children. The first had its real beginning in my own childhood reading, the second with the sometimes painful but always rewarding experience of being part of the development of our two sons.

These threads have become inseparable. I was in graduate school studying library science when I finally admitted to myself that our babysitters, who saw more young children than we did, might be correct when they observed that our sons were unusually bright. (At four, David was eagerly conversing with people of all ages, listening with intense curiosity, testing his developing ideas, and using a large vocabulary gained in part from his own reading. Before he was two, Mark was absolutely fearless with strangers, presaging his ease with all kinds of people as he grew to adolecsence and adulthood. From his earliest years, he spent happy hours working with his hands and his mind to discover why things — toys, clocks, people — work the way they do.)

We had not considered the joys and frustrations of rearing gifted sons. Once assured it was more than the flattery of overzealous babysitters, we turned to the serious business of dealing with giftedness, and a fitting education for them. My initial contribution was to learn all I could about giftedness. And so, I wrote a major paper on library services for gifted children.

Ten years later, I held two titles at the independent school our sons attended: librarian and director of the gifted program. I developed reading programs for gifted children from preschool through grade twelve. I followed their reading interests and found myself in an ideal position to observe both their emotional and their academic needs.

At the same time, my psychologist husband, recognizing that many of his adult clients are gifted, began to consider the benefits of coming to terms early with a high intelligence. He encouraged me to join him in developing a center to serve the psychological and emotional needs of gifted young people. While exploring this idea we met Dr. James T. Webb, founder of Supporting the Emotional Needs of the Gifted and now president of the American Association for Gifted Children, who suggested in 1984 that I write this book. Three years of researching, reading, theorizing, testing, discussing, reading more, and finally writing followed.

My professional experience includes years of leading discussion groups and teaching enrichment classes in literature for gifted children who had completed the school reading curriculum, as well as teaching library skills for all grade levels. Working in a school with a high proportion of gifted children from preschool through twelfth grade, I acquired a developmental view of these special youngsters and their reading, something I have tried to pass along in this book.

I have been fortunate to be able to work with groups of students both at Pathfinder School and in the summer program for gifted and talented students at Northwestern Michigan College, both in Traverse City, Michigan. Some of them asked if they would be named in the book, and some of them are. Here I want to thank all of them for their participation, and for their refreshing, sometimes breathtaking, honesty. I learned a great deal from them, and have revised my assumptions accordingly.

As background for these groups, I have researched the

current literature on bibliotherapy. Also helpful were conversations with Rosalie Brown, CPT, director of bibliotherapy at St. Elizabeths Hospital in Washington, D.C. and Doris Robinson, past chairperson of the Bibliotherapy Forum of the American Library Association's Association of Specialized and Cooperative Library Agencies. I thank them for their time and the information they shared.

In the past three years I have read and re-read several hundred books for children and young adults, and have culled the list to the 162 titles found in the bibliography. Some of these books are out of print, several are published in other countries, and not all are commonly found in small library collections. This effort would have been impossible without the enthusiastic help of the staff of the Traverse Area District Library, and I thank each one of them.

Other libraries have been helpful as well, especially the graduate libraries at the University of Michigan and the University of Chicago, including the Center for Children's Books. The staff of the Ann Arbor Public Library has helped with suggestions in person and through correspondence. Naomi Noyes of the New York Public Library serves as liaison for the American Library Association's Association for Library Service to Children and the American Association for Gifted Children; she has sent a booklist as well as other useful information regarding gifted children and books.

Gifted educators from universities, school districts, and individual classrooms around the country have been generous in providing suggestions for book titles and descriptions of their programs.

The entire project would never have been started without the original idea from Dr. James T. Webb. The suggestions and guidance that he and my publisher, Henry Saeman of Ohio Psychology Publishing Company as well as Editor Sanna Hans Longden have offered throughout the work have been very welcome.

Most of all I thank my family. My husband, David W. Halsted, has provided unfailing confidence, support, and encouragement which have been both highly gratifying and absolutely necessary to the completion of the book. Our sons, David and Mark, contributed in some ways they will recognize and many they will not. I thank them especially for many long conversations about books and about what it meant to grow up gifted.

— Judith Wynn Halsted

INTRODUCTION

Steven is a joy to his parents. Still a preschooler, he is bright, curious, cheerful, and friendly. He talks quite easily with adults and seems remarkably mature. His mother describes him as a sensitive child, usually happy, who is looking forward to beginning first grade. The nursery school teacher relies on Steven as the most responsible child in his group. Other children find his ease in acquiring skills puzzling.

Occasionally Steven expresses frustration, not understanding why his friends can't follow what he is saying. Sometimes it bothers him that they don't share his intense interest in the insects he likes to bring to his mother and teacher. He knows that adults will help him find information about insects in books, and he is beginning to be able to read about them himself.

Matthew is a bright but sullen high school junior. He has had some social difficulties along the way that have left their marks on him. These are most obvious in the discrepancy between his ability and his performance. His scores on the PSAT qualify him to compete for a National Merit scholarship, but his grades are not strong enough for him to apply to the better colleges. His school file contains notes from teachers indicating that he does not measure up to his potential, refuses to do homework, and doesn't study, particularly languages and math.

Matthew is defensive about his school record and confused about his future. He has been told so often that he is not measuring up to his potential that he has stopped listening. He wants to be part of the high school social life but doesn't seem to fit in; he feels that no one really understands him. He senses he has ability that he is not using, and this makes him uncomfortable, but he doesn't know how to "realize his potential." Matthew rationalizes that the world is in such a mess that no one can really change anything, so what he does with his life makes no difference.

He is depressed about his lack of direction, but the teachers see Matthew, who a few years ago was passionately concerned about national and international politics, as merely cynical and disinterested. They are concerned, but don't know how to help him.

Amy is also a high school junior. She is active in sports, student government, and the school newspaper, and she keeps her grades at an honors level. Her special interest is biology, and she has arranged with the biology teacher to do a year-long independent study as a supplement to the regular classwork. Her classmates notice that Amy is quiet about her own excellent grades and ready to help others who don't understand as quickly. In the summer she is a counselor at a local day camp where the children know that she is always available for ping pong or a pep talk.

Despite her full schedule and many friends, there are times when Amy feels truly alone. Her concerns about the future are so much more intense than her friends' that she has never attempted to discuss them with anyone. Although she worries about the future of the world, Amy's plans for her own future are nonetheless taking shape. She wants to go to a university with a strong biology curriculum, and is looking forward to visiting campuses.

If we were to ask both Matthew's and Amy's parents what their children were like as preschoolers, they would describe someone remarkably like Steven. What happened in those twelve years to turn a Steven into a Matthew rather than an Amy?

Steven, Matthew and Amy are all gifted. This is an

extra dimension in their lives, imposing on them certain emotional and intellectual developmental tasks in addition to those all children face. Little has been written about the steps that lead a gifted child from a bright and curious preschooler to a well-adjusted high school student with a promising future. Based on a background of experience with gifted children and adults, this book attempts one answer to the question: If I'm fortunate enough to start with someone like Steven, what can I do to help him or her develop into a confident, productive young adult who remains as happy and responsive as Steven is now?

Guiding Gifted Readers is written in the belief that books and reading can have a profound effect on the lives of gifted children. Adults who live and work with these youngsters can use books to guide the intellectual and emotional development of gifted children through book discussion and bibliotherapy — powerful tools for influencing the environment in which these exceptional youngsters grow.

Gifted preschoolers need to develop a positive self-concept and grow toward a strong sense of self. Early elementary youngsters must begin to understand that different people have different abilities, and to value others for whatever abilities they have. Although gifted children need friends who share their own capabilities they must learn to get along with all children.

Later elementary students are able to understand the term "giftedness," but may not be ready to apply the concept to themselves. Much depends on the attitudes of parents, teachers, and other children. At this age, gifted children often choose to acknowledge and follow their natural eagerness to learn, or to hide their abilities in order to fit in with their classmates. This is one reason why it is so important for preschoolers to develop a strong sense of self, a confidence in their own worth.

At this point, well-adjusted gifted children will enter junior high school with a good basis to withstand the turmoil for which that age is famous. If giftedness is part of their self-concept, they won't lose it as they try on various personae. Ideally, they will emerge from this stage knowing their capabilities, being at ease with their classmates, and having a few close friends.

Senior high students with this background, more aware of their individuality and responsibility for their own future, have a chance to accept and use their giftedness without self-consciousness. If we have been able to follow Steven to this point, we find him still happy, but far more self-aware, conscious of both his abilities and shortcomings. He recognizes his gifts with gratitude and a sense of responsibility that will lend direction to his life, although he doesn't know where it will take him. Although he realizes he is different, he feels the acceptance of those close to him. He accepts and values others as well. He has the self-confidence to take intellectual risks, and can accept failure and try again. Steven's healthy development is more likely to occur if his parents, teachers, friends, and school systems value and nurture giftedness, whether or not they formally identify it.

The question of formal identification is an important one. It is estimated that only about half of our gifted children have been identified. Those who have not are nevertheless gifted and have the characteristic intellectual and emotional needs of gifted children. In addition, there are many youngsters who may not be intellectually gifted, but who are talented or creative in special ways for which no identification is made and no programs are available in local school systems.

New developments in brain research are changing our definitions of giftedness. In *Growing Up Gifted* (1983), Barbara Clark defines gifted individuals as "those who are performing, or who show promise of performing, at high levels of intelligence (p. 6)." It is important that this definition include those who show promise but may be stifled by environmental conditions which can be changed. Even the term "intelligence" is changing, now including a variety of abilities rather than just the academic or intellectual ability the word has evoked for so long.

It will be some time before the new research is reflected in the procedures used to identify children for school gifted programs. It could be that the terms "gifted," "talented," and "creative" will eventually be recognized as labeling different aspects of a whole intelligence. For now, however, the terms differentiate among the gifted, generally those who have high intellectual ability and excel academically; the talented, who display special abilities in the arts; and the creative, who are divergent thinkers, "idea" people who do not see things the way most of us do and may not fit into a typical classroom situation. School programs for gifted children generally begin by meeting intellectual needs. Programs for the artistically talented and for creative thinkers may be added later.

While academic needs may differ for gifted, talented, and creative children, all of these children are subject to the range of emotional needs discussed in this book — whether they are identified or not. We are talking here about the multi-talented young person who comes to mind when we mention gifted children, and also about those who may have just one or two areas of special talent.

Unfortunately "gifted" is a value-laden word, inviting charges of elitism that make students, parents, and teachers uncomfortable. But it is the word we have at the moment; it does convey meaning, and it does label a phenomenon which we know exists. And we have plenty of Matthews to remind us that being gifted does not guarantee a happy, productive life.

This book recommends that the adults most concerned with the development of gifted children — parents, teachers, counselors, and librarians — consider very seriously the potential that books and reading have for helping gifted children understand themselves and become all that they can be.

Books for children are so plentiful, and gifted children find them so easily, that *planning* to use books can seem unnecessary; too often it doesn't happen. Teachers who struggle to keep up with curricular requirements have little classroom time to devote to literature and even less for their own reading. Parents may find it difficult to keep track of what their children are reading. Guiding children's reading appears to be one more unaffordable luxury in a busy world.

Yet books offer compelling advantages to those who would nurture the development of gifted children. They are abundant, often excellent, inexpensive, accessible sources of challenge and understanding. If just one avenue of enrichment could be open to these bright youngsters, books would be the first choice.

Merely providing books is not enough, however. A knowledge of both gifted children and children's literature is necessary to make maximum use of the benefits they offer. The hope behind this book is that parents, teachers, counselors, and librarians will see value in filling the gaps in their own knowledge so they can bring gifted children and books together more effectively.

This book has four parts and is divided into eight chapters. Part one offers background information on both the emotional and intellectual developmental needs of gifted children, and establishes a framework of categories of needs which is also used to organize the annotated bibliography.

Part two begins with a chapter about the reading patterns of gifted children and suggests two approaches for using books with them: enhancing emotional development through bibliotherapy, and promoting intellectual growth by guiding their reading and teaching them to be independent seekers of information.

In parts three and four the focus is on books. Criteria for selecting books for gifted children are given in chapter six, and chapter seven offers a brief course in children's literature. In part four an annotated bibliography lists over 160 books carefully selected for their usefulness in promoting the intellectual and emotional development of gifted children and young people.

There is nothing new about the idea that gifted children need good books or about the idea that books can be used to help children to build coping skills. There may be something new in the ideas presented here for using books with gifted children to help them to develop optimally as gifted people. For parents, teachers, counselors, and librarians, I have written the book I wish I had read 20 years ago.

1

The Heart of the Gifted Child: Emotional Development

Having recognized for years that gifted children have special academic needs, parents, teachers, and psychologists are now turning to the emotional characteristics of these children. A persisting myth has been that gifted children have no trouble with emotional and social development, or if they do have problems, they also have the necessary inner resources to deal with them. Sensitive adults who work with gifted children realize that this is not true and are focusing attention on how being gifted complicates the usual problems of growing up.

Gifted children face the same difficulties as all children, but being gifted adds an extra dimension. To understand their emotional needs, it is necessary to recognize the extras in the developmental tasks they face. Four areas in which giftedness affects the emotional development of a child are establishing an identity, needing time alone, getting along with others, and learning how to use one's own ability.

All children must establish their own identity; the gifted child must recognize and accept an identity that is different from the norm, which may not be popular or acceptable to peers or family.

> *Now beginning junior high, Matthew has already learned that some of his ideas seem strange to his classmates and even to his parents and teachers. Entering a new school, he is determined not to mention thoughts that others might not understand; he tries, in fact, to*

stifle them in himself. At an age when he should be establishing his sense of identity, he is attempting to deny a part of it to himself as well as to others.

All children must learn to be alone at times; however, gifted children may actually require time alone, and may need more of it than most people need or can understand. They may have to learn to cope with mixed feelings about their own need for time alone, aware that they also need time with other people, and uncertain how to balance these needs with the expectations of others.

Sara loves to read, to play the piano, and to sew — all solitary activities. After a day crowded with people at school, she enjoys coming home to these quiet pursuits. Her parents are worried, however, because she seldom invites friends to come home with her. Although Sara is happy with her friends at school and content with her activities at home, she senses her parents' concern and wonders whether there is something wrong with her.

All children must learn how to get along with others; gifted children must find a few good friends, and learn to value and respect others, even though they themselves may be rejected. Gifted people are unusually intense, and this characteristic is difficult for other children to understand. Gifted people also have heightened sensitivity to the comments and actions of others, so that being misunderstood or rejected is a more painful experience for them than for most. For gifted children the issues of friendship, so important to their healthy development, are much more complex than they are for most children.

Brian talks with enthusiasm to high school students and adults, but he can find no other grade school children who share his interest in biology. His sixth grade classmates are puzzled by the intensity that marks his oral science reports, and he mistakes their lack of understanding for rejection. In response, he is building a protective wall around himself, neither giving nor expecting friendship from people his own age. If he can be helped to respect his classmates' social or athletic skills as well as his own knowledge of biology — and if he can find just one or two friends his age who share his interest, perhaps at a community science center — he will avoid years of social isolation. Otherwise, Brian may not learn to make friends of his own age until he enters college.

All adolescents must make career and college decisions; gifted youngsters often have so many possibilities that choice becomes paralyzingly difficult. Unwilling to give up any and unable to choose among them, gifted teenagers and young adults may find it difficult to take the steps that will enable them to make full use of their abilities.

Alex is a superior math and science student and is considering a career in medicine. He also plays piano and guitar with a group that provided the music for high school proms for the last three years. Music is so important to Alex that he wants to delay entering college while he tests his ability to find work as a professional musician. He is concerned, however, that too much time away from science and math will dull his skills and damage his chances of acceptance to medical school. As he weighs the decision, college application deadlines are passing by, adding to his anxiety about his future.

Chapter 1 considers the emotional development of gifted children by further exploring each of these four aspects of development. Since this chapter serves as background for later sections, only brief mention will be made here of ways in which books can enhance that emotional development.

Establishing an Identity

The search for one's identity is a major task of growing up. For gifted children, a vital part of this task is to recognize and accept their own giftedness. This is made more difficult by the fact that giftedness can be more of a burden than a blessing in our society, as many gifted children sense even before they start school. They may not be able to avoid the knowledge that their abilities are above the norm, but to fit that knowledge willingly and comfortably into their self-concept, knowing how different it makes them, takes a degree of maturity that must develop over time.

Who They Are

Establishing an identity is a matter of discovering who we are, of learning what it is that makes us, like the Little Prince's rose, "unique in all the world." What gifted children discover may be a self that they know will not be popular. They may feel that they must choose between being themselves and being liked. Out of this conflict and the ways they choose to deal with it will emerge their identities.

Gifted children realize fairly early that they are different, and often feel that there is something vaguely unacceptable about this. Our society is ambivalent about difference, and children can easily develop the uncomfortable feeling that something is "wrong" with them. Usually they do not know what it is, or even why they are different. They only know that when they exercise their creativity or knowledge, they do not fit in. They then feel alone, wrong, even freakish; ironically, they may feel inferior to those around them.

At the same time, especially if their environment provides enough stimulation, they may experience the elation of the insights and awarenesses their giftedness makes possible. They can know the joy of discovering new ideas, new people with whom they can use their vocabularies fully, new stimuli such as museums, music or films that excite them.

They live with this paradox, and they must learn, in the "down" times when they are feeling different and alone, to trust that the "up" times, when they can enjoy the benefits of their extra measure of perception, will come again. Some of them must learn to make a little "up" time last over a long "down" period. One friendship established at summer camp may be what carries a child through the next school year; one understanding and stimulating teacher may keep another child going through two or three years with indifferent teachers.

Attending a high school that places more emphasis on sports than on academic achievement, Debbie finds her work with a statewide youth organization more stimulating than school. Although meetings occur only twice a year, the friendships she has made with other natural leaders, the creative energy she puts into planning conferences, and the experience of traveling to large cities around the state have compensated for her feeling of not fitting in at school. Gradually she is learning to integrate the sense of being different and alone at school with the sense of inner delight and satisfaction that her giftedness brings in another setting. Her identity includes both.

Middle-elementary children, just becoming aware of the concept of giftedness, may be ambivalent about having the label applied to them. If parents and teachers react positively and matter-of-factly to the idea of giftedness, children will probably do the same, accepting their giftedness and learning to use it with enthusiasm. If anything in their environment causes them to be uncomfortable with giftedness, however, their responses may range from what appears to be showing off to denying their giftedness with the responsibilities it implies.

Self-conscious about his lack of athletic ability, Derrick seeks approval by offering answers in class so eagerly and frequently that the other children think he is boasting about how much he knows. Meanwhile, Cheryl answers questions only when the teacher calls on her and even uses a doubtful tone of voice to give the impression that she knows no more than anyone else. Both responses indicate that these children need help in accepting who they are. Establishment of a healthy identity depends on that acceptance.

Who They Will Become

Establishing an identity means more than merely discovering who we are. It also means creating who we will become. This is done through imagination, exploring and choosing among available identities, and risking. Gifted youngsters may (and should) experiment with more identities than most children, displaying more imagination and less conventionality. Books offer possibilities they would otherwise not encounter and permit them to experience vicariously various roles and ways of living as they move through the process of creating a personal identity.

The search for identity raises some complex issues for gifted people. Some children deny the gift and avoid developing it fully. They risk becoming restless adults, moving without a clear sense of direction from one pursuit to another. Because they have not trained themselves to use their abilities, they are often dissatisfied with the limited opportunities available to them. We are happiest when we know that our talents are being stretched and used; we feel best about ourselves when we know we are being useful. To reach that point, gifted children must develop the potential that lies within them.

Christopher was identified as a gifted student in junior high. Although he loved to read and talked glibly about ideas, he never learned to focus his thoughts sufficiently to complete written assignments on time. After graduation, he held a number of restaurant jobs, intending to save money for college but delaying application because he feared that his lack of study skills would lead to failure. He married within two years, and supporting a wife and children took precedence over his education. Christopher might have become an excellent teacher, but his lack of training confines him to work that offers no security and does not require him to think. With less time for reading now, and no one with whom to discuss his ideas, Christopher is lonely and resentful.

Other children feel that superior ability implies a responsibility. They see a gift as something to be developed so that they can pass it on by giving to others. These youngsters represent a happy middle ground; they can learn to rejoice in their gifts and use them with humility and productivity.

Joyce grew up in a well-to-do family and enjoyed a fine education. After her marriage there was no financial need for her to work. However, from the time she was in junior high she knew that she wanted a career that would serve other people in some way. She stayed home with her young children, but she continued her educa-

tion as a part-time student while gaining experience as a volunteer in several community organizations. Fifteen years later she was ready to begin a career as a psychologist. Her present work includes helping gifted girls make appropriate educational and vocational decisions.

Still others, impelled by their own inner drive more often than by over-ambitious parents, take their abilities so seriously that they become perfectionists. They equate flawless performance with self-worth, and fear to attempt a task that they might not perform well the first time. Their perfectionism puts them under severe stress, and eventually can lead them to attempt only that at which they are sure to excel. To counteract perfectionism, they must learn to risk and learn that failure is not disastrous. They must think of themselves not as perfect, but as experimenters.

Lisa has always been a superb student, but now in the eleventh grade she has to work harder than she has in the past to maintain her A average. She spends extra hours on her homework, but she has less time for social activities. She has become tense and has frequent headaches. The debate coach has been looking forward to Lisa's joining the team this year, but Lisa is reluctant because she has never spoken in public and is not sure she will do well. If she does not join the team, she will be starting a pattern of narrowing her experiences at a time when she should be keeping her outlook and her options open. If she does join, she probably will make mistakes. But the necessity of managing her time more carefully may help her establish priorities, and she can learn that life goes on after a defeat. She may also learn that she is valuable for the contribution she makes to the team, even when she does not win.

Another issue facing these children is their potential for leadership. Many of them are natural leaders, and developing a sense of identity means finding ways to explore and use their leadership ability. In some, the talent for leadership is so strong that if it finds no positive outlets, it will express itself in negative ways. They need adults who can see past the negative expressions and offer guidance in the constructive use of leadership ability. Since books provide examples of both negative and positive leaders, book discussion is one way of providing this guidance.

> *Feeling unchallenged by his high school courses, Tad is not only refusing to do his assignments but is also loudly proclaiming to other students his low opinion of the teachers, the curriculum, and the school's requirements. In his small high school, Tad's voice carries some weight. The result is that this gifted student is using his talent for leadership to encourage others to neglect their work, too. Tad and the others will all be happier if an adult can see what is happening and help Tad plan ways of redirecting his abilities.*

As part of creating who they will become, many gifted children discover that they can do so many things so well that career choice is extremely difficult. They need to develop superior self-knowledge and excellent decision-making skills. Multi-gifted young adults must face the fact that they will not have time to bring all of their talents to full flower. Again, books can help, enabling them to explore various options without spending months or years on each, helping them to establish priorities and make vocational and avocational choices.

Dyssynchrony

While gifted youngsters deal with these issues, they may also face the enormous task of integration. Different parts of themselves may develop at different rates, with academic interest and achievement far outstripping other areas of growth. The disparity between intellectual maturity and social, emotional, and physical development has been called dyssynchrony (Ehrlich, 1985), a wonderfully descriptive term for what happens in children whose various developmental schedules are not in tune with one another. It simply expresses the fact that in gifted children intellectual development can move rapidly, while social, emotional, and physical growth remain tied to chronological age.

Dyssynchrony makes it difficult to know whether a child should be accelerated into the next grade. It is exemplified by the third grade boy who joined an enrichment class of fifth and sixth graders in the junior high library to work on a research project, but who had to tape record his report because his fine motor skills were not advanced enough to write all he learned. Dyssynchrony causes us to expect the unusually tall, unusually verbal ten-year-old to behave like the twelve-year-old she appears to be. We must consider dyssynchrony in choosing books to recommend for the second grader who is reading at the sixth grade level.

If a child's intellectual growth has far surpassed emotional and social development, there may come a necessary time of academic latency that allows social and emotional growth to catch up. This can happen during the high school years, after college, or any time in between. One young man who began kindergarten at four and then was accelerated another year in high school entered college at sixteen. When he graduated from college at twenty he was sure of two things: he wanted to go to graduate school, and he did not want to go to graduate school that fall. He spent two years working at various jobs, learning to be self-supporting while consolidating his career plans. Now in graduate school, for the first time he is studying with his agemates, still occasionally restless at the pace of coursework but adapting to it with a new measure of self-understanding and maturity.

Indeed, it may not be until the early twenties or later that the different aspects — intellectual, emotional, social, and physical — of a very complex person begin to come together. It will help the person living through this dyssynchrony, and his parents, if they can recognize what is happening and know that the prognosis is good.

Establishing a Healthy Identity

To establish a healthy identity as a gifted person means discovering and accepting who one is and creating who one will become, acknowledging and using giftedness unselfconsciously. In addition, the gifted person needs to develop a protective attitude toward her abilities. On the one hand, she must integrate giftedness into her self-concept, and on the other she must be able to see it, with humility, as a separate entity to be nurtured. Only when she can do this has she fully accepted herself as a gifted person.

How does a gifted youngster reach this point? By admitting that she has many of the characteristics of gifted people, including some that are unpopular or misunderstood, such as being hypercritical or talking too much in class or wanting more time alone than most people do; by understanding the positive and useful sides of those unpopular characteristics; by forgiving herself for having them and bringing them under control to make good use of them; by recognizing the advantages of being gifted and learning to enjoy them; and by realizing that high intelligence is useless without training and self-discipline.

These attitudes cannot easily be taught by precept. Example is far superior, and examples can come from role models, gifted people whose lives are based on these understandings. Such role models can be alive or imaginary: parents, teachers, and friends — or characters in books.

Of course, some gifted children have so many barriers in their way that developing a healthy identity may be beyond their reach. The fortunate ones will have a good chance of becoming what Abraham Maslow (1962) called self-actualized adults: giving, productive people who make full use of their potential and gain deep satisfaction from doing so.

Being Alone

"Being alone" is an ambiguous term. It can mean being alone and liking it, being alone and lonely, or being alone and different. A gifted child can experience all of these, and can also develop conflicting emotions about being alone.

His confusion is compounded by the reactions of other people to those who appear to be "loners." Human beings are social animals, and are suspicious about those who choose to be less social than the norm. The gifted child is aware of this, and his own feelings about being alone are colored by his assumptions of the feelings of others.

Being Alone and Liking It

Gifted children, and adults too, may need what seems to be an inordinate amount of time alone, and they can use it productively; in fact, they may well be far less productive if they do not have it. Those who gather large amounts of information require more time to assimilate it; those who are more creative require more incubation time. However, the gifted child who enjoys being alone may feel an underlying sense of guilt, secretly believing that something is wrong with her. Is she really alone by preference, or did she somehow send potential friends away? And yet it is so delicious to have quiet time to read, or build, or plan, or dream. Maybe tomorrow she will invite someone over. But she would really rather have this time to herself. Is that all right?

It *is* all right, of course, and she should be reassured about that. Caring adults should support this legitimate need to be alone. Parents must learn to be patient with a child who spends hours apparently doing nothing, playing with blocks, taking things apart, daydreaming seemingly without purpose while chores remain undone. One such child, now a college junior working on a medical research project at a major teaching hospital, contributes his ability to "play" freely with computers as he develops new ways to graph test results. He links this ability to the hours he spent happily alone in a garage filled with treasures, experimenting to learn how things worked — "useless" alone time that fathered his present productivity.

Gifted people who have developed a sense of innerdirectedness and a protective attitude toward their own abilities may sense that time spent with other people can hold them back. Their characteristic intensity may keep them at their work for long periods of time, and time spent socializing can seem to them to be wasted. It may take years for them to recognize the value of relaxed time with other people, and they may always struggle for a satisfactory balance between time alone and time with others.

Being Alone and Lonely

Adults who watch a child spend time alone often fear that the child is lonely. However, gifted children who are busy with books, collections, music, or other favorite pursuits may not feel lonely. Rather, they are likely to sense that they do not fit in with other children, and it is their response to this feeling of not belonging that adults must monitor and try to guide.

Gifted youngsters may respond by trying to fit in. Without guidance, however, these attempts often do not work. Some try, often successfully, to hide their ability by producing mediocre work in school. By the time they complete sixth grade, this can become a pattern — one that becomes difficult to change as time goes on. Girls are especially likely to lower their aspirations during the junior high years in ways that will profoundly affect their futures (Kerr, 1985).

Children who wish to belong to the group sometimes use another ploy: attracting attention to themselves. Capitalizing on their differences may be the only way they know to do this. For gifted children, this can mean showing off their knowledge or using sarcasm or condescension with other children — behavior that can cause real rejection.

> *Amanda was a mature second grader with the highly critical nature gifted children sometimes develop. Feeling insecure when she entered a new school, she adopted the role of class police officer, letting her classmates know when they did not measure up to her standards and too often informing the teacher, too, of their failings. What began as her own fear of rejection led quickly enough to actual rebuff from her new classmates.*

Such inappropriate responses to a feeling of not belonging are more likely to occur in gifted children who do not understand giftedness. Self-acceptance must precede acceptance of others. If parents and teachers cannot help gifted children to understand themselves, the children are hampered in developing self-acceptance, and may appear to be arrogant.

Other gifted children make no attempt to fit in, but withdraw instead. They may spend much time reading, which causes concern for adults. (The negative aspects of reading too much are discussed in chapter 3). However, spending large amounts of time reading is not necessarily unhealthy for gifted youngsters. They may use this time as part of their identity search, reading for various role models, identifying with different characters, working out the basic question: Who am I? They may identify with undesirable characters some of the time, but usually this is only temporary.

Children who do not feel part of a group can develop their social skills. This can be especially difficult for those who were rejected by other children or by parents when they were young, and learned to protect themselves by getting along on their own. Is is hard for these children to recognize that they do indeed need others, and that they can take the first steps toward being a friend. However, they can be helped by school gifted programs that devote time to discussion of friendship skills, and by parents who teach the concepts at home. The books listed under "Getting Along with Others" in the bibliography are recommended because they portray children learning how to be friends or, in the case of nonfiction, they directly teach about friendship.

It is most important for gifted youngsters to learn that they have some control over the time they spend alone. Once they know that both time alone and time with others are valuable, they can make either happen.

Being Alone and Different

Being alone and different — that is, standing apart, being alone because one is different, and quite deliberately being oneself — is something that almost all gifted children will have to accept at some time. They know that they are different, but they may not know, unless a trusted adult tells them, *why* they are different. Knowledge of their giftedness and acceptance of their differences are very important steps in the search for identity.

It takes courage to be oneself, to be different, to like oneself in spite of the difference. This courage takes time to develop, and it must be done during that stage in life when conformity seems most important. Some gifted children need a great deal of support from parents, teachers, and other adults to move through this period successfully. Their independence and autonomous style must be incorporated into their identities, while at the same time they must learn to get along with others. Fortunately, the worth of standing alone is a common theme in literature, and books can easily be found to promote discussion and guidance.

Getting Along with Others

For all of us, one key to emotional well-being is to strike a balance between knowing who we are as individuals, and how we fit into our society. This is harder for gifted people; yet they need as much as anyone the nurturing warmth of good relationships.

Gifted children often see things from unusual points of view that others cannot share, and so they are misunderstood. They are even different from other gifted children; people at the upper ranges of IQ differ from one another far more than do people in the middle and lower ranges.

At the same time, and despite their need for time alone, friends are extremely important to most gifted children. The eagerness to communicate with others can show itself very early. One gifted toddler would stand up in his stroller, wave his arms, and crow in delighted greeting whenever he saw another baby being pushed toward him. The response was usually a languid glance from the other child, yet until he outgrew his stroller, he continued his enthusiastic greetings.

Finding Peers

The special problem gifted children have in finding friends is not that they are loners, but that they need at least a few friends who can function on their level, with whom they can speak as equals. Although they differ markedly from one another, their greatest social need is for friendships with other gifted children. In fact, when given the opportunity, gifted children will choose friends of their own mental age, rather than their own chronological age. Without such friendships, they may shrivel emotionally and intellectually; with them, they can thrive.

Getting along with others, then, means first finding appropriate others. The stratified grading arrangement in most schools makes it difficult for gifted children to find one another unless special arrangements are made by their parents or teachers. A gifted child may need to belong to several different groups, not necessarily of her own age, that will challenge her intellectually and introduce her to people with whom she can share her passionate interests.

This can be demanding and exhausting for parents. For a junior high student to join an adult astronomy group, his mother drove him to weekly meetings at a planetarium an hour away, driving home between one and two in the morning. Another family drove a daughter five hours each way, every other week for two years, to allow her to play in a university youth symphony. These parents understood their children's need to make contact with others who shared their interests, and were willing to make the necessary sacrifices to provide it.

Other Children

Getting along with others also means getting along with those who do not share, or even understand or respect, one's abilities and interests. In a classroom in which there may be only one or two gifted students, a gifted child is likely to alienate his classmates because he can do schoolwork so easily.

A subtler cause of resentment may be the intense interest gifted children have in topics that do not interest their classmates. If they talk too long about their shell collections, or use words that are too big, they can bore and finally alienate other students without understanding why. What starts out to be lack of interest in seashells can quickly become lack of interest in Tim, who talks about seashells all the time. And even before this happens, Tim may feel that it has happened — that the rejection of seashells is a rejection of him.

Gifted children are usually extremely sensitive, and remarks that most children toss off and forget can truly hurt them. They do not understand how lightly other children may make a cruel remark, and others have no idea how long and deeply the gifted child may brood over what is said. But the gifted child, who may have been as eager for friends as the baby in the stroller, begins to build a wall of defense, making it even harder to develop friendships.

Moreover, some gifted children are not interested in sports; in addition, those who have been accelerated find that their physical coordination does not match that of their classmates. In most schools, a lukewarm attitude toward sports or lack of athletic ability is another wedge between gifted children and their peers.

So gifted children can begin to feel rejected for a variety of reasons. And since giftedness does not necessarily include social maturity, these youngsters react in the same ways that most children do to feelings of rejection: they withdraw or act out. Either choice brings further rejection, and a downward cycle begins.

To reverse this cycle, children must take several steps that require maturity as well as adult guidance: they must develop empathy with those who are not as quick as they are and learn to value their differing abilities, they must learn to cope with being misunderstood and teased, and they must recognize and modify the behavior that leads to rejection and teasing — all of this while retaining their own identities.

One serious consequence of emotional difficulties at school is the possibility of underachievement. Rejected for being out of step because of their intelligence, they can learn fairly early to hide their abilities in order to conform. After several years of not performing, they may miss some basic skills, so that they are not able to perform at all. Suspecting that they cannot do what is asked, they resist trying. (This is an oversimplified statement of a complex problem. For more on underachievement, see Rimm [1986] and Whitmore [1980].)

Parents and Teachers

Getting along with peers is the most obvious problem of getting along with others; however, gifted children can find themselves in other relationships that may cause emotional problems, both at home and at school. These youngsters are vulnerable, and the attitudes they perceive in significant adults can make a tremendous difference in their attitudes toward themselves and their giftedness.

Parents. Parents react in varying ways to the news that they have a gifted or creative child. Undeniably, parenting a gifted child properly places an extra strain on the parents' time, energy, and money. If parents have enough of these resources (and especially if they remember the difficulties of their own gifted childhood), their support can make all the difference. If a gifted child has difficulty in finding peers, his parents may be his best friends for a time. Parents who accept their child's giftedness may be relieved to have the school confirm what they have suspected, especially if a suitable program is available, and they may join other parents to support programs for the gifted students in the community. A child in such a family sees that giftedness is worthy of the effort needed to develop it.

Yet even in such an ideal situation, tensions can arise if parents put too much pressure on the child to perform — and it is difficult for parents to sense the line between encouragement and pressure.

> *Scott has studied piano for six years and his teacher is deeply pleased with his progress. When he enters ninth grade, however, homework, the soccer team, and the ski team all demand more time than they have in the past, and he considers dropping piano lessons from his schedule. His parents are proud of his musical talent, which they believe is greater than his athletic ability. If they urge him to continue with piano, are they pressuring him to work beyond his endurance or encouraging him to develop a talent that in thirty years will be a significant source of pleasure and relaxation?*

By contrast, some parents may resist the suggestion that their child be placed in a gifted program, believing that the school has made a mistake. They want their child to be like everyone else, and wish to ignore the evidence that she is gifted. This amounts to rejection of the child as she is, and insistence that she be someone else. It can also mean failure to provide opportunities for enrichment or college. The effect on the child's life can be devastating.

Giftedness may appear to some to be a "high-class problem," but parents of gifted children know that it is also exhausting, sometimes frightening, and always challenging. As awareness of giftedness grows, more books for parents are published. One in particular that helps parents meet the emotional needs of their gifted children is *Guiding the Gifted Child* by Webb, Meckstroth, and Tolan (1982).

Teachers. Gifted children can make themselves unpopular with teachers, especially with those who do not know much about giftedness or who are not sympathetic to their special characteristics and needs. One middle-aged woman still recalls with an inner cringe the scorn in her second-grade teacher's voice when she foolishly gave an answer from a few pages beyond the assigned reading. "You read ahead!" the teacher accused. Indeed she had, but she was not yet clever enough to know that in some classrooms, it is wise to conceal such behavior.

Some children invite displeasure with their divergent thinking, coming up with a variety of creative answers to a question that has a "right" answer. They can see to the heart of a lesson plan while the teacher is going slowly through the introduction for the rest of the class, and their enthusiasm — or their lack of tact — can make it difficult for them to keep their insight to themselves.

Consider, for example, the fifth grader who announced at one discussion group that the book they had read was so simple it would be easy to write a sequel. He then proceeded, on the spot, to outline a very plausible plot, making both the book and the proposed sequel sound laughably trivial. How to lead a serious discussion after that? The group laughed with him, of course, and the discussion waited until everyone had enjoyed his humor.

Even teachers who recognize and encourage gifted students find them frustrating at times. One such teacher told the mother of a gifted fourth grader of her exasperation after a day-long field trip: "He was at my elbow, talking, the whole day. I wanted to listen because everything he says is worth hearing, but I have to listen to the others, too!"

Many gifted children are analytic thinkers, highly critical of the status quo, and only too willing to express an opinion about how things are being run. It is especially important for them to learn early how and when to question authority, and how effective politeness and respect can be.

Teachers have the potential to be a great influence, positively or negatively, on gifted children. *Guiding the Gifted Child* can help educators as well as parents better understand the emotional characteristics and needs of these children.

Responsibility for getting along with other children rests largely with the gifted child, but the responsibility for relationships between her and her parents and teachers rests largely with adults. If they enjoy the positive characteristics of her giftedness, and can understand and help modify the negative ones, they can enhance both her self-acceptance and her ability to get along with others.

Using Abilities

Humanistic psychologist Abraham Maslow (1962) developed a framework he called the hierarchy of needs, which is especially relevant in considering the emotional characteristics of gifted people. Maslow arranged human needs into five levels, from those so basic that life depends on them to those so advanced that only a few can feel and meet them. He makes the point that these needs must be met in order: until the lowest ones are met, we are not free even to sense the higher ones.

Maslow's hierarchy lists physiological needs as the most fundamental. Safety and security needs come next. Only if we feel that we are safe and secure can we experience the next needs, belonging and love. When we are sure that we belong and are loved, we are ready to sense the need for self-esteem. Those who achieve a healthy self-esteem are able to move to the highest level of need, self-actualization, the full use of one's resources and fulfillment of potential.

As already mentioned, gifted children may have difficulty in feeling that they belong and in developing self-esteem. Self-actualization, the full use of their abilities, can also be an issue for them. The degree to which they resolve this issue has a profound impact on their level of satisfaction as adults, but the foundations for self-actualization must be laid in childhood.

This is done not only by meeting the four previous needs, but by making decisions that enable the child to keep developing his unusually high potential. Early decisions, seemingly minor at the time, have a cumulative effect on how well prepared a person will be to take advantage of opportunities in his college years and beyond.

Several years ago a junior high boy attending a weekend statewide church youth meeting felt out of place and wanted to leave early. A religious education director spent over an hour talking with him about his concerns, finally persuading him to stay through the weekend. By the next day, he was comfortable enough to volunteer for a minor position in the organization. After a year of involvement at the state level, he was chosen to attend a national meeting, where he was selected to serve on the national council. Holding leadership positions at two annual meetings gave him the confidence and experience to win a scholarship for a summer program in Japan before his senior year in high school. This experience helped him gain a merit scholarship at a highly-ranked university. Although much of this might have happened in any case, he still traces the rich experiences of the last eight years to a Saturday afternoon in junior high when he was persuaded to see the weekend through, and he still makes risk-taking decisions with that example in mind. These decisions have kept options open for him and have put him in a position to become a self-actualized adult.

Whether or not to use all of one's potential becomes

an issue early in the educational process. The second grader who read ahead was faced with a decision: Would she read ahead again? The fifth grader who becomes aware that she answers too many questions in class and begins rationing how many she will answer per day is dealing with this issue, although she does not see it that way. The junior high student who lets his grades slide because fitting into a social group is more important is facing decisions that ultimately affect self-actualization.

Does it matter? Why is it important that a gifted person should use all his resources? One answer, of course, is that we need all the talent we have available to help us solve the world's problems. For the gifted individual, it is more to the point to recognize that he will simply be happier, more satisfied — life will be much more interesting — if he learns to understand and manage his intensity and creativity. Little research has been done on the gifted adult, so we have no clear idea of the long-term impact of not making full use of one's abilities. But Maslow's hierarchy, affirming that self-esteem and self-actualization are needs, points up the importance of being accepted, useful, valued, and free to use whatever talent one has.

To do this the gifted child must first identify his talents, accept them, and then make a decision about whether to use them or not. The first steps in this decision can be made in the early elementary years. At this point the child begins to see some of the disadvantages of being gifted, some of the conflicts it brings him. He may also run into barriers, external limitations like the absence of educational opportunities, and make a decision (consciously or not) about how hard he will work to overcome them.

Whether a gifted child will use her abilities depends to a large extent on how successfully she establishes her identity, learns to be alone, and learns to get along with peers, family, and teachers. This is the crux of the matter: Can this person, who has the potential to become a self-actualized, fully functioning and contributing member of society, content with herself and giving to those around her — can this person actually do it? Can we guide our gifted children to grow up happy with themselves and prepared to give to others?

How Books Can Help

Books can help us guide our gifted children far more than intellectual discussion because they touch the emotions. The problems presented in this chapter happen to characters a skillful author makes us care about. If a book can "hook" a child emotionally, he may be far more receptive to the ideas than if they are presented in a lecture by a concerned adult.

A child who is unwilling or unable to talk about things that are bothering him, or perhaps even to admit them to himself, may be able to identify with a character in a book strongly enough to experience an emotional release, a catharsis "*He's* bored in school, too!" and then to acquire some insights into his own situation. This is the process of bibliotherapy, which is discussed in detail in chapter 4.

REFERENCES

Ehrlich, Virginia Z. *Gifted Children: A Guide for Parents and Teachers.* New York: Trillium, 1985.

Kerr, Barbara A. *Smart Girls, Gifted Women.* Columbus: Ohio Psychology Publishing Co., 1985.

Maslow, Abraham. *Toward a Psychology of Being.* Princeton: VanNostrand, 1962.

Rimm, Sylvia. *Underachievement Syndrome: Causes and Cures:* Watertown, Wis.: Apple Publishing Co., 1986.

Webb, James T., Elizabeth A. Meckstroth, and Stephanie S. Tolan. *Guiding the Gifted Child: A Practical Source for Parents and Teachers.* Columbus: Ohio Psychology Publishing Co., 1982.

Whitmore, Joanne Rand. *Giftedness, Conflict, and Underachievement.* Boston: Allyn and Bacon, 1980.

2

The Mind of the Gifted Child: Intellectual Development

Much more is known about the intellectual development of gifted children than about their emotional development, and much is being done to help them meet their intellectual potential. Tests and forms help determine their IQs and their learning characteristics; universities throughout the country prepare teachers in gifted education; curricula designed to tap the reasoning powers of gifted students appear in professional journals; programs like Future Problem Solving and Odyssey of the Mind fill their extracurricular time.

What does all this mean in terms of an individual child? And where do books fit in?

The individual gifted child, like all children, is a blend of emotions and intellect — with artistic, physical, social, and spiritual dimensions. Because the intellectual aspect stands out (as does the physical with athletes), school programming for gifted students has typically aimed at meeting intellectual needs. If, in the past, gifted programs have erred in ignoring other facets of children's lives, many teachers are now attempting to correct this.

This book is part of that attempt, taking the approach that intellectual development is just one part of the total gifted person; and further, that intellectual development is an emotional need of the intellectually gifted.

The Need for Intellectual Development

A gifted child has extraordinary abilities, and each ability implies a need: a need for the ability to be developed and used, and a need for the child possessing it to become creative and eventually able to produce something of value to himself or others. For gifted people, the impetus is not merely that where there is an ability, it is best to develop it. An intellectually gifted child will not be happy, complete, certainly not self-actualized, until he is using his intellectual ability at a level approaching his full capacity.

Imagining the physical frustration of an athlete denied the right to exercise gives some idea of the mental frustration of a bright child denied the chance to challenge her mind. Underachieving gifted students may not display such restlessness, but this does not mean they lack the need for intellectual stimulation.

It is important that parents and teachers see intellectual development as a requirement for these children, and not merely as an interest, a flair, or a phase they will outgrow. A painting student is quoted (Piechowski, 1979) as saying, "I have a hard time *not* painting. I paint about 10 hours a day. Painting is my life." Another student, in response to an interview question, says simply, "I read because I can't help it" (National Council of Teachers of English, 1983). Gifted adults who relax by playing a musical instrument, reading in a foreign language, or experimenting with computer programming are expressing the same drive for mental stimulation. These activities are not work for them; they are paths to being fully alive.

Recognizing intellectual development as a need can help parents cope with inevitable frustration caused by a child who reads or tinkers or practices an instrument for "too many" hours per day. It can help teachers find patience when a child insists on working endlessly on a project or report, threatening to hold up the progress of the rest of the class.

Intellectual Overexcitability

Another way of thinking about the drive to understand comes from Kazimierz Dabrowski's intriguing ideas about developmental potential. Based on his work, Piechowski and Colangelo (1984) point out that both gifted adolescents and gifted adults show "overexcitability" in three areas: imagination, emotion, and intellect. They respond, experience, and act with unusual intensity in these realms. Overexcitabilities are not always understood or valued by others, but they contribute to the development of the gifted individual.

The concept of intellectual overexcitability helps to describe and to identify gifted children, and helps also to understand why the need for intellectual development is so strong for them. Piechowski (1979) says that intellectual overexcitability has more to do with "striving for understanding, probing the unknown and love of truth than with learning per se and academic achievement (p. 34)." It is this extra sense of urgency about knowing that underlies the need of some gifted children for intellectual development, that causes them to say, "I read because I can't help it."

Piechowski lists characteristics of intellectual overexcitability that may be familiar to those who deal with gifted youngsters: probing questions, problem solving, curiosity, concentration, capacity for sustained intellectual effort, voracious reading and starting on difficult books at a young age, wide variety of interests, theoretical thinking (thinking about thinking, moral thinking, development of a hierarchy of values), independence of thought (often expressed in criticism), and processes of self-monitoring and self-evaluation.

Intellectual Needs as Emotional Needs

There is a sense, then, in which intellectual needs are emotional needs for gifted children. "Can you tell the readers," one young man said to me when he knew I was writing this book, "how awful it feels when you have to go for two days without reading?" A 19-year-old West German student describes why he is drawn toward a career in university teaching: "When I read about culture, then I am happy!" Both of these young men exhibit the unusual intensity which Piechowski terms "intellectual overexcitability."

For gifted people, meeting intellectual needs should not be seen as a purely intellectual task; there is deep feeling behind it for them, and should be for those who want to promote their intellectual development. Piechowski's description of intellectual overexcitability reinforces the importance of this effort. All of the characteristics he lists are part of the drive to learn, to know, to understand. To have curiosity satisfied, to experience a wealth of diversity in ideas, places, and people, to explore all of the world and find their place in it — all of that is truly a survival issue for gifted youngsters. They *must* be able to grow, to learn, to develop their capacities, or they will wither intellectually.

To the four categories of emotional development given in chapter 1, this chapter adds a fifth: for satisfactory development, gifted children must learn to acknowledge and satisfy their drive to understand.

The following discussion of intellectual characteristics and needs of gifted children demonstrates why book discussions are an ideal means of helping them achieve this.

Intellectual Characteristics and Needs

Many lists have been developed that describe intellectual characteristics of gifted children. These lists are typically used in conjunction with intelligence and achievement test scores to determine eligibility for school gifted programs. They offer more than that, however, if the intellectual characteristics are used as a springboard for identifying the intellectual needs they imply.

Following is a compilation of three of these recent lists (Clark, 1985; Ehrlich, 1985; Webb, Meckstroth, and Tolan, 1982). The listing here eliminates overlap and groups intellectual characteristics of gifted youngsters into three categories: verbal, thought-processing, and performance characteristics.

After each list of characteristics is a list of related intellectual needs, derived in part from Clark's examples of problems that may appear in work patterns or in getting along with others if the needs are not met.

Verbal Characteristics and Needs

Gifted children in general display the following verbal characteristics:

They have a large vocabulary and are able to use advanced terminology correctly.

They read early and may be self-taught; they read enthusiastically and widely, often above grade level; they select reading material purposefully and enjoy challenging books.

They understand language subtleties and use language for humor.

They write words and sentences early, and they produce superior creative writing (poetry, stories, plays).

They display verbal ability in self-expression, choice of colorful and descriptive phrasing, and ease in learning a second language.

To challenge verbal abilities, gifted students need to:

Use their full vocabulary and develop it further with intellectual peers.

Read books at an appropriate intellectual and emotional level.

Be introduced to books that represent a variety of literary conventions and styles and that use language gracefully.

Express ideas verbally and in depth by writing or speaking with others who challenge their ideas, thereby helping refine them.

Thought-Processing Characteristics and Needs

As a group, gifted children display the following traits in thought processing:

They enjoy experimenting and can generate original ideas and solutions.

They give evidence of divergent thinking.

They accept open-ended situations and questions at an early age, and do not require immediate solutions; they can accept ambiguity.

They enjoy complexity and may try to create it, for example, by adding rules to games.

They have unusual power to process information, using logic, abstract thinking and symbolic thought.

They show flexibility of thought, seeking alternatives; they are able to see all sides of an issue.

They synthesize well, seeing relationships others miss; they transfer past learning to new situations and draw generalizations.

To develop thought-processing potential, gifted students need to:

- Consider alternatives and possible consequences of choices in an accepting environment.
- Be exposed to a great variety of vicarious experiences.

- Test new ideas without required conclusions or products.
- Discuss ideas with intellectual peers.
- Be exposed to many ideas at different levels.

- Take plenty of time for incubation of ideas.

Performance Characteristics and Needs

The following performance patterns are characteristic of gifted children:

They show great curiosity and unusual persistence in efforts to gain answers.

They have a wide range of interests and information.

They comprehend new concepts rapidly at an advanced level; they have little or no need for drill.

They display creativity and imagination, enjoy fantasies and science fiction, may have an imaginary playmate in their preschool years, can develop a variety of solutions to problems, and generate original ideas.

They are persistent and goal-directed; they have a long attention span and may want to spend more than the time allotted to complete a project.

They show unusual intensity regarding school projects, political or environmental issues, religion, world events, intellectual inquiry into an area of special interest, interpersonal relationships, and abstract values.

To enhance performance characteristics, gifted students need to:

Have curiosity met with exposure to varying styles of life, values, and approaches to problems.

Be exposed to new information and new issues.

Be presented with material at their own rate of learning.

Develop skills in creative thinking and problem solving.

Pursue interests beyond the time desired by most students.

Learn skills for dealing with intensity by exploring ways in which others cope with it.

How Books Can Help

A glance through these lists of needs will verify that one effective way of meeting them is with reading and book discussion. Many schools offer programs designed to meet most of these intellectual needs. Teachers looking for suggestions on the use of books with gifted children will find information in later chapters about children's reading patterns and literature, as well as bibliotherapy and reading guidance with gifted students. In addition, parents and teachers who work in a less complete gifted program can use books to enhance their efforts to promote the intellectual development of their children.

Many gifted individuals suppress awareness of their need to learn, and that suppression may be unintentionally reinforced by parents, teachers, and peers. Teaching these children to use books is one way of implying adult acknowledgment that learning is important to gifted students, and that books are important to their lives. Arranging book discussion groups for gifted students tells them that such activities are appropriate for them, and that books and the ideas they contain are important and worth their time.

Where special programs for gifted children are unavailable, concerned adults will find that the wise use of books can be a real contribution to children's growth. Few offerings are as rich, available, and rewarding as a well planned reading program. The quality of the books chosen and the content of discussions can support gifted young people in experiencing their own need to know, and exposure through books to a wide variety of ideas can alert them to those they wish to pursue further, helping them satisfy that need.

Chapter 5 details techniques for using books to meet intellectual needs, and the section of the annotated bibliography called Drive to Understand lists recommended books.

REFERENCES

Clark, Barbara. *Growing Up Gifted: Developing the Potential of Children at Home and at School.* 2d ed. Columbus: Merrill, 1983.

Ehrlich, Virginia Z. *Gifted Children: A Guide for Parents and Teachers.* New York: Trillium, 1985.

National Council of Teachers of English. *Your Reading: A Booklist for Junior High and Middle School Students.* New ed. Urbana, Ill.: National Council of Teachers of English, 1983.

Piechowski, Michael M. "Developmental Potential." In *New Voices in Counseling the Gifted,* Nicholas Colangelo and Ronald T. Zaffrann (eds.). Dubuque, Iowa: Kendall/Hunt, 1979.

Piechowski, Michael M. and Nicholas Colangelo. "Developmental Potential of the Gifted." *Gifted Child Quarterly*, Spring, 1984.

Webb, James T., Elizabeth A. Meckstroth and Stephanie S. Tolan. *Guiding the Gifted Child: A Practical Source for Parents and Teachers*. Columbus: Ohio Psychology Publishing Co., 1982.

3

Reading Patterns — What to Expect

The emotional development of gifted children can be promoted through bibliotherapy (chapter 4) and their intellectual development through reading guidance and book discussion (chapter 5). Using these techniques effectively requires an extensive knowledge of children's literature (chapters 6 and 7). And fundamental to all of this is a knowledge of what children *like* to read at what ages — the reading patterns of children.

In working with books and gifted children, it is also helpful to understand the patterns of gifted children who are avid readers and those who resist reading. Approaches for working with resistant readers are suggested later in this chapter. Gifted children have the potential to become "mature readers" as adults; a discussion of this concept, which is useful for work with gifted teenagers, concludes this chapter.

Characteristics of Gifted Readers

As they grow from preschoolers to high school seniors, from nonreaders to independent and voluntary readers and perhaps even to mature readers, children's interest in reading as a leisure activity ebbs and flows in predictable patterns. In addition, many studies over the past forty years have sought to determine the reading interests — the preferred subjects and types of literature — of children at various ages. A few of these studies consider the points at which gifted readers differ from the average.

Gifted children read earlier, better, and more than average children. In what they choose to read, however, differences are not so great. Gifted youngsters read a greater variety, and they may be more adventurous in exploring different types of literature, but in general their reading interests closely parallel those of average children their age (Hawkins, 1983).

They read three or four times as many books as average children, and some continue to do a great deal of reading after the time when most children's reading tapers off (Russell, 1961; Whitehead, 1984).

> *When Melissa was in fifth and sixth grades she typically read a book each day. In junior high, reading longer and more demanding books, her reading diminished to an average of three books a week. Now in senior high, most of her friends find no time for unassigned reading, but Melissa still reads a book every week or two; in the summer she systematically lists the books she plans to read, and she finds time to read fifteen to twenty adult books in addition to working.*

With these special characteristics of gifted readers in mind, it is possible to consider the broad picture of children's reading interests and know that generally it applies to gifted children as well.

Reading at Different Grade Levels

Research in children's reading over the years shows a clear picture of the types of literature and topics that appeal at different ages, so that it is possible to say, for example, that third graders enjoy fairy tales and sixth graders prefer mysteries. (More information about the general reading interests of children from preschool through senior high is given later in this chapter.)

However, recent articles caution that reading interest research produces generalities that may not apply to a specific child. To learn the reading interests of a group of children, teachers and parents should poll them, rather than assume that generalized research findings apply to their youngsters.

The best way to learn what any child likes to read is to ask, but a direct question may not elicit clear information. A bit of probing may be necessary. What does he do with leisure time? What are his favorite television programs? The last good book he read? Identifying his own reading interests is part of each child's learning who he is, and that takes time. The third grader probably doesn't yet know what he likes to read; the ninth grader may, if she is lucky enough to have been introduced to a variety of good books and has had some intelligent, perceptive reading guidance.

When using an informal interview to determine a child's reading interests, it is important to remember that she cannot be interested in literature she hasn't met. It does not mean much if a fourth grader says that he doesn't like fantasy, if he hasn't read or heard anything that he recognizes as fantasy. It is necessary to learn not only what he has enjoyed, but also what kinds of books he has in his background.

One research finding that may surprise us in this liberated age is that at about eight or nine, the reading interests of boys and girls begin to diverge. Reading studies have shown this divergence for a long time. It might be expected that the pattern would have changed in recent years, but Glazer (1981) and Hawkins (1983) found that this is not the case. Studying a group of gifted children, Hawkins found, for example, that girls in the upper elementary grades chose biography, poetry, fairy tales, and animal stories, while boys selected science, science fiction, and "how-to" books.

On the other hand, enlightened teachers and librarians are disproving the old belief that while girls would read "boys' books" (books in which boys are the main characters), boys would not read "girls' books." Teachers who read girls' books to a class — Jean Fritz' *Homesick: My Story,* or Jane Langton's *The Fledgling,* for instance — report that boys' interest equals the girls'. It is relatively easy to build on this response to encourage boys to read on their own some of the fine literature about girls. Adults choosing books to use for discussion with gifted children should not worry too much about the gender of the main character.

Preschool

Few school districts provide programs for gifted preschoolers. Therefore, the characteristics and needs of these children are not as carefully documented as those of school age children. Yet, more people are becoming aware of their special needs.

It is clear to all who study preschoolers that it is important to have a loving person read aloud to them. This is especially so for gifted children, who need the stimulation and the exposure to new ideas that reading aloud can provide. Nothing can quite match the warmth of being held and read to, and if the one who is reading loves not only the child but also the literature and the experience of sharing it, so much richer are both reader and child. Since the child's attention span is short at this age, it is best if there can be several brief "story hours" a day.

It is impossible to overemphasize the importance of reading aloud to children of any age, but especially to preschoolers. Any parent who doubts this, or cannot find time for reading aloud, should read *Babies Need Books* (Butler, 1985), an eloquent statement of the pleasures and advantages of growing up in a family where reading aloud is valued. Butler can make a believer of anyone, and she gives plenty of suggestions for books to help those unfamiliar with children's literature.

There are studies to document the fact that children who are read to as preschoolers are better prepared for learning to read when they enter school. Since their language skills are superior, they do well in any area that depends on language, and what area does not? Some parents read to their preschoolers specifically to build language and pre-reading skills. Books such as *Getting Ready to Read* (Boegehold, 1984) offer ideas on reading aloud to preschoolers for this purpose.

In addition, parents may read to their preschoolers simply to enrich the children's store of knowledge. An ever-increasing supply of information books for young children makes this an easy project, one which is sure to interest the parents as well as the child. In the process, they are teaching the child that books are an infinitely varied source of fascinating information.

But a more fundamental reason for making time to read to a preschool youngster, several times a day if possible, is to instill the sense that reading is a source of pleasure. By sitting with a child, cuddling, enjoying a good story and lovely illustrations, by talking about the pictures and characters and imagining what if this child were in the story, or had the same choices to make, adults lay the foundations for a lifetime of reading for pleasure and information. Reading at its best, even for adults, is an emotional response to the art of literature. The openness to the emotional response begins here, in a loving environment, when children's imagination is most accessible and flexible. Children who miss books at this age will never be able to make up entirely for the loss, because never again will they be so receptive.

In addition to having loving adults who enjoy reading to them, preschoolers need to attend a library story hour where they can experience literature with other children. The children's librarian knows the range of children's literature, and understands how to make it live. Skilled librarians use music, puppets, and storytelling as well as reading aloud, and they involve the children as participants, making the literature an immediate experience.

This approach is perfect for preschoolers, who are still delighted with the sheer joy of language and who will respond well to cumulative tales like "The House That Jack Built" or the nonsense syllables in Mother Goose or the rhythms in Dr. Seuss. Stories that allow the children to join in the repetition are favorites, as are books without words that allow them to tell the story themselves. For content, preschoolers enjoy stories about themselves and their daily lives, and about "things that go" such as trucks, trains, and cars. They like stories with talking animals or toys, and they are ready to begin hearing folklore like "The Three Billy Goats Gruff," "The Little Red Hen," and "The Gingerbread Boy."

Teaching Preschoolers to Read. Some gifted children of this age teach themselves to read, sometimes to the alarm of their parents, who have been told not to push them. If the children have indeed only been encouraged and not pushed, but have learned apparently spontaneously from television or from being read to, there is no cause for alarm. As many parents have learned, there is not much a parent can do to prevent a child from teaching herself to read if she is ready.

The harder question is whether parents should respond to the obvious interest of a gifted child by teaching him to read. This is one of the unresolved issues in education; teaching preschoolers to read is frowned upon by some educators and encouraged by others. The parent of a gifted child may reason that knowing how to read could keep the child occupied in school while the teacher works with slower learners, and prevent some of the disruptive behavior that accompanies boredom. Certainly it is difficult to withhold information from a child who clamors for it.

A mother who admits with some reluctance that she taught both of her children to read when they were three and four recently asked her younger son, now in college, how he remembers feeling about his reading lessons at the time. His surprising answer was that it was confidence building for him, not because he would start school already in possession of this vital skill, but because the time she spent teaching him was proof that "I was worth being taught to read." He knew that she was passing on to him a life-enhancing ability; for him, learning to read was a rite of passage, a welcome into the circle of his reading family.

It is possible for parents to teach their own gifted children to read without undue pushing. The question to answer before making this decision is that of motivation: Are the parents truly hoping to meet the child's need, or is a secret need of their own being met? For most parents, answering this question honestly will require some soul searching. One clue to underlying parental need is this: have they imagined a conversation in which they tell a friend or relative that Jennifer is now reading? The brief pleasure of that conversation is surely not worth risking the possibility of turning reading into a chore for Jennifer.

If parents conclude that their motives are pure and begin to teach their child to read, they should continue to monitor their own behavior. Lessons should be very brief, and if there is any hint of impatience or stridency in their voices or in the child's, they should stop. The only really good criterion for judging the value of preschool reading lessons at home is joy. Is there joy in the doing of it, for the child and the parents? If not, it would be better not to bother. Continue to enjoy reading aloud, continue weekly trips to the library, and wait for nature to take its course.

Reading Aloud. No matter when their children learn to read, parents should continue reading aloud to them. Unhappily, most parents stop this practice by the time youngsters are in the primary grades (Mendoza, 1983). The story hour at home remains important for the warmth, for the exposure to the more advanced books parents will read, and for the opportunity for children to read aloud to parents.

Books listing literature that is especially good for reading aloud include *For Reading Out Loud! a Guide to Sharing Books with Children* (Kimmel and Segel, 1983), *Books Kids Will Sit Still For* (Freeman, 1984) and *The Read-Aloud Handbook* (Trelease, 1985).

The longer parents keep up the tradition of story hour, the better, both for the quality of family life and for the intellectual development of their children. Some families continue reading aloud until the children are in junior high. How much would have been missed if they had stopped when the children learned to read!

Early Elementary (Grades 1-3)

These are the years when most children learn to read, that is, learn the techniques of interpreting the words on a page. As they gain reading skills in the classroom, they come to the library eager to find books. A group of first or second graders appears to swarm over the shelves of easy readers, selecting a wide range of books, some of which they can read themselves but most of which they will have to find an adult to read to them. Whatever the library's limit on books per child, they will come to the circulation desk with that number or more.

As they become independent readers they become more selective. They learn to use the "five finger test," reading a page and putting one finger down for each word they do not know. If by the end of the page fewer than five fingers are down, probably the book is close enough to their reading level for comfort. They begin to recognize author's names, and may want to read all of the Encyclopedia Brown books, or all of Beverly Cleary.

Gifted children often become independent readers earlier than most, and they should have free access to books at their reading level in the school library. It is a proud day when a second grader comes home to announce, "I can read chapter books now!"

As they become independent readers, primary children choose realistic animal and nature stories as well as adventure and mystery. They continue to enjoy folklore of increasing complexity, and they love fairy tales, especially at about third grade.

Their enthusiasm for the library story hour is undiminished, and as important as it is for parents to continue to read aloud at home, it is also important for teachers to find time to read aloud daily to the class. One primary teacher greets the children as they return from their library time and selects one book that has been checked out for immediate reading to the entire class. Then, all the children have quiet time to read their library books. These children look forward to library hour as one of the most important times of the week.

Upper Elementary (Grades 4-6)

A surge in reading begins at about fourth grade and carries through into junior high. Most children's reading is done between fourth and eighth grade, and these few years are vital in forming the reading patterns which will continue in adulthood. If at this time they have access to good books, time to read, and an enthusiastic adult, gifted children in particular have an excellent chance of joining that fortunate group of adults whose lives are immeasurably enriched by the pleasure they find in reading.

Fourth graders, mostly independent readers by now, are beginning to identify favorite authors and ask for their books in the library. The gender split occurs here: boys start to look for sports and war stories, while girls still enjoy fairy stories and begin an interest in books about interpersonal relationships. For both boys and girls in the upper elementary grades, mystery stories are the most popular literature.

Most young readers become interested in fantasy and science fiction at this age, often introduced to it through C. S. Lewis's *Narnia* series. A few children will show an interest in biographies or historical fiction. One study (Swanton, 1984) indicates that gifted students are more likely than their classmates to select fantasy, science fiction, and history.

By the fifth grade, the reading habit is becoming well fixed. Fifth and sixth graders may add the Greek and Roman myths and the legends of King Arthur and Robin Hood to their list of interests. Adventure, mystery, and fantasy remain on the list for gifted and average students alike.

Problem Novels. At this late elementary stage, children begin to read contemporary realistic fiction, including the "problem novels" books about problems they or their friends may be experiencing. There are books for this age group about young people coping with physical or mental disability, divorce, drugs, aging, and death, as well as books that deal with the typical questions and concerns of growing up, finding friends, moving through puberty, and developing a sense of one's own identity. An excellent source for such reading is *The Bookfinder: A Guide to Children's Literature about the Needs and Problems of Youth Aged 2-15* (Dreyer, 1981) which contains over 1,000 listings, each summarized and cross-referenced according to topic and feelings exemplified in the book's story.

Sometimes the "problem" cannot be stated succinctly. For a period of several weeks, a fourth grade boy asked his school librarian each time his class visited the library for "Jewish books." Randy could not explain further what he wanted, but in the limited collection she found something about Judaism, some history, and several legends. Each week it was clear to her that these books were not entirely satisfying his curiosity, but he would not say more about exactly what he was seeking. She understood why when she discovered from Randy's classroom teacher that he had just learned several of his family members were Jewish. Unsure of what it meant and living in a community that included very few Jews, he was turning to books to learn more about himself.

Young people know that they can read about people their age coping with problems they themselves face, and this may cause gifted students to turn more readily to books for an understanding of difficulties related to being gifted. Ironically, however, there is some evidence that gifted students do not perceive books as a source of problem solving as much as average students do (Martin, 1984). It is possible that because they choose books at a higher reading level, they don't see those that deal with problems of people their own age. Reading guidance can point them to useful books they would otherwise miss.

Unfortunately, some gifted children lose their interest in reading as a leisure activity sometime during these years (Martin, 1984). There seem to be two major reasons for this. One is that some youngsters become deeply involved in computers, fantasy games, or sports and do not want to spend time reading; the other is that gifted students may resent being forced to read material not of their own choice. They want "interesting" and "exciting" reading, and their opinion of what is interesting and exciting often does not coincide with the material to be found in elementary reading texts.

Reading guidance to help them find appropriate books can help, along with open-ended assignments that encourage them to read books and also allow them some choice. It's a good idea to begin with books about computers, fantasy, or sports, so that reading can complement their interests rather than compete with them. And it is still important, difficult as it may be, for the teacher to find time in the school day to read aloud, and for the students to read silently.

Junior High (Grades 7-9)

At the beginning of this period, youngsters may still be at the peak of interest in reading, exploring every field of literature. By the end of it, however, other activities and interests take over, and most young people find little time for unassigned, leisure reading. What happens to young adolescents in other aspects of their lives occurs in their reading lives too: they are leaving childhood and the literature appropriate to it. If they are going to continue to read, they will choose adult literature, and their interests will become so individualized that general statements no longer apply. Anyone hoping to guide or influence their reading will have to know them as individuals, and know their reading background as well.

Although reading tapers off for most students in the junior high years, gifted students are more likely to continue reading avidly. One study (Carter, 1982), designed specifically to determine leisure reading interests of gifted junior high students, reports that the gifted students studied read more than twice as much as the students in the control group.

The gifted students in Carter's study read more science fiction and fantasy than the students in the comparison group, and they read fewer problem novels and a wider range of historical fiction. Of the students in the study, only the gifted showed the pattern of moving toward reading adult fiction; this shift began to occur at the end of the eighth grade.

As they move to adult literature, young people need reading guidance more than at any other time. Perhaps surprisingly, gifted students are no more skilled than others at selecting excellent literature without adult guidance.

Girls are likely to discover the more simplistic, sentimentalized romantic adult novels, while boys discover sensationalized, violent adventure. Without direction, they may never find the superb adult literature that can fill their present need for romance and adventure, while enhancing their taste for good literature. If they don't learn the difference between sentimental or sensational novels and good literature at this age, chances are dim that they will eventually develop into mature readers of fiction.

Senior High (Grades 10-12)

By the sophomore year, the reading peak is past for most students, and those who still read choose books focused on very specific, individual interests. Their motivation is likely to be related to their interest in philosophical issues and their attempts to formulate their own opinions and value systems. For gifted high schoolers, this may raise special considerations that are discussed in chapter 4 under "Goals of Bibliotherapy with Gifted Students."

Senior high students read such a wide variety of both fiction and nonfiction that it is no longer possible to make general statements about their reading preferences. To learn the reading interests of any student requires an individual interview. Effective reading guidance for these students demands a very broad knowledge of books as well as a good understanding of the individual student.

It is also helpful for the purpose of reading guidance to think of these students, particularly of high school juniors and seniors, as being nearly adults. This applies especially to gifted students.

In the foregoing survey, reading guidance has been mentioned only briefly. Chapter 5 includes a more detailed discussion of reading guidance with gifted students at different ages.

Avid Readers and Resistant Readers

As readers, gifted children can be considered in two groups: those who pick up a book in their free time, and those who find something else to do. Members of the first group seem to have copious reading as a life goal. Reading comes naturally to them, and when tasks must come first, they feel distracted and annoyed. Those in the second group usually *can* read quite adequately (unless there is a learning disability); they simply do not choose to read *much.*

Avid Gifted Readers

Voracious in the pursuit of books, avid gifted readers often keep several going at once. For a period of several years, Kevin could be traced through the house by the open books spread face down on the floor of each room he had left. He exemplifies those who learn early how to use the local library and the school library, soon becoming personal friends of the librarians, who, in turn, are delighted with such enthusiastic "customers."

Such children may read with amazing speed and incredible comprehension, or they may pore over a passage, savoring the beauty of words. They know how to skim and when to study. These are often the early readers, teaching themselves before they start school, or being taught by parents who respond to their interest.

It is important to remember that "read" in the early stages can mean something closer to "decode." Children can understand the words, pronounce most of them, and glean meaning from the sentences and paragraphs. They may be able to read a book of a hundred or more pages and summarize the story at a time when most of their classmates are still reading the early readers with controlled vocabularies.

However, these young readers may not be emotionally ready to comprehend what they read — to understand the symbolism, or grasp everything the author says about human relationships.

> *Seven-year-old Andrea is reading at the sixth grade level. Therefore, she can read* The Witch of Blackbird Pond. *While she can follow the story line and answer fact questions about the plot, Andrea is not ready to*

> *understand why the old Quaker woman who lives at the pond is feared as a witch, or appreciate the courage shown by Nat and Kit in befriending her.*

Children like Andrea, especially those who know how proud their parents are of their reading ability, need guidance to help them find appropriate reading. In some cases, it seems that more than anything else they need permission not to stretch too far, to enjoy the books that are appropriate for their level of emotional development.

In working with gifted readers, there are three potential problems. One is that they may push themselves, or be pushed by their perception of the pride others take in their reading, to read whatever they can decode before they have developed the emotional readiness to comprehend. They may then not read a book when they are emotionally ready for it because they have already "read" it. They do not realize, of course, that it would be an entirely different book for them at the right time. Such children in the sixth grade sometimes choose books normally read by third graders, perhaps trying to catch up on what they missed three years ago, when they were in such a hurry.

A second problem is to know what books to suggest. It is a great challenge to find a book for a second grader who reads at the sixth grade level. In general, it seems best to match fiction with his emotional level, while guiding him toward nonfiction at his reading level.

> *In the second grade Doug is reading Mary Norton's* The Borrowers, *E. B. White's* Trumpet of the Swan, *and George Selden's* The Cricket in Times Square. *At the same time he is pursuing his interest in computers and lasers by reading books on these topics written for middle school children. By the time he is in the upper elementary grades, he will be able to find more challenging fiction.*

Good sources for recommendations of intellectually challenging books are *Books for the Gifted Child* (Baskin and Harris, 1980) and "Gifted Child Bibliography K-3," a pamphlet published in 1980 by the Ohio Library Association, 40 S. Third Street, #230, Columbus, Ohio 43215.

A third concern for those who work with gifted readers is to recognize that constant and prolific reading may not always be desirable. Occasionally the motive is not thirst for information or enthrallment with the world of the imagination, but simply the need of a gifted child to fill time he would prefer to spend playing with neighborhood children, if he only knew how to be accepted. When Kenneth's mother expressed concern that he was not spending enough time with friends, Kenneth responded, "I don't know a better friend than a book!" The defiance in his voice and the anxiety in his eyes told how he really felt.

It is best to respond to this situation positively. Don't tell the child he is reading too much or playing with others too little, but subtly and persistently help him increase time with other children to achieve a better balance. It's quite likely that this child sees himself as a "reader"; that is, "I am a reader" is a positive part of his self-concept. Anything that makes him feel guilty about the time he spends reading may convince him that reading is somehow wrong; he may also begin to believe that he himself is not quite acceptable as the reader he is. Therefore, no connection should be made between time spent with other children and time spent in reading. Each should be valued independently.

How much is too much time spent in reading? That varies with the child, of course, and parents or teachers will have to judge, basing their evaluation on how much time she spends with other children, how content she seems to be with herself, and how happily she spends time alone. If reading is an escape because interpersonal skills are lacking or because of depression or fear, then some intervention — perhaps professional — should be considered.

However, in our socially oriented society, it is quite possible that adults are overly zealous to see children relate to others. If a child relates well with other children when she does play with them, and seems happy with herself in general, then it probably should not be of great concern if she spends less time with other children than adults think necessary.

Resistant Gifted Readers

Some highly intelligent and able children, gifted or not, simply don't choose to spend their leisure time reading. They may be quite capable of reading to gain information, and they certainly have the potential for success in college and career, but they aren't people who enjoy literature as an art form. In the long run, this is no more alarming than the fact that some children never learn to enjoy music or dance or theater, or participate in sports or car repair. No matter how much we want our children to be well-rounded, they retain the right to develop their own interests. All we can do is to expose them to the world around them and accept the total package the child represents, without unduly imposing our values as we watch them make their choices.

Nevertheless, in the short run it is to the child's advantage to read, both to hone the skill and for the vast amount of information he can gain. Therefore, adults should avoid the tendency to view the middle-grade child — and to allow him to see himself — as a nonreader. It may help to understand what is going on if adults recognize that the roots for his resistance to reading may have been established long ago, in the preschool years, especially if an older sibling has preempted the reading role.

Consider the plight of the two- or three-year-old younger child growing up in a reading family. It is known, of course, that parents who are readers are good models for their children. Children growing up in homes where reading is valued are more likely to be good readers themselves than those in homes where little reading is done. But for this child, whose older siblings are also reading, there is a negative side: everyone in her world takes pleasure from an activity not yet available to her, inevitably ignoring her in the process. Frequent read-aloud sessions can only partially atone, and if the older children read when she wants to play with them — as they will if they are avid readers — it seems natural that she will resent reading to some degree. She learns to capitalize on what she can do, and so may begin her self-image as one who does rather than one who reads. Regardless of this child's ability to read by the time she is a third grader, the doer identity will have had a significant head start over the reader identity, and the reader may never catch up. A mother of such a child tells this story:

> *Jessica's parents and her older brother, Michael, had open books in every room. She, too, was included in the reading orgy, having been read to in the womb and the crib long before she could pick out her own books in the library. But if she wanted Michael to play with her, his invariable response was, "Jessica, I'm* READing.*" When she wanted her mother's attention, it was "When I'm through with this chapter," and Dad's was an absent-minded, "That's nice, dear," as he turned a page.*
>
> *So Jessica began to draw. Her wallpaper still shows evidence of her early interest in art. Then she turned to clay and from there, as a teenager, to beads. While her family read, she sat among them working with tiny crystals and wires. Her giftedness found its outlet in the handiwork of her fingers as she created beautiful, intricate designs for necklaces and earrings. At twenty, she has already sold her work at local art fairs and planned a career in jewelry design. While she enjoys reading, she spends leisure time with beads, not books.*

Jessica is proof that gifted resistant readers can be productive and happy. Nonetheless, reading is so important a skill for success in school that adults in reading families should not give up on their young children as potential readers, particularly during the peak reading period in the elementary grades.

At School. Because many of these children read when reading is assigned, it is critical that teachers include the reading of full books in the curriculum as well as fragments of literature. If this is not happening, it may help if parents ask the teacher to do what they cannot do at home — assign a book.

The assignment may be all the incentive necessary, and it need not add to the teacher's burden. A simple notebook in which the children record the titles they have read may be enough to keep them going if the teacher has no time for more elaborate book reporting procedures; in fact, this is something that not every child in the class would have to do. The book assignments should be free choice, from a list of recommended titles for quality control. Suggestions for the list can come from the school librarian, the bibliography in this book, or from *Books for the Gifted Child* (Baskin and Harris, 1980).

There are many ways in which a teacher, with the help of the school librarian, can bring children's literature into the classroom. But when there are too many children and not enough time to meet the pressing curriculum requirements in every subject, literature may seem like a luxury. In these classrooms, it is especially important that reading be assigned to nonreading gifted children.

At Home. Parents can also gently build reading time into the schedule. One common way of doing this is to set bedtime a half hour earlier than necessary, with optional reading time. Limiting television is commendable for a variety of reasons; reading at bedtime is an excellent substitute.

If parents are aware of the child's reading, occasionally reading one of his books and talking with him about it, asking his opinion, and listening well, they will find several advantages. The child will begin to think of himself not only as a reader, but as one who can respond to books and make judgments about them. In addition, the parents may find themselves truly enjoying some of his books. Moreover, books may become a bridge for more real communication than would otherwise occur. The elementary years are the ideal time to build these bridges — they will be needed during junior high school!

Reading Aloud. Both parents and teachers can help keep gifted children from prematurely deciding that they do not enjoy reading by continuing to read aloud. This, too, may seem like a luxury in a frenetic world, but it can answer a crucial need: unhurried, quiet time for reflection.

One advantage is that children will happily listen to adults read literature that they themselves would not choose. Slower-paced books of real quality lend themselves to reading aloud. *Old Ramon,* by Jack Schaefer, is a quiet book about a wealthy boy's relationship with a shepherd as they take the sheep to the high ground one summer, a trip arranged by the boy's father precisely so he could have a chance to learn from the wise, unlettered older man. This is not initially an exciting book, and children of an age to want adventure will not choose to read it themselves; however, fifth graders will sit silently day after day and listen, coming to love the book and identify with the boy, and they will be sorry to have the story end.

Older Resistant Readers. As gifted resistant readers reach junior high, there is still a chance that they will begin to enjoy reading, if never as much as avid readers. It will help if reading continues to be assigned. When these youngsters understand that a background in literature is part of a good education, some highly motivated gifted students, avid readers or not, will read from lists of classics or suggested pre-college reading during the summers simply to gain that background. Some will turn to reading even later: her mother reports that Jessica is now reading Dostoevski.

Some children will never be avid readers, and those of us whose business or interest it is to push books will do better if we can accept that gracefully. They can grow into happy, productive adults anyway, and there is nothing to be gained if they feel guilty about their lack of interest in reading. If our goal is simply their joy in the literature that we have been able to introduce, and if we achieve that, it is enough.

Mature Readers

The gifted child has an opportunity to develop into what is known as a "mature reader." Mature readers consider reading an integral part of life. It is not something they do only to relax or to escape or if there is nothing good on television. It is something they plan for in each day, and if the day develops so they have no time for it they may become restless, rather like joggers who miss their run. Some, busy mothers for example, stay up late at night to read their daily quota after the house is quiet.

The time spent reading each day may not be measurable in hours, especially for individuals leading active family and professional lives; however, the reading material will be carefully chosen with a long-range goal in mind, if only vaguely so. Reading will be a fairly important part of their pursuit of needs or interests they have identified, and the material they read will be appropriate to that pursuit.

They read about a variety of subjects, but with particular depth and perception in one or more interest areas. They recognize the value of reading as a tool for individual growth, and their reading is purposeful, not random or accidental. While not everything they read is on a high level, most of it is, and their competence in the skill of reading is superior at all levels.

Mature reading can be a useful concept in the guidance of gifted children, especially in career guidance. Facing the problem of their multipotentiality, some of them will one day make a choice among interests, keeping one as a vocation and the others as avocations. It can be easier to give up the full-time pursuit of a favorite interest if one understands that he can continue to follow it through reading. In fact, he may make a career choice partly on the basis of which interests are most accessible through a program of planned and deliberate reading.

Therefore, the concept of mature reading should be introduced to gifted students in high school, so they can consider how to make use of it in their lives. It will be helpful if they realize that mature reading is an acceptable and enjoyable life pattern. With this reassurance, gifted readers who have reached the age when few of their peers still enjoy leisure reading can avoid any concern about their own continuing interest in books.

REFERENCES

Baskin, Barbara H. and Karen H. Harris. *Books for the Gifted Child.* New York: Bowker, 1980.

Boegehold, Betty D. *Getting Ready to Read.* New York: Ballantine, 1984.

Butler, Dorothy. *Babies Need Books.* New York: Atheneum, 1985.

Carter, Betty. "Leisure Reading Habits of Gifted Students in a Suburban Junior High School." *Top of the News,* Vol. 38, 1982.

Dreyer, Sharon S. *The Bookfinder: A Guide to Children's Literature about the Needs and Problems of Youth Aged 2-15.* Circle Pines, Minn.: American Guidance Service, 1981.

Freeman, Judy. *Books Kids Will Sit Still For.* Hagerstown, Md.: Alleyside, 1984.

Glazer, Joan L. *Literature for Young Children.* Columbus: Merrill, 1981.

Hawkins, Sue. "Reading Interests of Gifted Children." *Reading Horizons,* Vol. 24, 1983.

Kimmel, Margaret and Elizabeth Segel. *For Reading Out Loud! A Guide to Sharing Books with Children.* New York: Dell, 1983.

Martin, Charles E. "Why Some Gifted Children Do Not Like to Read." *Roeper Review,* Vol. 7, 1984.

Mendoza, Alicia. "Elementary School Children's Preferences in Literature." *Childhood Education,* Vol. 59, 1983.

Russell, David. *Children Learn to Read.* Boston: Ginn, 1961.

Swanton, Susan I. "Minds Alive: What and Why Gifted Students Read for Pleasure." *School Library Journal,* Vol. 30, 1984.

Trelease, Jim. *The Read-Aloud Handbook.* Rev. ed. New York: Penguin, 1985.

Whitehead, Robert J. *A Guide to Selecting Books for Children.* Metuchen, N.J.: Scarecrow, 1984.

4

Emotional Development Through Books: Bibliotherapy

Chapter 1 made reference to the myth that gifted children have few problems. On the surface it appears that they have everything going for them, that they can handle any difficulties on their own. Gifted children themselves help to perpetuate this myth: they are quick to perceive what is expected of them and to produce it, so that even alert adults may not be aware of their specific problems.

The discrepancy between a carefree appearance and painful reality was demonstrated by Beth, a bright, happy sixth grader. Telling about being accelerated into a fifth and sixth grade reading group when she was in fourth grade, she cheerfully recalled, "They hated me." Her voice revealed nothing of the pain of rejection by older children.

What prompted her comment was a discussion of *(George)*, a book in which Ben Carr, a seventh grader whose imaginary playmate, George, still lives inside him, is accelerated into a science class with seniors. With older students, he encounters an ethical situation that temporarily proves to be too much for his level of maturity. Discussion about the book led naturally to a conversation about how it feels to be accelerated, and reminded Beth of her own experience.

Books like *(George)*, and discussions about them with understanding adults, can become catalysts to help gifted children recognize and talk about some of the experiences — joyful and painful — that are part of growing up gifted. Such discussions offer adults a low-key method of informing children about their giftedness and the problems they may encounter. As with Beth, such reading and discussion can also lead to an understanding of experiences they have already faced.

Books in which characters struggle with some of the same problems the reader has experienced can give assurance that someone else has had similar difficulties, and the reader can solve the problems vicariously with the character. If a trusted adult reads the same book and then discusses it with a child, an intimate problem can be discussed at third-person distance. If it is a group discussion, the child can benefit from the experiences of other children.

Many gifted children, for instance, try to hide their intelligence as Henry does in *Henry 3*. Although they may not wish to admit openly that they do this themselves, they can talk freely about why Henry does. In a group discussion, Patrick may recall that in first grade (now comfortably in the past) he pretended he couldn't read. Patrick's revelation surprises Holly, who thought she was the only one who had tried to conceal her ability. Holly may not add a word to discussion, but she feels less alone as a result of it and perhaps, too, more willing to answer difficult questions in Patrick's presence.

Individual or group discussion can lead to fresh insights that will help the child cope with difficult situations in her own life. This process is especially useful for gifted children because they face specific developmental issues in common with one another, and because so many of them are enthusiastic readers.

It is not simply a matter of handing a child a book about a problem he is facing himself, however. A book is not a pill that will cure if administered at the proper time; it is a starting point. To be most effective, the reading must be followed by discussion with a concerned adult who has also read the book. This statement cannot be made too strongly: *the adult must read the book too,* and be prepared with his or her own response to the literature, and a few key questions to promote discussion.

Most of the books listed in chapter 8 can be read in

three hours. The delightful surprise in store for adults unfamiliar with current children's literature is its high quality. There is no need to settle for the mediocre; there is plenty of the good and the excellent, and it is not boring, no matter what the age of the reader.

The rewards are in the reading, in the discussion, and most of all in the response from the children. After a series of four discussions, Heather said, "I learned that being gifted is important." She had made a start toward accepting the label.

But the label is not so important as the developmental needs. The many gifted children who have not been formally identified have the same emotional needs as those who have been labeled, and they too can benefit from discussions that will help them to establish an identity, recognize their need for alone time, learn to get along with others, and develop their full potential. This chapter offers theoretical and practical information on using books to enhance the emotional development of gifted children through bibliotherapy.

Bibliotherapy

The use of books to generate discussion with gifted youngsters about the emotional aspects of being gifted is a form of bibliotherapy. *Webster's Third New International Dictionary* defines bibliotherapy as "the use of selected reading materials as therapeutic adjuvants in medicine and in psychiatry; also: guidance in the solution of personal problems through directed reading." Cornett and Cornett (1980, p. 8) quote one of the classic definitions among those who use bibliotherapy: "a process of dynamic interaction between the personality of the reader and literature — interaction which may be utilized for personality assessment, adjustment, and growth."

Webster's reference to medicine has a long and honorable history. Libraries in the ancient world bore inscriptions such as "Medicine for the Mind" in Alexandria and "The Healing Place of the Soul" in Thebes. In America, the use of bibliotherapy goes back at least to Dr. Benjamin

Rush, who recommended the reading of books as part of a treatment regimen for hospital patients in the early part of the 19th century.

The two definitions in Webster's point out the ambiguities in the word. In fact, three types of bibliotherapy are recognized: institutional, clinical, and developmental (Rubin, 1979). As the name implies, institutional bibliotherapy is used in hospital settings, following the lead of psychiatrist William Menninger in the 1930s. Institutional bibliotherapy uses literature designed to teach, and the discussion that follows the reading is typically between an individual patient and his doctor. This type is less commonly used at present than the other two (Rubin, 1979).

Clinical bibliotherapy may be used in hospitals or in the community. The literature is primarily imaginative rather than instructional; discussion is typically in groups of clients who have emotional or behavior problems. Doctors and librarians consult with one another in planning the groups, and either may lead them. The best known examples are the program at St. Elizabeths Hospital in Washington, D.C. and the Santa Clara County Free Library in San Jose, California, which provides a community-based program of clinical bibliotherapy.

Developmental Bibliotherapy

Developmental bibliotherapy, offered in schools and public libraries, is more common today than either of the other types. It serves not patients or clients but ordinary people who can benefit from bibliotherapeutic discussions for a variety of reasons. Participants may be in a group assembled by a school counselor to help students cope with a current crisis situation such as parental divorce, or by a public librarian to help patrons meet a new life stage such as aging. They may be a classroom of children whose teacher believes they need to gain empathy for a handicapped classmate and who uses a story to try to move them to awareness, possibly without recognition on her part or theirs that they are experiencing bibliotherapy.

Developmental bibliotherapy attempts to anticipate and meet needs before they become problems, helping people to move through life's predictable stages with information about what to expect and examples of how other people have dealt with the same developmental challenges.

Several psychologists have created lists of developmental tasks that all people face. In an article about bibliotherapy in public libaries, Lack (1985) summarizes Zaccaria's (1978) compilation of such lists:

Infancy — Achieving a sense of trust
Middle childhood — Achieving a sense of initiative
Late childhood — Achieving a sense of industry
Adolescence — Developing a sense of identity
Early adulthood — Achieving a sense of intimacy
Middle adulthood — Achieving a sense of generativity
Late adulthood — Achieving a sense of ego integrity (p. 29)

Those who are interested in the development of gifted children will see immediately how important are the tasks for middle childhood, late childhood, and adolescence. A sense of initiative, industry, and identity are essential to enable gifted youngsters to avoid underachievement and develop their abilities to their own full satisfaction. Yet for some gifted children, the response of others to their giftedness makes it especially difficult for them to move through these developmental stages with complete success.

Todd showed a sense of initiative when he asked his fourth grade teacher for harder math problems. Busy with thirty-two other students and unable to believe that Todd wanted to work harder, she brushed aside his request.

When her sixth grade class studied ancient Egypt, Kirsten became so interested that she persuaded her family to travel to a nearby city one weekend to visit the museum, delaying the completion of her report. Her parents encouraged Kirsten's sense of industry; the teacher, who would not accept a late report, discouraged it.

Jason knew that he was unusually bright, but because his parents wanted their son to be "just normal, like everyone else," he had difficulty accepting his own ability. It was a junior high teacher, patiently working with Jason as he built a project for a science fair, who enabled him to enjoy his talent and develop a sense of identity that incorporated his intelligence.

Todd, Kirsten, and Jason exemplify the impact of adults' responses to gifted children's attempts to establish a sense of initiative, industry, and identity. The reactions of other children can also encourage or thwart the healthy growth of these children. Developmental bibliotherapy can help make the difference.

Typically, when used by teachers and school counselors bibliotherapy focuses on events that are difficult for a child to comprehend such as death or divorce, or tasks that every child faces in the process of growing up, such as making friends or accepting differences among people. But developmental bibliotherapy can also be used by teachers, librarians, counselors, and parents to help gifted youngsters recognize and articulate their feelings, and to prepare them for the particular spins that being gifted puts on the normal developmental tasks faced by all children.

Therefore, in this book bibliotherapy is seen more specifically as a way of helping gifted children understand and cope with growing up gifted in a world that is geared to the average. It can be used to help them anticipate difficulties as well as give them a basis for self-understanding when they feel alone and misunderstood, or are reluctant to use their abilities because it is not popular to be smart. Through bibliotherapy, adults hope to encourage them to build a strong enough self-concept to develop their full potential in spite of the inevitable pull toward the peer group, or to resist pressures from inside and outside toward perfectionism. Developmental bibliotherapy can be part of a planned effort to help them meet their childhood and adolescent tasks.

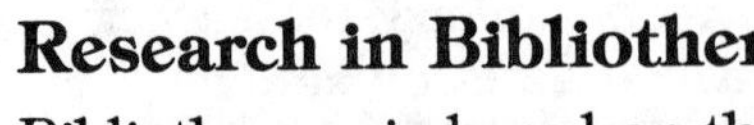

Research in Bibliotherapy

Bibliotherapy is based on the belief that our lives can be changed by what we read, particularly if there is an opportunity to discuss what we read with others. Although difficult to document, this belief persists, perhaps because of the inner certainty of those who love books; we may feel that we do not need scientific proof of what we so surely know. Each of us has identified so strongly with a character that we made him a part of ourselves or adopted his attitude toward a situation. We have all been comforted by knowing that an author has perfectly described our innermost feelings; and developments in psychology over the last two decades have shown that group discussion can be a therapeutic process.

Nevertheless, it is impossible to predict how a particular book will affect any one person. Therefore, bibliotherapists must proceed with caution, with respect for the infinite variability of human nature, and in the knowledge that they are practicing an art and not a science.

Bibliotherapy is an emerging discipline, and there are not yet enough scientific studies to confirm the theories behind it. Although many articles have been published on the subject, most of them are case studies or theoretical descriptions of the process. Some research studies have been published, but inconsistencies in definition and method weaken the collective impact of their findings. Nearly every article on bibliotherapy closes with a plea for more research.

While little research has been done on the effectiveness of institutional bibliotherapy, in recent years more interest has been shown in developmental bibliotherapy. Summarizing findings of research in bibliotherapy, Haney, Harris, and Tipton (1976) reported:

1. There does seem to be a growing body of evidence supporting the idea that bibliotherapy is effective with normal children. And while this is occasionally contested (Kimmel, 1973), the evidence is definitely cumulating in support of the efficacy of bibliotherapy. Furthermore, advances in the theory of bibliotherapy are also being made (Ulibarri, 1970).

2. Bibliotherapy appears most effective with children of average or better reading ability, although note the

presence of other findings (Hynes, 1972; Livengood, 1961).

3. The effects of bibliotherapy are greatly enhanced by follow-up discussion and/or counseling (Madden, 1970).

4. Bibliotherapy must be constantly viewed as an adjunct to other developmental relationships rather than as an alternative or independent form of therapy. (pp. 197-198)

In the 1970s there was great interest in whether reading had the power to change attitudes, specifically attitudes of white children toward black children who were being bused to white schools. Schrank and Engles (1981) and Schrank (1982) reviewed the research studies of that period and reported that while the effectiveness of bibliotherapy in some other areas was not supported, "research in this category suggests an overwhelming Yes to the question of whether bibliotherapy is effective" (Schrank and Engels, 1981, p. 144).

A careful reading of articles (see also Tillman, 1984) that review earlier studies reveals the difficulties of using them to make final statements about the effectiveness of bibliotherapy. More consistent research must be done. For example, some studies have gathered information simply through a checklist that asks students how reading has affected them. In others, the effect of reading on attitudes is studied by administering a pretest, a reading, and a post-test. In these types of research there is no discussion of the book or of students' reactions to it, although other studies do include discussion as a part of bibliotherapy.

As difficult as it is to draw general conclusions from studies that employ a variety of methods, it is the results of these studies that provide the limited knowledge presently available on how bibliotherapy works, and how well. If the definition of bibliotherapy includes a follow-up discussion of the reading, as it does here, then research will have to attempt to assess the entire process. Further, research investigating the use of bibliotherapy with gifted children is needed.

Therefore, current studies can point toward but not confirm the effectiveness of using carefully selected books and well planned discussion to help gifted students cope with giftedness. At present, only the experience of educators and children support the assertion that bibliotherapy is valuable for gifted students. Children probably say it best when they affirm, time after time, that they would want to be in a discussion group again and that it is definitely worth the time it takes from their regular schedule — typical responses when they are asked to evaluate the experience at the end of a discussion series.

Continued and expanded use of developmental bibliotherapy with gifted youngsters should be encouraged. The research we do have indicates that the process has potential; connecting gifted children with books and giving them a chance to talk about their responses makes intuitive sense. From the knowledge now available, it seems safe to assume that developmental bibliotherapy is a promising technique still in the theoretical and experimental stages.

This section must also close with a plea for more research. Meanwhile, adults who work with books and gifted youngsters can do so with the knowledge that they are creating a new method of guiding gifted children.

Training for Bibliotherapists

Do parents, teachers, or librarians have the expertise to lead a bibliotherapeutic discussion? Opinion varies from the assumption that anyone can practice bibliotherapy to the conviction that it should be used only under the guidance of a trained psychologist. This book takes the view that many parents, teachers, and librarians are already practicing bibliotherapy in various degrees, perhaps without knowing it and almost always without formal training. The more they can learn about what they are doing, the more effective they will be.

Those who are interested in doing bibliotherapy probably already have some of the qualifications. In a book that outlines a course of training for bibliotherapy, Hynes and

Hynes- Berry (1986) list the personal characteristics required of a bibliotherapist:

> Maturity: self-awareness, self-acceptance, tolerance of others
>
> Integrity: respect for self and others that enables the therapist to avoid exploitation of emotions
>
> Responsibility: an attitude of responsiveness as well as willingness to guide group participants through even difficult discussion
>
> Adaptability: the ability to adjust plans to meet the needs of the group at the moment, and to allow participants their own interpretations

In addition to these inherent characteristics, the authors point out that the bibliotherapist must acquire and develop therapeutic attitudes:

> Empathy: the ability to understand another person's feelings without actually experiencing them
>
> Respect: the recognition of the value of another person's feelings, and of his or her inherent worth and uniqueness
>
> Genuineness: sincerity, spontaneity, openness; awareness and acceptance of one's own inner experiences

For those who use developmental bibliotherapy with gifted children, it is also necessary to know and enjoy children's literature, to understand child development in general and that of gifted children in particular, to have the trust of the children with whom they are working, and to know something about counseling and discussion techniques.

In spite of the interest in developmental bibliotherapy and the number of people doing it (as shown by articles in education, counseling, and library science journals), there are presently only two places in the country where formal training is available.

St. Elizabeths Hospital in Washington, D.C. offers a training program in clinical bibliotherapy that is intended also as a basis for developmental bibliotherapy. Currently it is a two-year program; applicants must have a bachelor's degree, preferably with a concentration in health sciences or group process. There is no degree or certification in the broad field of bibliotherapy, but graduates of the program can apply for the rating of *certified poetry therapist*. Transfer of control of the hospital from the federal government to the District of Columbia may result in changes. Information on this program can be obtained from the Director of Bibliotherapy, Circulating Library, St. Elizabeths Hospital, Washington, D.C. 20032.

At the University of South Florida in Tampa, the School of Library and Information Science offers courses and a practicum in bibliotherapy as a part of the sixth year (post master's degree) program. The course work provides background in developmental bibliotherapy, and the practicum offers experience in VA and children's hospitals as well as in schools and public libraries. It is possible to enroll as a special student to take the courses, but students must be in the degree program to be eligible for the practicum. Graduates of the program have an educational specialist (Ed.S.) degree. Those interested in this program should contact the School of Library and Information Science, HMS 301, University of South Florida, Tampa 33620.

Although these are the only training programs, institutes in bibliotherapy are occasionally offered around the country, and some graduate schools in library science offer courses in bibliotherapy. A good source of current information on such offerings is The Association of Specialized and Cooperative Library Agencies (ASCLA) of the American Library Association, 50 East Huron Street, Chicago, 60611.

For those who cannot take a course or attend an institute, the Hynes and Hynes-Berry book, *Bibliotherapy: The Interactive Process: A Handbook* (1986), offers a thorough and thoughtful explanation of the process and is highly recommended. Hynes established the St. Elizabeths training program, and while her book emphasizes clinical work, it also provides a good basis for developmental bibliotherapy.

The Bibliotherapeutic Process

Present theories about what happens in bibliotherapy go back to 1949 when educator Carolyn Shrodes studied the relationship between bibliotherapy and psychotherapy for her doctoral dissertation. She identified three phases of the bibliotherapeutic process, corresponding to phases of psychotherapy: these form the basis of subsequent concepts of bibliotherapy.

The three stages of bibliotherapy are identification, catharsis, and insight. A fourth phase, less often mentioned but especially interesting for work with gifted children, is universalization (Slavson, 1950), the recognition that our difficulties and sense of difference are not ours alone.

Bibliotherapy depends on the dynamics set up among the reader, the literature, and the discussion. In *identification,* the reader identifies with a character in the book, recognizing something of herself and so coming to care what happens to that character. If the reader admires the character, her own self- esteem may improve (Spache, 1974). If she is having some of the same problems with which the character is challenged, she may experience the sense of universalization.

It may sound improbable that identification with a fictional character can be a powerful experience. Book characters are real people to most readers, however, and they remain real people even under the close scrutiny of discussion.

Catharsis occurs as the reader follows the character through a difficult situation to a successful resolution. Spache (1974) defines catharsis as:

> . . . sharing of motivations, conflicts and emotions of a book character. Defined in psychological terms, catharsis is an active release of emotions, experienced either first-hand or vicariously. Catharsis goes beyond the simple intellectual recognition of commonalities as in identification. . . . It involves empathetic emotional reactions similar to those that the reader imagines were felt by the book character. Or, in another sense, the reader relives, insofar as his own emotional experiences permit, the feelings he attributes to a character in a story. (p. 242)

One quiet summer morning years ago I was working contentedly in the kitchen, the children still in bed upstairs, when from Mark's room came the sudden heart-stopping sound of deep sobbing. He had been awake for some time, reading *Julie of the Wolves,* and had reached the cruel and emotionally painful point in Julie's conflict between two cultures. Anyone who knows that book will recognize that Mark was experiencing catharsis. It is not a bad thing, after all, to be able to cry over a book.

Insight is the reader's application of the character's situation to her own life. If identification and catharsis have occurred while reading the book, insight may occur during discussion or even later, as the reader reflects on the story. She may transfer her understanding of the character's personality and motivations to herself, increasing self-understanding and bringing her own options into sharper focus.

Insight does not necessarily lead to immediate action, nor does it need to. The discussion leader may not even always know whether it has occurred. Assumptions can be made, however. What insights might have resulted from Mark's reading of *Julie of the Wolves*? A confirmation of his sensitivity to cruelty and his tender-heartedness toward animals; a reluctant recognition that true endings are not always happy ones; and the new-found confidence that he could accept this fact, if with sadness. A growing experience for a ten-year-old!

This process, of course, does not take place with every reader and every book. A discussion leader can help to bring it about by asking questions that focus first on identification with one or several characters; then on the critical situation, the way the story character handled it, and the feelings stirred in the reader in response; and finally on ways in which all this relates to the reader's own life. A demonstration of this process will be found in the sample questions given later in this chapter.

Nor do all of these steps necessarily fit neatly into a half-hour discussion session. Many readers continue to mull over books long after they have finished them. If there is not a good response to one of the deeper questions during the discussion, a seed may nevertheless have been planted that will lead to thought later on. Like parents and teachers, bibliotherapy discussion leaders will know only a small portion of the impact they have on children's lives.

Caution with Bibliotherapy

As with any helping relationship, bibliotherapists must exercise caution, always aware of the possibility that deeper problems may be present. Remember that developmental bibliotherapy is meant to help prevent problems, not to cure them. Anyone who encourages children to discuss their feelings should know when to refer a child to a mental health professional. Children may exhibit any of several warning signals that the bibliotherapist should discuss with the child's parents or a psychologist.

There may be potential problems if the child or the family appear to be denying giftedness. If the child shows unusual reluctance to be placed in the gifted category, or if the parents are unable or unwilling to allow the child to participate in enrichment activities, there is some cause for concern. Comments from the child may indicate prejudicial treatment at home, such as "If you're so smart, why can't you remember to take out the trash?"

If a child seems unable to relate to the purpose of the book discussion group, or unable to relate meaningfully to at least some of the other children in the group, there may be a problem.

> *Bruce gave clear signals of his resistance to participating in a discussion by slumping in his chair, glowering, and looking at the floor except when spoken to directly. He made only minimal contributions to the discussion, including one comment that revealed very low self-esteem. After three sessions he stopped attending, and after the discussion leader called his mother for a conference, the mother made arrangements for individual sessions for him — a much more appropriate arrangement in this instance than group discussion.*

Responses can indicate much more than low self-esteem. There is reason to be concerned about students whose responses reveal excessive anger, aggression, anxiety, depression, fear, preoccupation with sexuality, inability to have empathy for others, little or no social life, or inordinately high or perfectionistic standards for themselves. School performance that is far below ability level, or a lack of investment in achievement in any area, even those of high ability, are further signals of underlying problems that might be helped by therapy.

Anna has been invited to join a bibliotherapy discussion group because her test scores indicate that she is gifted. Her academic performance has never measured up to her potential, and teachers hope the group will bring about changes in her behavior. Although the other students in the group are her friends, Anna does not join in the discussion. It is clear by the second session that she has transferred her attitude toward schoolwork to the group; she will not read the books not because she is too busy but because she has decided not to participate. Recognizing that the bibliotherapy group is not appropriate for Anna, the leader refers her to the school psychologist.

Of course, a leader must be concerned about a student who gives evidence of physical or psychological abuse or neglect, who shows signs of drug or alcohol abuse, or who is carrying a weapon. She may be alerted in discussion by a student who strongly defends the right of individuals to use drugs.

A bibliotherapist must also be aware of the possibility of serious depression or even potential suicide, particularly among gifted adolescents. Indications of depression include insomnia or other sleep disturbances, lack of interest in life or in any number of activities that formerly were motivating and exciting, emotional outbursts, noticeable weight gain or loss, and changes in clothing and dress standards. Be alert for direct mention of suicide or a strong defense of suicide as a desirable choice.

These warning signals do not occur often, but bibliotherapists should be aware of them and realize they are in a unique position to help. A discussion leader's best contribution to some children may well be a referral to a competent psychologist.

In addition to watching for signs of deep emotional problems, discussion leaders should be careful to control the depth of the discussion. It is not necessary that everything be explicitly said; trust the participants to take and use what they can. If a discussion at greater depth seems potentially beneficial, a teacher or librarian could ask the school guidance counselor or psychologist to serve as co-leader. Discussion leaders without training in psychology should not attempt to invite self-disclosures that would make participants feel exposed without a mental health professional present.

Setting Up Discussion Groups at School

When teachers or librarians use book discussion with gifted students, they are most likely to do so with a group, although they may occasionally hold informal discussions with individual students. Parents do not need the detailed information given here on selecting children to join discussion groups and on setting a place and time, but the information on choosing books will be useful to them. Later sections on planning and leading discussions are specific enough to be used in school programs, and can be adapted for use at home.

Before a leader can sit down with a group of youngsters, all of whom have read the same book and are eager to discuss it, there is much work to be done. Setting up a group means bringing appropriate children and appropriate books together, in sufficient numbers of each, at a time and place that will suit everyone's needs. The advance planning will vary considerably, depending on such factors as how the school identifies gifted students, the academic structure of the program for them (if any), the flexibility in the schedule, and how important the faculty and administration feel it is to deal with the emotional needs of gifted youngsters.

The Children

It is easier to hold effective discussions if the children are close in age. Students from two grade levels can meet together, but a wider age range makes it difficult to choose literature that will appeal to everyone.

They should also be relatively close in ability level. Like academic programs for the gifted, a book discussion group that combines students in the superior range with those who are highly gifted will probably fail to meet the needs of the highly gifted members; it would be better to have a separate group for them if possible.

Remembering that highly gifted people differ from one another more than do people in the superior or average ranges, the leader for this group should keep the individual characteristics of each reader in mind while selecting books. For the same reason, discussion should be specifically planned for the individual students rather than for the group in general. In addition, the books chosen for them should offer examples of highly gifted people.

With any discussion group for gifted children, the leader should know how much the children understand about giftedness and their own selection for the group. How comfortable they are with the term will depend largely on how it is handled within their school. It may be a good idea in the first session to discuss how members will describe the group for children who are not included. The leader can help them avoid hurting others without downplaying their own abilities: "We're going to read books and talk about them. It's a group for good readers who like to read a lot. We're going to learn ways to think about a book after you've read it, and how to discuss the ideas in the book."

The leader should consider whether the self-concept and personal strength of each potential member is sufficient to allow participation in the group without inappropriate self-revelation or hypersensitivity. If the leader knows that a child has a specific problem that may be discussed and that it is so close to the surface that the student will be unable to think or speak about it objectively, then for the protection of the child an individual discussion would be preferable to a group experience.

> *Tracy's parents have recently divorced, and her mother has asked Tracy's school counselor to include her in a support group for children of divorced parents. In talking with Tracy, however, the counselor has learned that she is not yet ready to discuss her experience in a group of peers. Rather than participate in a group discussion of* A Girl Called Al *or* The Boy Who Could Make Himself Disappear, *both about children dealing with the emotional aftermath of divorce, Tracy should be given the option of meeting individually with the counselor for a time.*

Unexpected self-revelation will of course occur during group discussion, and the leader can deal with it at that time through reassurance, redirection of the topic, or by offering to talk about it after the meeting; it is better if selection of group members can minimize its occurrence. Members of a book discussion group designed to help them cope with developmental issues of giftedness should be children not currently in crisis. If a leader wishes to develop a group for children in crisis, it should be planned and led differently, probably with a counselor as co-leader.

A group size of six to eight is optimum. Even with eight, there may be some who will be able to remain silent because the group is large enough for them to do so. With fewer than six, the group can become ineffective if two members are absent or have not read the book.

Should group membership be optional for those eligible to join? If it is, there will be better potential for good discussion. However, if required, the group may include students who would not otherwise join, but who may benefit greatly once they are involved. Those who know the students best should make this decision.

Consider forming a group specifically for those who would not join if given a choice, such as future scientists who scorn fiction and do not think of themselves as readers. Certainly this would benefit leaders who are nonscientists who could do with some stretching in that direction, and it would help create a participatory rather than authoritarian leadership style. A good start might be to ask potential group members for suggestions of book titles, including biography as well as fiction, from which to develop a book list.

Another issue is what to do about students who come to the discussion without having finished the book. One way of alleviating this problem is to request that the classroom teacher accept books read for group discussion as book reports to meet the curriculum quota, so the books do double duty.

The Books

In some contexts, bibliotherapy is practiced with little regard for the quality of the literature chosen. The only requirement is that the subject of the literature be appropriate to the goals of the discussion. For a couple of reasons, this cannot be the case in bibliotherapy with gifted students.

First and most practical, inferior literature will not lend itself to discussions that will touch and challenge these very bright children. They may not recognize the technical differences between good and bad literature, but they will certainly recognize (and mention with notable lack of grace) when a book is "bor-ing." Discussion about boring books is bound to be boring itself, at any age.

Second, it is a disservice to gifted children to encourage them to spend their time on less than the best. Of course they will experiment with escape literature from time to time, but they can learn to recognize it and how to find good literature when they want it. Parents and teachers who are guiding them in the larger sense of helping them develop their potential must have the courage to differentiate the inferior from the good, and must take the time to find the best for them. There is plenty of excellence in literature for children and young people as well as for adults.

To find good literature, make use of as many sources of book lists as possible. Teachers and librarians should have access to *Booklist, School Library Journal,* and other selection aids librarians use in considering books to buy.

Journals about parenting and educating gifted children often have book review sections. Even newsletters of local associations for parents of gifted children may have suggestions of good books.

Browse through the education section of bookstores; there are always books to help adults encourage children to read. For discussion purposes, however, look for publications that focus on books to read rather than on the process of reading or on reading readiness. There is a partial list of these at the end of chapter 6.

Develop the habit of reading reviews of children's books, keeping in mind the criteria in chapter 6 for books that meet gifted youngsters' emotional needs while challenging them intellectually. Good ideas come from other gifted educators and from children, too. As discussion leaders gain experience with excellent literature, they will recognize trusted authors and good writing so they can browse effectively. Before long, by reading just a page or two they can sense whether a book is appropriate for use with gifted children.

After gathering lists of suggested titles, leaders need to find the books for preview. If they are not available they can be ordered. Because several copies will be needed, cost considerations may limit the choices to paperbacks. Remember that it can take four to six weeks for books to arrive.

In addition, thanks to library networking developed in the last twenty years, any title can be located through interlibrary loan at most public libraries. In some cases, a small charge is assessed. In my research for this book, almost every library book I requested has been located in Michigan or a nearby state, and they have arrived faster than I could read them.

Students may wish to buy their own copies to build personal libraries, or borrow copies from local libraries. The most efficient way of ensuring that each student has a copy is for the school to provide multiple copies of the titles selected, keeping them in the school library for use in future years, and making them available in the meantime to other students.

Try to select titles that most of the students have not read. This is a challenge, but it is pleasant when the titles are announced to hear more children say, "Oh, I've heard of that one!" than "I've read that one."

An issue that always arises in assigning reading is that of free choice. Children prefer to read books of their own choosing, and obviously, unless everyone in the group has read the same book it will be difficult to establish common ground for discussion. Compromise seems to be in order here, with required books for the first few discussions, to give them a chance to see what it is all about, and then free choice from a pre-selected group of books for later sessions. An advantage of free choice is that having every child read a different book saves the expense of multiple copies while giving children exposure to more good books.

Discussion of free-choice books will be more open-ended, perhaps with each student answering a core question in whatever way it applies to his or her book. Perhaps there could be simply a series of brief oral reports from the students, including an explanation of why they think the book they have chosen is or is not suited to discussion about issues of giftedness. Since these sessions will not be as focused as those based on required reading, it is better to establish a ratio of more required than free-choice books; save the free-choice books for the end of the series.

Place and Time

Privacy is important when choosing a place for the discussion group. A special room or corner of the school library would be best if the library is empty at the time. A corner in the classroom is not a good place to discuss feelings the participants would not want all classmates to hear; in fact, such a spot will probably limit the effectiveness of the discussion.

The difficulty in scheduling a time will depend on whether children are coming to the group from more than one class, and on what degree of priority the school gives to the gifted program. It is not a good idea to schedule this group at a time that requires the students to miss recess, physical education, or lunch. The most logical time would seem to be during their classroom reading time, with a librarian or team teacher leading the group.

For children in grades three to six, a series of four sessions may be adequate, spaced one week apart. Junior high students may need more time to read their books; biweekly sessions might be better for them. For high school students, book discussions could be held once a month throughout the school year.

Book discussion groups can also be offered as part of summer enrichment programs. These sessions may be spread over a period of two to three weeks, with two or three meetings a week, assuming children have more time in the summer. These groups can incorporate gifted students from different schools, granting them an anonymity that may make it easier to talk.

Bibliotherapy at Home

In a less structured home setting, parents may accomplish less in a given amount of time, but they have the advantage of being able to continue over a period of several years. In addition, they will bring such a wealth of family experience to the conversations that in the long run they may well be able to accomplish much more.

> *The Miller family began reading to their children in the nursery, and both Jon and Laurie began reading early. When they were three and four Dad would push back his chair from the dining table in the evening and say, "I feel a little Pooh coming on," and they would pile into his lap for a chapter or two of* Winnie-the-Pooh. *The family read aloud on vacations and camping trips, and it was a natural step to begin talking about the books the children were reading.*
>
> *Usually, Mother had read the books they read, and when she asked Laurie what she thought of* The Wolfling *the discussion expanded to include Dad's and Jon's thoughts on why higher education is important for someone like Robbie Trent — and Jon and Laurie. Laurie's excitement over* Anno's Medieval World *led to a family*

discussion that helped Jon understand superstition and scientific thought in a new light, an understanding that he tucked away for further attention as he pondered budding career ideas. When Laurie showed evidence of feeling uncomfortably different and out of place in her new junior high school, Mother reminded her of Jess in A Bridge to Terebithia, *who did not fit in his family or his school but who did have one friend and one teacher who understood. Over the years, their love of books led to productive conversations and mutual understanding for the entire family.*

What a parent does in bibliotherapy will be much the same as what a teacher or librarian would do, except he will usually be talking with an individual instead of a group. He can use the same procedures in planning and discussing that are outlined for use with a group, modifying them to his situation and child.

Motivation may be slightly different for a parent. With an avid reader, Mother may need do no more than mention that she would like to read a book he is reading; when both have finished the book, they can talk about it over dishes or while driving home — whenever there are fifteen or twenty uninterrupted minutes. Once a pattern of discussing books is established, the parent can reciprocate by recommending a book to him, and they will be on their way.

With a resistant reader, a parent may have to be more assertive. It will help if reading time has been built into the daily schedule from the early years, and it will certainly help if the parent is a reader. Some parents find that they can strike a deal with their child: they will read what the child recommends to them, and she will read what they recommend to her.

The discussion itself will be slightly different from one with a group. If one child is doing all of the responding, she is more likely to become involved in the discussion than if she could leave some of the work to others. On the other hand, she will miss the reinforcement of ideas from peers; the parent may need to compensate for that by bringing up the points of view that other children might mention if they were there.

With these few differences, parents can apply the following ideas to the reading program they create at home.

Planning

Whether working informally with a child at home or setting up a series at school, some planning is necessary before discussing a book with a child.

Reading the Book

The first step is to read the book. For those not familiar with children's literature, this may at first sound like a tedious task, but good children's literature will hold adults' interest too. In fact, a book that does *not* hold the leader's interest should be reconsidered before being recommended for gifted students. One way to test for good writing is to read a passage aloud: if the tongue feels stiff and stumbles over the words, the book simply may not be well written. Look for books that glide along, flowing from word to word and from thought to thought when read aloud. But above all, read the book!

The leader must plan discussion questions related to the book; this will be easiest if she thinks about them as she is reading. She must also keep in mind the child or children with whom the book will be discussed, and the purpose in discussing it with them. She can use as a bookmark a three-by-five slip of paper on which she jots down page numbers and key phrases that strike her as potential discussion material. When she goes back later to write questions, she will have an overview of themes in the book that will be useful for discussion.

It is a good idea to allow a day or two after finishing a book to let it "settle in" before writing questions. During this incubation period, the leader will be subconsciously working on the book, and when she does sit down to write, the questions that come will be a distillation, probably of better quality and drawn more from the true heart of the book than if she had begun to write immediately. What she is doing in that dormant period is allowing the book to sift down into deeper levels of her own understanding, so that her responses will contain some measure of wisdom as well as intellectual analysis.

Busy students will probably not have the time for a similar incubation period before they come to the book discussion. It can't hurt, however, to suggest it to them.

Adults may find that their immediate response to a book is that it can't possibly be used with gifted children. When they sit down with pencil and paper they may still think the book has nothing to offer. But if they go on with the physical act of writing, beginning with a summary of the plot, the potential of the book begins to unfold and usually questions will occur as quickly as one can write them down. Sometimes, of course, this does not happen; the book truly is unsuitable for this purpose. In this case it is worth taking the time to clarify exactly why it is unsuitable; this bit of discipline helps in the ongoing definition of what the leader is looking for in books to use for bibliotherapy with gifted students.

Preparing the Questions

As any teacher or discussion leader knows, productive questioning is an art. Two systems of questioning likely to be familiar to those working with the gifted are the one resulting from the work of Benjamin Bloom (1956), and the one taught to leaders of Junior Great Books discussions. The procedure used in both of these systems — identifying and using questions of lesser and then greater complexity — is also used to develop questions for use in a bibliotherapeutic discussion.

The annotated bibliography of this book suggests core or interpretive questions, intended for the meat of the discussion. It is best to lead up to them with a few fact questions to ascertain the general level of understanding and response to the book. These introductory questions also provide a warm-up period, a chance to recall the impact of the book and to build to the emotional level called for by the core questions.

After a few fact questions have helped the students turn their thinking toward the book, it is time to move on to interpretive questions. Here is a list of general interpretive questions that can be adapted to specific books:

1. What is the central character's biggest problem?
2. How do you think (he) (she) feels?
3. What strengths does (he) (she) have that help (him) (her) cope?
4. Do you know anyone who has ever been in the same situation?
5. What would you have done?
6. If you were (his) (her) best friend, what advice would you give?
7. How would that help the situation?
8. What effect do the people in the book have on one another?

In planning interpretive questions for a bibliotherapeutic discussion, keep in mind the stages of bibliotherapy — identification, catharsis, and insight — and structure questions that will lead the students from one to the next. Questions may come more easily if the leader thinks of these stages in terms of actions he wants to guide the students to take, and changes the terms accordingly. Identification, catharsis, and insight are excellent terms for conceptualizing the process, but for writing questions it may help to think of guiding students toward *recognizing, feeling,* and *thinking.*

As an example, here is a list of questions used for a discussion of Constance C. Greene's *A Girl Called Al,* which can be used with gifted third or fourth graders. The questions progress from encouraging identification with Al to generating insight into the reader's own life.

Identification (Recognizing)	Describe Al; describe the narrator (who is never named in the book).
	Whom are you most like, Al or the narrator? Why? (Al is a leader; the narrator a follower.)

In what ways does Al have extra trouble because she is bright? How are things easier for her because she is bright?

Catharsis
(Feeling)

How do you know Al is lonely, even though she never says so?

What happens in the book to help Al overcome her loneliness?

What effect does Mr. Richards have on Al? Do you know anyone who is as important to you or to someone else as Mr. Richards is to Al? What effect will his death have on Al? On what do you base your answer?

How does Al feel when Mr. Richards dies? How do you know? Do you know anyone who has trouble showing feelings as Al does?

Insight
(Thinking)

When do you hide your real feelings? What are the advantages of doing so? Why is it hard to show real feelings?

Why does showing real feelings make people feel less lonely?

These questions pursue just one of the themes in the book: loneliness. An equally productive theme is Al's defiant nonconformity. To follow that theme, a discussion leader might use the same identification questions, and then continue with these:

Catharsis
(Feeling)

Why has Al chosen to be a nonconformist? How do you think she feels about it?

Think of nonconformists you know, or even yourself, if you are one. What feelings (good or bad) do you think compel people to be nonconformists?

How do you imagine nonconformists feel about themselves generally?

Insight (Thinking)	When do you choose not to conform? Why?
	What are different ways to be a nonconformist?
	When is nonconformity destructive? When is it productive?

These questions assume identification with Al more than with the narrator. If a child in the group is more likely to identify with the narrator, the leader may want to develop different questions, perhaps with the purpose of encouraging understanding of what the follower brings to a leader/follower relationship, or of developing empathy for nonconformists from the point of view of those who find it easier to conform.

For a thirty-minute discussion with middle or late elementary children, a list of twenty questions is more than enough. Each interpretive question can carry the entire discussion, if it catches the imagination of the students. Having more questions than needed gives flexibility, preparing the leader to go in any of several directions when student interests become apparent. And for beginning discussion leaders, it builds confidence to know there is more than enough material to fill the time.

These questions are only suggestions to get started. As leaders gain experience, they will want to use their own insights and questions. As students gain experience, they also will be able to generate their own questions. When they can do this, they are learning enough of bibliotherapy to be able to use it independently. It could become a skill they will be able to use even in adulthood.

Motivating the Children

Before it is possible to discuss a book with a group or with a child, they must have read the book, too. This may be no problem at all, or it may be a matter of some difficulty, depending on the level of interest they already have in reading and on the way in which the whole idea is presented to them.

It clearly seems better to appeal to their interest in the content of the books and the discussion itself, than to approach it from the view of working on gifted people's problems. That will come up later as a natural part of discussion, and will be more authentic as a result. The best aid in motivating children to read specific books is the leader's enthusiasm for the books, and his ability to convey it to them.

For the teacher or librarian planning a discussion series at school with a group of gifted children, motivation is done according to good teaching practices. The leader gathers the group for an initial meeting and outlines his plans: duration of series, meeting time and place, how many books are to be read, how this group will fit into their reading program, their responsibility to read the books on time and be prepared for discussion, etc.

Agreeing to participate in the group should constitute agreement to read the books on schedule. This seems to be a bit more difficult, and the leader should know ahead of time how he will deal with those who have not finished a book by discussion time. May they participate or not? One solution is to allow participation, but to try to change the parameters of the group to prevent recurrences. Allowing more time between sessions may help; so may providing more classroom reading time, as well as counting the reading done for this group toward required book reports, to provide a deadline external to the book discussion group.

With the logistics out of the way, it is time to present the first book to be read. This can be done in a brief book talk, in which the leader

> hints at the plot or conflict in the book: "In *Jacob Have I Loved,* Louise's abilities are unrecognized, and all the family's meager resources go for voice lessons for her musically gifted twin, Caroline";
>
> mentions ways in which it might relate to their own experience: "Louise grows up believing that her family loves Caroline more than they love her";
>
> tells enough about the characters to initiate the reader's identification with them: "Louise is hard-work-

ing and resourceful, but not much interested in schoolwork or in her own future until circumstances force her to make a decision";

tells why he likes the book enough to think they would like to read it too: "I like this book especially because I like each of the characters — even Caroline, by the end of the book."

Any difficulties in the book might be mentioned, also: the structure of Konigsburg's *Father's Arcane Daughter,* for instance, may be discouraging to some readers unless it is pointed out that the book has flashbacks that will become clearer as they read. *Across Five Aprils* will start slowly for some; the leader might pass along the judgment of one sixth grader, that the book does not get interesting until page 64!

It is probably best to introduce just one book at a time, rather than giving a reading list for the whole series. Avid readers may read all the books immediately, and then the stories will not be fresh in their minds for the later discussions. Closing each session with the introduction of the next book is one way to keep motivation high.

Leading the Discussion

Whether leading a group or talking about a book with a single child, there are certain techniques that will help to make the book discussion as meaningful as possible:

1. Confidentiality is important. Group members should understand that what is said in the group should not be repeated elsewhere. Even if the leader is her father, the child will want to know that he will not talk about the discussions to others without her permission.

2. Confidentiality will be difficult for some children to maintain. Therefore it is important to help children avoid giving information they will later regret. Children may not yet have a firm sense of how much personal revelation is appropriate. Use the "capping" technique, especially in a group. Be alert to those

times when a child may be saying too much, and divert attention to another question and another child, effectively "capping" the overflow of emotion and self-revelation. (The leader may speak to the child later, giving him a chance to continue the discussion individually.)

3. Encourage children to share any ways they have found useful for coping with common problems. Some of the more mature children may have simply adopted attitudes that enable them to transcend difficulties, at least part of the time, and it will be helpful for others to hear about these.

4. Let the conversation flow where the group or the child wants to take it. The leader may understandably be eager to get to her prize question, the one that for her gets to the heart of the book or the problem; however, if she forces the discussion in that direction, her wonderful question may fall flat. This is not to say that she should allow the discussion to wander away from the book; rather, that the children may select another theme they are more ready and able to discuss.

5. Outline good discussion techniques with the children before beginning, and remind them of these when necessary. Some rules to establish are that everyone must have a chance to talk, that only one person will talk at a time, and that there are no right or wrong answers.

6. Remember that the leader's role should be not too intrusive. She is not there to be sure they understand her interpretation of the book, but to moderate and to facilitate their own understanding.

Begin the discussion with a few quick fact questions, and move as soon as possible into the more interpretive core questions. In a thirty-minute session with elementary school children, it is enough if only the middle twenty minutes are spent on real discussion of issues. At first it is only natural that the leader will be concerned about pacing, and about getting her questions covered in the time remaining. As she gains experience it will be possible for her to become more involved in the discussion herself, giving real answers to the children's comments and validating their emotional responses. She can close with a review of the major points that have been brought out, or ask the group to do this, then introduce the book to be read for the next meeting.

Goals of Bibliotherapy at Different Stages

How much a child understands about what it means to be gifted is determined partly by the child's age and partly by the degree to which adults have discussed giftedness openly. In turn, the child's level of awareness will determine the character of the book discussion.

Preschool and Early Grades

A conversation about books with preschoolers or early elementary children will be just that: a conversation, not a discussion in the sense of a series of questions and answers. Accordingly, this book does not suggest discussion questions in the bibliography for this age group, but merely lists concepts found in the book that would be useful as the focus of a conversation.

Reasonable goals with this age are to introduce concepts, label feelings, and develop frames of reference so that when an event in the child's life recalls a story read together, the concepts can be reinforced. This process establishes the importance of books as windows into various life experiences, builds foundations for years of discussion based on books, validates the child's feelings and assures him that talking about feelings is not only permissible but also a positive way to release emotions.

For early elementary children, a combination of conversation and deliberate questioning can be used, still with an individual child rather than with a group. Watch for signs of fatigue or restlessness and be prepared to stop as soon as they appear. This is still a preparation time for true discussion; the emphasis should be on the warm relationship between adult and child, with books as the catalyst for occasional conversation but not yet the focal point.

Upper Elementary

It is in the later elementary years, grades 4-6, that intellectual differences among the children become apparent to them. In many schools, this is also the age when gifted programming begins. Many children hear the term *gifted* applied to them for the first time; however, they may not know what it means or how they are expected to react. It makes sense at this stage to discuss giftedness openly with them. Since these are the peak reading years, it is a particularly good time to begin book discussion groups.

A realistic goal for discussion groups with gifted children of this age is to help them become aware of the word gifted and gain some understanding of what it means. They may not yet be comfortable applying it to themselves, but they can recognize some of the problems that gifted children in books have and how they cope. They can also begin to recognize the importance of empathy and respect for all people who are different, in whatever way.

Gifted fourth graders who had read *Mrs. Frisby and the Rats of NIMH* talked about why other rats edged away from the superintelligent ones who had escaped from NIMH. The students agreed that they have felt others pull away from them, and they discussed how they respond to that: by trying to be more like other people. Later, when they evaluated the series, one gain they mentioned was "learning not to edge away until you know a person better."

Junior High

For junior high students, social needs are paramount. The major contribution of a book discussion group may lie in simply bringing gifted students together, to allow them to belong to a group of peers. They need to blend with their social group while retaining their own identity, which includes their giftedness. One goal will be to remind them from time to time of this part of their identity, so that it will be available to them to build on when they emerge from this period. Books with gifted characters can help to keep them aware of their potential.

Some gifted adolescents, in both junior and senior high, become poignantly and cynically aware that adults have failed to realize the potentials that life has to offer. They may begin to question the meaning of life, and given the intensity that characterizes gifted youngsters, may carry this questioning to the point of an existential depression. Be prepared to refer to a psychologist any student who shows signs of depression.

Senior High

During the senior high years, students become increasingly concerned about the decisions they must make for the future. Gifted students of this age are working on college and career choices, very often struggling with the issues raised by their multipotentiality, and the reluctant realization that they must choose from among several abilities and interests. It is important now that they face the fact of their own giftedness, accept it, become comfortable with it, and begin to recognize some of the responsibilities that giftedness may imply.

A major goal of book discussion with senior high students is to help them consider these issues. The books chosen will be mostly adult literature, and at times the discussion may be very like a discussion with a group of adults.

An Author's View

When Stephanie Tolan, the author of *A Time to Fly Free* and other books for young adults, was asked what she would say to potential bibliotherapists, she answered that discussion leaders should realize that the purpose of writing literature is not to prescribe solutions to problems. The author is trying to create a world that is real and true, not to teach. Discussion, she said, should be open-ended, helping the child to see why things work out as they do in *this* book. The author is not saying that this is what should happen, only that this is one way it could happen. It is not the only answer.

If we look from the author's point of view, we see that stories as they are being written are organic, developing in their own ways, and that other ways are possible. There is always the question, "What if . . . ?" Realizing this will help to derive the widest possible meanings from the story, and the most flexibility in relating a book to a child's own life.

In books in which characters make life-shaping decisions, such as *Shadow of a Bull* and *Jacob Have I Loved*, the possibility of other options is especially clear. Each reader can respond to these books by making the decision for himself, adding components from his life that the author did not include in the book. Thus the book continues to live in the reader, informing his future decisions. With healthy development, gifted children as they grow create lives that are real and true, even though they differ from the world the author creates.

Bibliotherapy: An Affirmation of Strengths

To most people, giftedness doesn't sound like a source of trouble at all. Those of us who call attention to potential difficulties for persons whose very label implies they have been blessed could be accused of making up problems where there may not be any and generally holding too gloomy a view of the lives of gifted children. It may appear that we have forgotten that gifted children have strengths and joys as well as vulnerabilities and loneliness.

For now, however, it is vastly important that the emotional needs of gifted children, and the fact that they do have problems peculiar to them and their giftedness, be recognized. Once that recognition is commonly accepted, those who discuss the social and emotional needs of gifted children will be free to place more emphasis on their strengths and capabilities.

In the meantime, bibliotherapy can be used to affirm and develop those capabilities. The fact that it is a vehicle for discussing problems should not cloud the fact that it is also a tool for calling upon the strengths of gifted children and young people. Bibliotherapy is a process uniquely designed to do just that, as Hynes and Hynes-Berry (1986) point out:

> . . . the emphasis on strengths plays a fundamental role in the bibliotherapeutic process. In the first place, the initiative for each step of the process lies with the participant. The facilitator can guide, but it is the individual participant who must recognize, examine, juxtapose, and integrate the feeling-responses and the understandings. . . . Moreover, progression from the first to the final step calls increasingly on the individual's strengths. . . . including (1) some ability to analyze issues, (2) sufficient honesty to look at the inner self, (3) enough objectivity to view a feeling or behavior pattern from another perspective, and, finally, (4) adequate self-confidence and hope to feel that change is possible and that one is personally capable of making such a change.
>
> Another way of making the same point is to say again that bibliotherapy is a process of *self-actualization*. Moreover, we consider the self-actualizing process to be one that not only enhances existing strengths but also corrects discrepancies. . . . (p. 58)

For gifted children at home or at school, in groups or as individuals, bibliotherapy is a way of building on the strengths of their reading abilities, analytical skills, and heightened sensitivity. It uses and enhances their ability to see relationships, draw conclusions, synthesize and evaluate. And it can give direction, focus, and purpose to their introspective self-awareness. Bibliotherapy should be seen not as a remedial step but as a positive, forward thrust toward the full use of the strengths these children possess — and, eventually, toward self-actualization.

REFERENCES

Bloom, Benjamin, ed. *Taxonomy of Educational Objectives: the Classification of Educational Goals.* New York: McKay, 1956.

Cornett, Claudia E and Charles F. Cornett. *Bibliotherapy: The Right Book at the Right Time.* Bloomington, Ind.: Phi Delta Kappa Educational Foundation, 1980.

Haney, R., Michael H. Harris and Leonard Tipton. Impact of Reading on Human Behavior: The Implications of Communications Research. [Part] VI. Bibliotherapy: Reading in a Therapeutic Context. In *Advances in Librarianship,* Melvin J. Voigt and Michael H. Harris (eds.). New York: Academic Press, 1976.

Hynes, Arleen McCarty and Mary Hynes-Berry. *Bibliotherapy: The Interactive Process: A Handbook.* Boulder: Westview Press, 1986.

Lack, Clara Richardson. "Can Bibliotherapy Go Public?" *Collection Building,* Spring, 1985.

Rubin, Rhea J. "Uses of Bibliotherapy in Response to the 1970's." *Library Trends,* Fall, 1979.

Schrank, Frederick A. "Bibliotherapy as an Elementary School Counseling Tool." *Elementary School Guidance & Counseling,* Feb., 1982.

Schrank, Frederick A. and Dennis W. Engels. "Bibliotherapy as a Counseling Adjunct: Research Findings." *Personnel and Guidance Journal,* Nov., 1981.

Slavson, S. R. *Analytic Group Psychotherapy with Children, Adolescents, and Adults.* New York: Columbia University Press, 1950.

Spache, George D. (1974). Using Books to Help Solve Children's Problems. In Joyce Rhea Rubin (ed.), *Bibliotherapy Source Book.* Phoenix, Oryx Press, 1978.

Tillman, Chester E. "Bibliotherapy for Adolescents: An Annotated Research Review." *Journal of Reading,* May, 1984.

Zaccaria, Joseph S., Harold A. Moses, and Jeff S. Hollowell. *Bibliotherapy in Rehabilitation, Educational and Mental Health Services.* Champaign, Ill.: Stipes, 1978.

5

Intellectual Development Through Books: Reading Guidance

In chapter 2, the point was made that for optimal intellectual development, gifted students must acknowledge and satisfy their desire to know. This chapter explores several ways in which adults can use books to help them accomplish this, all under the general heading of reading guidance. A major part of the chapter is devoted to the advantages of reading and discussing books, either with individuals or groups, to meet the intellectual needs outlined in chapter 2. The final section provides suggestions for teaching gifted students to satisfy their curiosity by becoming independent seekers of information.

Reading Guidance

Reading guidance may be defined as "the right book for the right child at the right time." It means being aware of what a child is reading, in terms of quality, content, and age-appropriateness, and being ready to offer suggestions for further reading that will move that child along with good literature at each stage of development.

Practicing reading guidance means watching a child read through the Hardy Boys series and being ready at the right time with a suggestion that he might also enjoy Alfred Hitchcock's short stories, and several years later a Leon Garfield novel and then Edgar Allan Poe — all filled with suspense but moving up the ladder of literary quality. Or noticing that a third grader has reread Laura Ingalls Wilder until it may be time to tell her about *Caddie Woodlawn*, and then the historical fiction of Scott O'Dell and Betty Baker. Later she might enjoy *Johnny Tremain* or *Across Five Aprils*, and eventually Willa Cather's novels of the American West. In addition, she could be encouraged to try biography or fiction about the history of other countries.

Parents are in the best position to offer such long-range reading guidance; teachers and librarians usually see only one to six or seven years of a child's development. They must work harder early in their relationship with a child to learn what he has enjoyed reading so that they can make suggestions that will interest and delight him and keep him coming back for more good literature.

Reading guidance involves stretching — always trying to suggest a book that will meet the child where she is now in the hope that when she finishes it, she will have grown a little. Those who guide reading do not deny the use of escape literature, but want the child to recognize it and know when she wants it and when she wants something more challenging — and then be able to find the more challenging literature.

The goal of reading guidance is to help students determine the kinds of literature they enjoy, use books to find information, and eventually guide their own reading independently.

For Gifted Readers

Guiding gifted readers is particularly important, because they have the potential to gain so much from books. They are also likely to respond enthusiastically, which makes helping them especially rewarding. Reading patterns of gifted youngsters (chapter 3) indicate the importance of guiding their reading early:

> They may teach themselves to read before they start school.
>
> Whether or not they are reading in kindergarten, they are probably independent readers by second grade at the latest.

By third grade, they may have identified their favorite authors.

By fifth grade, the habit of reading is well established, if it is going to be.

By sixth grade, their reading may diminish if they are among the many gifted youngsters who become involved in sports, computers, or fantasy games.

By late junior high, extracurricular reading may well have disappeared, although it may reappear later.

Adult influence on gifted children's *interest* in reading is limited primarily to the four years from second grade to sixth. Adult influence on the *quality* of children's reading lasts perhaps two more years — the important junior high years (longer for those who continue to read). Thus, time is precious indeed, and there isn't very much of it to introduce them to the wealth of children's literature. These are crucial years to stimulate imaginative thinking, to ensure that they will know some of the classics when they enter college, and to help them establish a pattern of reading to last a lifetime. Those early years are a time for subtle intervention, for suggestions, for sharing and passing on the enjoyment of reading. It is no time for well-intentioned adults to watch passively as mediocre reading habits unfold.

Reading guidance takes many forms. It can be so informal as the casual mention of a title or an author a parent has enjoyed, or the "floor work" that librarians do, talking with students as they browse the shelves. It can be a book talk carefully planned by a librarian or a teacher, or even a list of books from which students are required to select five to read each semester for an English class.

Although she is now the mother of teenagers, Ginny has warm memories of summers spent reading when she was a child and adolescent. Her mother had always enjoyed reading, and she was ready each year with suggestions of books Ginny might enjoy that summer. They were books she might otherwise have missed: Too Late the Phalarope; My Name is Aram; Madame Curie; Wind, Sand and Stars; A Death in the Family. *Some were in her mother's library; she found others in the public library at her mother's suggestion. She has less time now, but reading is still a source of immense pleasure for Ginny, in part a result of her mother's gentle reading guidance.*

The relationship between the student and the guiding adult is important for the success of reading guidance, as is the genuine love of the adult for books and the natural wish to share this pleasure. If these are present, then an adult can establish a reading guidance relationship with gifted students even without a formal program. Any adult who listens to a student talk about books she is reading, and is ready with suggestions for more good reading at appropriate times, can provide all of the advantages discussed in the next section.

What Books Can Do for Gifted Students

The needs listed in chapter 2 suggest that for optimum intellectual development, gifted children should be offered these experiences:

1. Challenge them to use their intellect effectively.
2. Expose them to a wide variety of people and ideas.
3. Provide flexibility, allowing for their individuality as people and as learners.
4. Give them opportunities to talk with intellectual peers.

There are many ways in which creative librarians, teachers and parents can provide an environment for gifted children that offers such experiences. Books can enrich that environment immeasurably, especially if students have an opportunity to talk about them.

Using Intellect Effectively

Many gifted children are able to move easily (not to say lazily) through the elementary grades without learning to make effective use of their intellectual abilities. They can listen with half an ear and pick up enough to stay up with the class. If this continues too long, they develop neither study skills nor thinking skills.

Daniel was a very bright child in elementary school and he shone in high school, graduating near the top of his class. No one was surprised when he was accepted at one of the most academically demanding eastern universities. However, he is not doing well there, although he is the same serious, purposeful student. He knows why: he has not learned to think analytically or to examine his assumptions. In grade school and high school, his answers were correct so often that few listened critically to what he was saying. Now, in a class of many other outstanding students, Daniel's lack of study and thinking skills is hampering his progress. His intellectual ability is not diminished, but he has not learned to use it effectively.

Expressing ideas freely. Their own interest in learning to use their abilities will be stimulated if gifted children are provided opportunities to talk about ideas in more depth than is possible in the usual classroom discussion or casual conversation. By using their vocabularies without restraint, and by sharpening their thinking in talks with knowledgeable others who can spot flaws and helpfully point to discrepancies in their reasoning, they will be encouraged to develop their verbal abilities.

Since gifted children have the ability to think critically, evaluate, and reason out unusual solutions to complicated situations, they should be able to voice opinions and ideas in an environment that respects divergent thinking, where their different approaches will be accepted and heard, rather than drawing negative responses from others.

During the Vietnam era, a fourth-grade class discussed sending bandages and soap to the people of South Vietnam. Jeff suggested that probably the same staple commodities were needed in North Vietnam. Could the class not send packages to both? This was so serious a departure from the norm that Jeff's father (mother would not do) was called in to discuss the situation.

Obviously, this was not a safe environment in which to express divergent opinions.

The sense of safety is terribly important to children whose intellectual abilities drive them to express thoughts which others may think are strange. It is, in fact, essential to their further intellectual growth.

Books provide ideas on which in-depth discussions can focus. In a discussion about a good book, children can follow up on the ideas the book has generated, feeling safe enough to express even half-formed ideas without fear of ridicule. With an understanding adult or in a group with other gifted children, they can feel free to exchange views without toning down their vocabularies and be enriched by these opportunities for regular dialogue with intellectual peers and bright adult friends.

Precise thinking. Too often, careless use of language and the lazy thinking it permits are accepted both in school and at home. Children must be free to speak the way their peers do, of course, but adults can do gifted children a great service by creating a milieu in which they can practice the exact expression of incisive, critical thought. In the process, they will be learning to think with improved precision. Just as they should learn the difference between "good" and "escape" literature, they should learn the difference between casual conversation and productive discussion of ideas so they can use each when appropriate.

In individual or small group discussions, the leader has opportunities to probe for exact statements, demanding penetrating thinking which produces greater understanding. This kind of questioning can be used in any context, but books provide an especially productive opportunity for it.

In a discussion of Sperry's Call It Courage *the leader asked, "Why is someone in the book alone or lonely?" When the response was a retelling of the events of Mafatu's childhood, she said, "You are telling the whole plot. I only asked, Why is someone in the book alone or lonely?" Nine-year-old Andy immediately answered, "Mafatu was lonely because he was afraid of the sea and everyone else was courageous," eliminating all extrane-*

ous information and zeroing in on exactly what the question asked.

Higher levels of thinking. In Bloom's (1956) taxonomy, the lower levels of information gathering and processing are knowledge, comprehension, and application. The more advanced levels of thinking, that gifted students should be encouraged to practice continually, are analysis, synthesis, and evaluation.

To develop the use of analysis, synthesis, and evaluation they should work with these processes, identifying each level of thinking as they use it. Open-ended book discussions conducted in an atmosphere that promotes respect for individual opinions can be rich training ground for higher levels of thinking.

For example, in leading a book discussion series with a group of sixth graders, their teacher might talk to the students about analysis, synthesis, and evaluation. As she asks questions about the books, she labels each one so the students know when they are analyzing, when synthesizing, and when evaluating. For the last meeting in the series, she may ask the students to bring three questions for discussion, one of each kind. The books provide the focus and the discussion group provides the opportunity for the students to clarify the meaning of each process and learn to use them independently.

Providing Wide Exposure to People and Ideas

When trying to describe the constant need of gifted children for new information, parents and teachers often find themselves using metaphors for food. "I've never known a student so thirsty for knowledge." "She is so hungry to learn." "He is a voracious reader." These are not just clichés; they reflect the impressions that eager gifted students make on observant adults. Indeed, knowledge, information, and new ideas are nourishment for their minds, and (perhaps unconsciously) they sense they are in danger of intellectual starvation without them.

Children can be exposed to people and ideas in many ways — through good television and movies, through plays and concerts, through travel in this country and others. While books cannot substitute for everything, they can offer an efficient and cost- effective way of exposing gifted children to a wide range of information, alternative ways of doing things, and different kinds of people.

Information. It is clear that gifted children should have access to many more subjects and concerns than are typically covered in the standard curriculum. The extensive range of nonfiction available for school libraries makes this an easy need to meet.

However, fiction is useful in this regard, too. Literature introduces children to times and places they will never see, and to lives they will not be able to live. It can expand their awareness of the variety of human concerns, styles, emotions, and ways of relating to others, and do it in a way that makes them care, opening doors to topics ranging from the Holocaust *(The Upstairs Room)* to the plight of migrant workers *(Roosevelt Grady)* or the struggle for education for blacks *(The Tamarack Tree)* — subjects that might not seem real if read only in history books or newspapers.

Alternatives. Gifted children enjoy a capacity for thought processing that includes the ability to think in alternatives, sense consequences, and make generalizations. To turn these abilities into skills, they must play with a variety of ideas, including some that may not be familiar to most people in their schools and neighborhoods. Opportunities to experiment with these ideas in exploratory conversations build both their abilities and confidence.

For example, during the reading of *The Arm of the Starfish,* a group of eighth graders might be directed to stop reading at designated points and write down whether Adam should side with Dr. O'Keefe or with Kali and her father, along with reasons for and probable results of their decision. They will then have the makings of a discussion that enables them to test their judgment and decision-making skills against the outcome of the book and against the ideas of their peers.

Books are laboratories for bright students, a proving

ground where they can reason out solutions to complex problems, examine the consequences of their decisions, and then try something else. Good fiction reflects life truly and, as in life, the outcome of the story can depend on one small decision or a series of events beyond one's control. There are always turning points that lead to the question, "What if . . . ?" Book discussions that consider "what if" invite the expression of divergent thought.

By suggesting books that approach an issue from several angles, adults can introduce new ways of looking at it and help students toward a broader point of view. Gifted children respond readily to this expansion of vision; through their broader awareness of human potential, they will learn what is possible for themselves.

Tolerance of others. A less obvious reason why gifted children need to be exposed to a variety of people is expressed by Clark (1983) when she says that gifted children have "an evaluative approach to themselves and others (p. 93)." She is tactfully saying that they can be highly critical, even intolerant, of people, including themselves, who do not measure up to their standards. They need to be aware that there are different abilities and talents, and different ways of solving problems. Exposure to a variety of people can help them develop tolerance, empathy, understanding, and acceptance of human weakness in others and perhaps also in themselves.

The world of literature not only provides an infinity of characters who exhibit human weaknesses and learn somehow to accept them, it introduces these characters in ways that make children care about them. Readers are drawn emotionally to them, or in bibliotherapeutic terms, they identify with them. From that identification gifted children can learn to accept human weakness as well as to celebrate human strength. Both the identification and the acceptance of weaknesses can be reinforced in a well planned discussion.

Providing Flexibility for Individual Needs

Gifted children are so different from one another and from other children that any home or school program must have enough flexibility to allow for their individuality. By encouraging voluntary reading and discussion, teachers introduce flexibility to the standard classroom format, meeting individual needs by allowing for accelerated thinking, slower processing, and delayed closure — all within gifted learners' capabilities.

Accelerated thinking. The thinking processes of gifted children are faster than normal, so the pace of a typical classroom discussion makes it an agonizing experience for many of them. It is a welcome relief for their pent-up frustration and boredom if for at least part of the time they are able to acquire knowledge at their own rate.

One of the wonderful aspects of reading is that it is a thoroughly self-paced activity. Skimming and rereading by turns, readers can move at whatever pace they choose. A reading program increases the amount of self-paced learning available to gifted children as soon as they become independent readers.

These youngsters should not only be able to learn at their own rate, but also be able to talk, at least part of the time, with others who also process at an accelerated pace. Book discussions provide this opportunity. For some gifted youngsters, it may be the only such opportunity available in this period of their lives.

> *Entering a new school at the beginning of sixth grade, Aaron found that both the curriculum and the pace of instruction were unchallenging and that the other children were slow to accept him. He spent as much time as he could in the school library, where the librarian soon identified him as an enthusiastic reader who responded warmly to her suggestions. She recommended books such as* Anthem, *that stretched Aaron's thinking. He began asking questions about the books when he returned them. Throughout the year, the books she recommended and the brief discussions after Aaron had read them enabled him to learn at his own accelerated rate despite the slower progress in the classroom.*

Slower processing. At the same time, gifted people are capable of comprehensive synthesis and can benefit from a rather long incubation period to integrate new ideas.

Some gifted children process information more slowly and deeply — and thoroughly — than others.

Reading and book discussion, if properly arranged, can accommodate this slower processing better than the typical routine of classroom assignments. If an adult discusses the concepts of incubation and slower processing time with these students, they can gain useful knowledge about their own work patterns and can learn to provide incubation time for themselves, for example, by planning to finish a book a day or two before meeting to discuss it.

> *Cindy is in the gifted program, but she is not sure she belongs there. While most of her classmates are racing to be first with the right answer, she is quietly going over information in her mind, connecting new ideas with already acquired knowledge. In book discussion, however, she is ready to speak with the rest and her well-formed opinions are respected by the group. When the teacher mentions that Cindy makes good use of incubation time, she begins to understand and appreciate the advantages of her slower processing.*

Delayed closure. Earlier than most, gifted children show the ability to delay closure, to accept a situation for which there is no immediate solution. Therefore, questions with single, final answers are not always appropriate for them. They are more likely to want to wait until all the information is in, to spend time looking at all sides of a question.

To develop this ability, they should be allowed to pursue their ideas and integrate new ones into their thinking without being forced to make final decisions or judgments immediately. They need open-ended discussion and open-ended situations to discuss.

In a book discussion final judgments are never necessary; in fact, one result of a critical book discussion will be the new insights it evokes. The process of interacting with the book may only begin with the discussion.

Further, some children's literature provides open-ended situations; such books do not come to final conclusions in order to let readers consider possible endings.

These books often have characters who are able to delay closure, and provide excellent discussion material.

The Beethoven Medal presents such an open-ended situation. Throughout the book Pennington displays first one and then the other side of his personality: the talent and discipline of the promising professional musician and the aggression and temper that have left him with a jail record. A second unresolved theme in the book is his relationship with Ruth. Gifted students can accept the lack of resolution and benefit from discussion of the complexities of human nature that the book presents.

Talking with Intellectual Peers

We all need friends with whom we can speak comfortably as equals. It is hard for gifted children to find such friends, even harder than for gifted adults, and it is impossible to measure what a difference it can make in their lives.

> *During the summer between seventh and eighth grades, Ben spent two weeks on a college campus at a summer program for gifted teenagers. He had never before been exposed to so many people with exciting ideas and the eagerness to talk about them. When the program ended, his parents and younger brother picked him up and took him out for dinner and then to a nearby campground to begin a family vacation. Ben was so stimulated by the campus experience that he talked about it nonstop through dinner and all the time they set up camp. He woke up the next morning still talking; it was late that afternoon before it was completely out of his system. Ben had discovered something momentous: There are other people like him. A new confidence began to replace Ben's long-standing sense of isolation.*

One reason the summer experience had such an impact on Ben is that it included older students. With comprehension advanced beyond their contemporaries', gifted children need contact with their intellectual peers of any age. It is essential for them to be able to talk with people who can challenge and stimulate them, and who respect their ideas. They do not need this all the time, but they must know that it is available to them often enough to make a difference. Adults who talk about books with them can provide intellectual peership during the awkward years some gifted children experience before they attend a high school or college where opportunities for finding intellectual peers of their own age improve.

These young people are socially aware, sensitive, and concerned with values and ideals at a surprisingly early age. They need to know others who can help them put these concerns into perspective so that they can develop a positive focus rather than becoming negative or cynical.

Parents, teachers, and librarians can suggest books that deal with social concerns and depict committed people taking positive action. Discussion about such books may help students to see serious issues from a problem-solving point of view rather than from one of hopelessness. Such perspective-building is a major benefit of discussion, especially with students in junior and senior high.

Meeting Intellectual Needs at Home through Books

Although parents cannot usually provide a group experience at home, they can meet many of the same needs through a loosely structured program of reading and conversation.

Moreover, by providing a favorable environment at home, parents can offer a haven to their children, a place where they can know they are safe to express their thoughts, ideas, and opinions without risk of censure. Parents can offer the psychological security that schools cannot guarantee.

Several books offer suggestions to parents who want to provide enrichment (Alvino, 1985; Graue, 1982; Moore, 1981; Saunders, 1986). However, although these publications mention the value of reading, not much is said about book discussion. By adding discussion to the reading, parents can use books not only for the pleasure which is their primary reason for being, but also to respond to their gifted children's intellectual needs and as a focus for thoughtful family conversation.

When parents encourage reading and promote book discussions at home, they will be doing their part to meet the intellectual needs mentioned in the preceding section and discussed below.

Using Intellect Effectively

At home a child should feel free to use the full range of her growing vocabulary, trying out new connotations as she tests the full meaning of words she has read. If she makes a mistake in pronunciation (common for children who pick up new words by reading as well as by hearing them), she can be corrected gently.

Parents can allow divergent thinking, recognizing that children need to try out ideas by talking about them. In this trying-out period, children may sound more convinced than they really are, and the parental role is to listen calmly, ask thoughtful questions, and offer their own opinions as something the child might want to consider. Books that provide facts and narratives of others' experience can help to direct discussion.

If enough time is allowed, book discussion leads to opportunities to consider ideas in depth. By asking follow-up questions ("What do you mean by that?") and identifying meaningless slang expressions when a child uses them, parents can help children think carefully and use language more precisely. Moreover, by asking questions that require analysis, synthesis, and evaluation, parents can challenge children to deeper thinking.

Without encouragement, gifted children may stop voluntary reading by the end of the elementary years. Family book discussion promotes intellectual growth merely by giving a reason for continued reading.

Providing Wide Exposure to People and Ideas

Parents who routinely take children to the library and help them select books expose them to a new world of people and ideas, particularly when they help choose books that open up new topics and points of view. When discussing these books, parents can guide children to think of alternatives so that they can predict and examine the consequences.

For children who have "an evaluative approach to themselves and others," parents may make a special effort to find books that promote sympathy for people in difficult situations. Librarians are always glad to make suggestions.

Providing Flexibility for Individual Needs

Simply by helping a child find books that interest her and are on her reading level, not necessarily her grade level, parents are helping to meet her needs.

Parents can consider with their children the meaning of an incubation period, and help them learn to recognize their own patterns of processing information. This self-knowledge will be useful in scheduling book discussions at home, and can be transferred to the scheduling of school assignments.

By allowing open-ended discussion and not expecting a conclusive answer, parents can give their children experience in considering diverse approaches to problems, confirming the value of different responses, and encouraging individuality.

Talking with Intellectual Peers

In a discussion of a book that both participants have read, the importance of age differences tends to diminish. If a parent has a genuine desire to know what the child thinks rather than a need to give his or her own opinion, then parent and child are starting the discussion as peers.

Parents who lack time for or interest in book discussion may find a relative or friend who can act as reading partner for their children. Although this means the loss of family interaction, it could be a mutually enriching relationship and a very satisfactory solution.

In a book discussion, whether group or individual, there is alway a triad: the leader, the child(ren), and the author. As gifted children grow older, they will find authors who can play the role of intellectual peers. Thus, parents who foster book discussion at home are setting the stage for continually introducing their children to potential peers.

If book discussions are offered at school, parents can reinforce them at home with their unique knowledge of their children. If not, home may be the only place where gifted children have the advantages of reading and talking about books.

Discussing Books with Gifted Students

In chapter 4, the focus is on book discussion designed to promote the emotional development of gifted children; here it is on promoting intellectual development. Goals and approaches differ, and there are special considerations in selection of children and books.

Reading Guidance with Individuals

Reading guidance in the form of book discussion with individual students can commonly be traced to a special relationship between a teacher or librarian and a student. The student may have come to her attention because of his reading — either the quality or the quantity, or both. Informal conversation about what he has read reminds the adult of a similar book which she enjoyed, leading naturally to suggestions of what the student might like to read next.

Often parents also provide reading guidance this way, particularly if they remember their childhood reading with pleasure. It is even more useful if they enjoy keeping up with recent juvenile literature so their suggestions include current titles as well as childhood classics.

Reading guidance with individuals that remains at this informal, casual level is valuable and can be a source of pleasure for both adult and student; however, it is usually sporadic. The adult might consider adding a bit of structure merely by asking the student to let him know when he finishes his present book so they can talk again. If it seems desirable, eventually meetings can be arranged on a fairly regular basis. For some gifted students these meetings, even if they continue only for a few months, could be a highlight of the school experience.

Book Discussion Groups

When I was in high school, one English teacher invited a few, maybe six, of us to form a small reading group. We met above the study hall in a loft used mostly for storage. At that time, the senior high did not even have a library; we stopped by the public library on our walk home to borrow the books we read for the group.

The group met for just part of one year, and I have only two specific memories of it: one girl said that her mother had told her that *Gone with the Wind* is not great literature (this was news to me) and we had to ask our parents' permission before we could read *Grapes of Wrath*. All the parents consented.

In spite of my sparse memories, I am sure that good things happened in that group. No one called it a group for gifted students; no one identified gifted students then, just before Sputnik. But it stands out in my high school experience along with the memories of sitting in the classrooms of superb teachers among whom excellence was the common thread. In that group, students truly were a part of excellence — trying to match the thinking of great authors with our own best thinking. Even under fine teachers, that did not happen in English class.

This group was an experiment in my high school, and I don't know whether it was considered a success, or even whether it was continued. Probably if I could listen now to one of the sessions, I would be disappointed in the quality of the discussion, but the sense of touching excellence has remained with me. Book discussion groups have the power to convey that sense, and they have that power even when they may seem not as successful as the leader would like.

Pulling gifted students together for a book discussion presents discouraging logistical problems. Teachers and librarians who attempt it and administrators who must approve the use of time for the groups will want to know that it is worth the effort. Some conclusions reached by Clark (1983) may help. After charting intellectual characteristics of gifted children, the needs they imply, and possible related problems, she offers organizational patterns and strategies. Her suggestions emphasize that gifted students need educational programs that offer small group discussion, flexibility, respect for ideas, time for reflection, and opportunity to compare communication and decision-making processes with academic peers. Adults concerned about appropriate use of valuable school time should be delighted to realize that small groups of students assembling to discuss books are meeting all of these requirements simultaneously.

Setting up discussion groups. Many of the suggestions for setting up bibliotherapy groups in chapter 4 apply to organizing groups for reading guidance discussions and do not need to be repeated here at length.

Even for groups designed for intellectual rather than bibliotherapeutic discussions of books, the selection of children should depend on their emotional development as well as on their reading ability. For younger children accelerated into older reading groups, it is especially important that their emotional level be weighed against the material to be read.

If children are pulled out of a regular classroom for a book discussion group, the leader may need to help them explain the group to their friends. The necessity for explanation depends on attitudes in the school about gifted children and specialized groups.

Other questions — group size and whether participation should be required or optional — are the same for these groups as for bibliotherapy groups.

The books, however, are not the same. Unconstrained by the goals of bibliotherapy, the leader of a reading guidance discussion group can choose from an array of books limited only by the desire to present books of the highest quality and intellectual challenge. The usual requirements for finding appropriate books apply: knowing children's literature and what makes a book especially appealing to gifted children, examining reviews, and prereading all books before recommending them.

The problems of having enough copies available at the right time remain the same, as does the question of free choice of reading for group members.

Place and time must also be considered. Privacy is not as important as it is in a bibliotherapy group, but quiet is necessary. The discussion should be in a place where students feel free to become thoroughly involved and to voice opinions with passion.

Timing the discussion is the same as with a bibliotherapy group, especially planning so students will not miss lunch, recess, or physical education.

Planning. This kind of book discussion group can incorporate drama, art, music, guest speakers, and projects along with discussion. The leader may plan for the group in the same way a teacher develops a lesson plan, introducing the children to the criteria for good literature so they can begin making their own informed judgments about books. The format the leader chooses will dictate the kind of planning necessary.

Questions for an intellectual discussion of a book should be as carefully prepared as they are for a bibliotherapeutic discussion, even though the stages of intellectual book discussion are not so thoroughly documented. Teachers and librarians may have their own procedure already developed, or they may use or adapt one of two well-known systems, Bloom's taxonomy or Junior Great Books.

Benjamin Bloom's *Taxonomy of Educational Objectives* (1956) lists the higher levels of thinking, those which book discussion with gifted children should emphasize, as analysis, synthesis, and evaluation.

Analyzing a book involves questioning some of the author's decisions. Why did he choose that form, setting, or organization? Are there inconsistencies or inaccuracies? How does he make the characters seem like real people? These questions may be difficult for children until they are in the late elementary or junior high years, when they reach the stage of thinking called "formal operations." Analysis questions might begin with phrases such as:

What are the parts of . . .

Which steps are important in the process of . . .

If . . . then . . .

The difference between . . . and . . . is . . .

The solution would be to . . .

What is the relationship between . . . and . . .

How would you have . . .

Synthesis means connecting elements from a book to each other or to knowledge the students have acquired, to create a new way of looking at the issues. Synthesis questions might begin with:

Can you retell this story from the point of view of . . .

How is a character from this book like . . . in . . .

Can you write a similar story that would . . .

Change . . . so that . . .

Develop an original plan for . . .

Good background music for a tape of the story would . . .

Evaluating a book or a decision requires making a judgment about it based on established criteria. The criteria can be developed in group discussion before the children are asked evaluative questions. Beginning phrases for such questions include:

What solution do you favor and why . . .

Appraise the chances for . . .

Which characters are best developed . . .

Which character would you like to be . . .

Which of these stories is the most believable . . .

Rank these books on the basis of quality of language . . .

Which situation required the most courage . . .

Although the Junior Great Books program was not originally developed for gifted students, it develops a seriousness of purpose in reading and offers a structured discussion format that makes it useful for such programs.

Junior Great Books discussions are offered either as an extracurricular activity or as part of the language arts curriculum, and are led by parent volunteers or by teachers. The two-day training course, offered in many locations around the country, prepares leaders to create the reflective, interpretive questions on which the discussions are based.

Trained teachers and parents are certified as Junior Great Books leaders and then may order the collections of books, which are not available in bookstores. There is a Junior Great Books series of twelve readings for each grade from second through twelfth, with two series each for grades three, four, and five. More information is available from The Great Books Foundation, 40 E. Huron Street, Chicago 60611.

Using the Library

Using books to foster the intellectual development of gifted children includes guiding them toward good literature, offering opportunities to discuss it, and teaching them to find the books they need independently. If gifted children are to learn how to use books to satisfy their craving for knowledge, they must be able to use libraries effectively.

Library skills don't have to be boring and tedious for teacher and learner. No one has to turn cartwheels to make library skills exciting, but there is one major trick: teaching at the right time. Teach each skill to children young enough so that what is being taught is at the cutting edge of their knowledge. This does not push them if skills are presented in small segments, and it avoids boredom for them and the teacher. No skill is so simple that it is dull when taught to an enthusiastic learner.

Library skills are dry only when taught in isolation. Teach each skill when students know they need it: how to use the card catalog when they first begin wanting to find their own books, for example, or the use of appropriate reference books when a report is assigned.

Teach developmentally, a little each year rather than waiting until students are old enough to grasp the entire concept. If gifted fourth graders learn to use the *National Geographic Index,* a good introduction to indexes because it refers to just one magazine, the concept of indexes to articles in magazines is a familiar one when they begin using *Readers' Guide to Periodical Literature* a year or two later. Learning to write bibliographical entries for magazine articles is just one more small step in junior high.

Certainly, ninth graders can learn to use the *Readers' Guide* all at once; but they will have missed the earlier opportunity to gain self-confidence in using the library, to have pride in understanding one more part of the adult world, and to enjoy the sense of independence that comes from knowing how to proceed — a reservoir of positive feelings about libraries and their own place in them.

The ideal time to teach children to use the library is during the elementary years, when they regard the library system as both a code which they can break and an exciting challenge. By junior high, the system appears just easy enough to be boring and if introduced for the first time at that age, few students pay enough attention to master it.

Unfortunately, elementary libraries sometimes lack adequate staffing. Too often a single professional librarian oversees the libraries in several elementary schools, leaving only library aides to assist when children come in. It is at the secondary level, where accreditation standards apply, that professional librarians are more frequently found. Parents who have gifted children in elementary schools without a librarian should learn how much they are being taught about library skills and ask for help at the public library if necessary.

What They Need to Know and When

If the basics of library use are taught in the elementary years, secondary students can focus on using the more sophisticated reference sources and learning correct bibliographic form, so that all of this comes naturally to them by the time they enter a college library with the assignment for their first freshman paper in hand. That is the real goal of teaching library use: to enable students to enter any library with confidence, free to concentrate on the information they are seeking rather than on the process by which they get it.

Early elementary. Primary children as early as kindergarten can learn that picture books are on the shelves according to the author's last name, making the connection between the letter on the spine of the book and the label on the shelf. First and second graders differentiate between fiction and nonfiction, and learn where these sections are in the library, as well as the location of magazines, encyclopedias, and dictionaries. They also learn the parts of the book (author, title, illustrator — actually the preparation for later bibliographic work) and how to select a book they can read.

Third and fourth grades. These are the busiest years in the library for gifted children. Third graders are ready to learn that nonfiction is in order numerically by subject, and that fiction is arranged alphabetically by the author's last name, and they begin to search purposefully for both.

After three years of watching the librarian go to the card catalog when they request a book on a specific subject, they are eager to use it themselves. They learn how to locate a card in the catalog, to find the call number on the card, and to decode the call number to find the book on the shelf. They discover various reference books in addition to encyclopedias. Folklore and biography are introduced as special forms of nonfiction, and they learn where biography is on the shelf. Third graders learn also where their favorite authors' books are shelved.

Gifted children can make a quantum leap in their ability to use the library during the fourth grade. Using the card catalog, they learn to identify the author, title, and subject cards and to follow the peculiarities of library alphabetization, and they can read a catalog card for bibliographic information. They learn the major classes of the Dewey

Decimal system and locate the books on the shelves, and learn how to use long encyclopedia articles effectively.

They can also use indexes in books, and in connection with a class project, use the *National Geographic Index*. And they begin to use the vertical file.

Fifth and sixth grades. Fifth and sixth graders begin to use cross references in the card catalog and can write author-title bibliographies for reports. They learn the finer points of the Dewey system, including how the decimal works (after they have had decimals in math) and where biographies, with only letters for their call "number," fit into the system.

Reference work branches out at this age. In connection with a class assignment, these children can use the *Readers' Guide,* following up by finding magazine articles on microfiche or in print form. They also use geographical and biographical reference sources and *Facts on File,* a compilation of information from magazines which is published every two weeks.

Junior high. Junior high students become more familiar with the *Readers' Guide* and learn the tricks of using the subheadings on the subject cards, looking up geographical and historical information in the card catalog. They can write complete bibliographical information for books. If they have not already done so, they should begin to use the public library as well as the school library.

Senior high. Gifted high school students who have newfound mobility and may begin using larger libraries should be introduced to the Library of Congress Classification system, as well as to the value of Sears and Library of Congress subject headings lists for research. They can branch out from the *Readers' Guide* to other, more specialized indexes for art, biography, science and technology, education, and the humanities. They are able to recognize and use more sophisticated catalog cards than the familiar author, title and subject, and they can write correct and complete bibliographies for books, encyclopedias, and magazine articles.

They should have the experience of writing at least one major research paper in high school. If it is possible for them to use a large college or university library for some of the research, that would be a fitting culmination of the process that began in kindergarten. They are ready to use any library in the country to satisfy a lifelong need to continue learning.

REFERENCES

Alvino, James. *Parents' Guide to Raising a Gifted Child: Recognizing and Developing Your Child's Potential.* Boston: Little, Brown, 1985.

Bloom, Benjamin, ed. *Taxonomy of Educational Objectives.* New York: David McKay, 1956.

Clark, Barbara. *Growing Up Gifted: Developing the Potential of Children at Home and at School.* 2d ed. Columbus: Merrill, 1983.

Graue, Eliza Brownrigg. *Is Your Child Gifted? A Handbook for Parents of Gifted Preschoolers.* San Diego: Oak Tree Publications, 1982.

Moore, Linda Perigo. *Does This Mean My Kid's a Genius?* New York: New American Library, 1981.

Saunders, Jacqulyn. *Bringing Out the Best: A Resource Guide for Parents of Young Gifted Children.* Minneapolis: Free Spirit, 1986.

6

Selecting Books for Gifted Children

Selecting books for children merits thought and effort. It is easy for them to pick up inexpensive books nearly everywhere they go. Some of them are excellent, but paperback racks in bookstores, groceries, and drugstores also display books of poor quality with enticing covers. Parents who monitor their children's television carefully may pay no attention to what the children are reading; they may not know what is good and what is not. (Monitoring reading, incidentally, is much more fun than monitoring television, because there are so many more alternatives to bad books than there are to bad television programs.)

In library work with children, a perennial issue is the quality of their reading. The premise "it doesn't matter what they read; if they only read, that's enough" has reason for defenders, but it does not apply to gifted children who have the capabilities to read books of substance and great literary value. It is the responsibility and pleasure of adults who guide their development to supply them with the most meaningful. Part of the pleasure is that there is a wealth of children's literature.

But what makes certain books especially appropriate for gifted children? Like the children themselves, the books they cherish have a special spark that adults can learn to recognize. This spark has been analyzed and codified so that it is possible to list the characteristics most desired in books for gifted children.

This chapter brings together ways to identify books that are not only good literature, but also appeal to gifted readers.

For Emotional Development

Finding literature that speaks to the emotional world of the gifted child requires knowledge of that world (such as the categories in chapter 1: establishing an identity, being alone, getting along with others, and using one's ability and intelligence) and knowledge of the ways in which books can reflect that world. Here are components of the spark that gives a book emotional appeal for gifted readers:

1. The characters are coping with one or more of the same problems the readers are facing, such as establishing an identity — learning how to be human in their own particular way. While few children are in exactly the situation of Laura, who learns that she is psychic in *And This Is Laura,* they can recognize her growing sense of who she is and what it means for her relationships with others.

   Characters may be in the process of accepting themselves as people who enjoy being alone, like Arvid, the introspective young king in *In the Time of the Bells.* Or finding friends as in *Jennifer, Hecate, Macbeth, William McKinley and Me, Elizabeth,* where Jennifer displays her own rather unusual method of making a friend when she needs one. Or making choices about their commitment to school work, practice time, or to their own talent, a theme which is especially well developed in stories set in a time when school conflicted with farm labor, like *Across Five Aprils* and *The Wolfling.*

2. The characters are not necessarily gifted themselves, or at least not labeled as such, but they stand alone or in a small group for their convictions. In *The Cat Ate My Gymsuit,* Marcy takes a stand against an administrative decision at school and

then finds herself, for the first time, part of a group as students who agree with her speak out.

3. A character may be different from his peers and learning to cope with the difference, which could be an interest, a family situation, a handicap or anything that sets that person apart. For Joshua Taylor in *A Time to Fly Free,* the difference is his extreme sensitivity to his classmates' cruelty toward living creatures. Through the understanding and support of his parents, he is able to work with an older man who helps Josh learn to use his sensitivity and to temper it with realism.

4. The characters may be learning to accept someone else who is different, as in *Summer of the Swans.* This is the story of a sister's affection for a mentally handicapped younger brother, affection not always shared by neighborhood children.

5. Adult characters should be present and supportive in at least some of the books. Much contemporary literature for adolescents depicts adults who are weak or absent, giving the young people more control over their own lives. They still need adult concern, however, and it is comfortingly present in books such as Garner's *The Stone Book,* in which Mary's father introduces her to her family's heritage, recorded in a cave she must enter alone.

6. Some **characters** should be gifted adults who lead productive and enjoyable lives, and in general function well as gifted people in the adult world. Tom Curtis in *Jazz Country* finds such people, jazz musicians as well as his father, who act as mentors while he works toward a decision for his own life.

7. Some of the child characters should clearly be gifted themselves, so that the reader can say "He's like me; I feel that way too; maybe I'm not the only one who thinks this way!" Several books in the annotated bibliography meet this criterion. A good example is *Willaby:* Willaby is so engrossed in her draw-

ing that she forgets what the assignment was. She is not called gifted in the book, but her intensity can be recognized by readers who understand what it is to be lost in their own projects.

8. Giftedness need not necessarily be labeled, but may be implicit, that is, comfortably accepted, and life goes on from there. It is clear enough in such stories of warm, lively, and supportive families as *Cheaper By the Dozen* and *May I Cross Your Golden River?*

9. Characters should be people to whom the reader can relate: open-minded, questioning, with a passion for learning everything or devoted to one subject of intense interest. Junior high boys with a strong interest in science and nature can easily understand why Mike Harrington, the amateur biologist in *A Heart to the Hawks,* cares so much for the pond near his home that he tries to fight the construction that threatens it.

10. Some books for gifted readers should depict characters struggling with issues of personal or moral courage, personal values, and moral and ethical choices. *The Witch of Blackbird Pond,* in which Kit Tyler, newly arrived from Barbados, befriends an old woman who is thought by the people of her village to be a witch, shows Kit's courage and also the greater moral struggle of her Puritan uncle.

11. Some books should have humor of a high level: spontaneously arising from a situation, springing from a character's way of looking at the world, based on intelligent use of language. An example is *A Day No Pigs Would Die.* The character Rob's humorous use of language is unconscious, but the author Robert Newton Peck clearly knows what he is doing. In her books about the Bagthorpes, a family of British eccentrics (*Ordinary Jack* and others), Helen Cresswell uses every opportunity to add a zany twist.

Of course, no one book can be expected to meet every item on this checklist, but a collection can. The goal is to keep the criteria in mind while gathering as many books as gifted readers have time to read. With the list as a guide, and experience and exposure to a number of excellent books, it is possible for guiding adults to develop an instinctive sense for books that will catch and hold gifted readers' interest and give them something to think about long after the books have been read.

For Intellectual Development

A fifth category of developmental needs for gifted children was added in chapter 2: for optimal intellectual development, they must learn to acknowledge and satisfy their need to know. Books that will help them achieve this goal must both satisfy and whet their curiosity, and be intellectually challenging. But just what does make a book intellectually challenging?

Two valuable books on this topic are Polette's *Picture Books for Gifted Programs* (1981) for young children, and Baskin and Harris' *Books for the Gifted Child* (1980) for readers from beginning levels to late junior high or early senior high.

Picture Books

Following the child development theories of Jean Piaget, Polette recommends looking for books for preschoolers and early elementary children that will help to develop visual, language, and thinking skills, and that will promote both productive thinking (fluency, flexibility, originality, elaboration, and evaluation) and critical thinking (planning, forecasting, decision making, and problem solving).

At first these expectations may seem unrealistically high for a picture book, but the best of them have much to offer, and a rich assortment will contain all of these elements. Picture books for gifted children should have the following characteristics:

1. Illustrations should be vibrant and original rather than stereotyped, and should not merely accompany the story line but complement and enhance it. Good examples are the books by Maurice Sendak, in which the expressions on the characters' faces tell the story from their own point of view.

2. Details of the illustrations should be so fascinating that a child can look repeatedly, and always find more: a surprise or a bit of humor, a private joke between the illustrator and the attentive child. Books by Anno and by Scarry are prime examples. *Anno's Alphabet* invites adults to join the game, challenging them to identify the plants and animals woven into the borders of each page.

3. Some books should be provided that offer abstract illustrations which, while recognizable, still require mental exercise to be understood. Anno is a good example here, too; his *Topsy-Turvies* offers optical illusions that engage the mind.

4. Illustrations should not supply all the details or information, so that some imaginative effort on the part of the child is needed to complete the picture. The *Look Again . . . and Again, and Again, and Again Book* supplies four challenges to the imagination on each page, as the child turns the book and rearranges the picture in her mind.

5. Books should introduce new and fascinating words, satisfying to the tongue as the child learns to say them, mixed in plentiful measure among the familiar words. Cuteness and condescension to the child's verbal level are neither necessary nor welcome; what is needed is respect for the child as an intelligent, learning person. Authors of good children's books about dinosaurs, for example, make the correct assumption that four-year-olds can pronounce Ichthyosaurus and Tyrannosaurus Rex.

6. Authors who obviously take delight in the use of language, whose books demonstrate a playful, joyful

sense of fun with words, appeal to gifted children. Dr. Seuss books encourage children to experiment with words, making them up as necessary and bending them slightly to create a rhyme.

7. Books should depict characters, whether animal or human, who display real emotions, feelings, and relationships the child will recognize. In *Alexander and the Terrible, Horrible, No Good, Very Bad Day,* for instance, Alexander displays frustration, anger, and finally resignation toward the kind of day he is having — a day in which ordinary, everyday disasters happen to him all day long, as they sometimes do to everyone. A similar example is *The Sorely Trying Day* — a title one earnest child turned into what seemed to him more appropriate: *The Trying-Hard Day.*

8. Plots that are not completely predictable allow for conjecturing and discussion between adult and child as the book is read. *Time to Get out of the Bath, Shirley* presents two plots, one about Mother and one about Shirley. Shirley's story is much the more interesting, full of surprises to anticipate.

9. Stories, pictures, and characters that are outside of the daily experience of the child can help to expand his world view. Ceserani's *Marco Polo* tells the story of Polo's journey supported by illustrations that are filled with detail and interest, presenting not only other countries but another time.

Books for Older Children

Baskin and Harris point out that books for readers (as differentiated from not-yet-readers), whether beginners or advanced, can be judged in terms of language, structure, and content. In all of these areas, books appropriate for gifted readers are complex rather than simple; rich and varied rather than predictable; and open-ended and thought-provoking rather than neatly contained.

In book selection as in curriculum, it is helpful to remember Maurice Freehill's insight that gifted children are "challenged by the unfinished and the misunderstood" (Freehill, 1961).

Look for the following characteristics in books that provide intellectual stimulation for gifted readers:

1. Language is on a high level, making strong demands on the reader's vocabulary. In Garfield and Blishen's retelling of Greek myths, *The God Beneath the Sea,* the level of language serves to ennoble the text. In *The Phantom Tollbooth,* humorous, pun-filled language is part of the message of the book: that language itself is a source of delight and challenge. In both cases, the language does more than present the story; it becomes an essential part of the reading experience.

2. Pronunciation guides are helpful for gifted readers (though they are rare, and a pleasant surprise when found) since so many of them know words only from reading and therefore mispronounce them. One excellent teacher of gifted high school students calls this "The Calley-ope (calliope) Syndrome."

3. Books for gifted readers can display the full complement of literary devices that enrich the fabric of literature and the reader (whether he recognizes them by name or not): metaphor, simile, paradox, symbol, allusion. Poetry does this by nature; one example in prose is *The Bat-poet* by the poet Randall Jarrell.

4. Look for masterfully-chosen descriptive words that stimulate strong visual imagery. Pearl Buck's books on China, for instance, including *The Exile,* help the reader to create a clear picture of a different time and a foreign place.

5. As with picture books, books for gifted readers should be written by authors who delight in the use of language as a tool for expression of nuances of thought and feeling, and who use it with skill. Joyce Carol Thomas's *Marked by Fire* is remarkable for

the way in which language — prose and poetry — evokes place and mood, moving the story along on an emotional level.

6. Language patterns and vocabularies from other times and places, used without apology or explanation, encourage the reader to glean the meaning from the context. Examples abound: Garfield's *Smith,* which evokes 18th Century England; the language of remote corners of modern Wales, as in Mayne's time-warp fantasy, *Earthfasts;* a language of the future as imagined by Ayn Rand in *Anthem;* or even a supposed language system of the past, as in *The Clan of the Cave Bear.*

7. The structure of a book can put the mind to work — flashbacks, narration that shifts from one person to another, or the use of journal format. A good example is Konigsburg's *Father's Arcane Daughter,* in which each chapter is introduced by a dialogue between unidentified characters, adding to the mystery while simultaneously supplying clues for the surprise ending.

8. The settings of some books allow children to experience vicariously lifestyles that are not their own; an example is the detailed descriptions of African village life in *Thirty One Brothers and Sisters.* Children growing up in small towns or rural areas can learn something of great art museums and of life in New York City from *From the Mixed-up Files of Mrs. Basil E. Frankweiler,* or gain a darker view of New York street life from *Slake's Limbo.*

9. If it is true that the gifted are challenged by the unfinished and the misunderstood, at least some of the books they read should present problems that are unresolved, even at the end of the book. Plots should cause the reader to look at a situation from different perspectives, and then reach some conclusion. At the end of *The Beethoven Medal,* for instance, it is still unclear whether Pennington will be able to con-

> trol his self-destructive impulses and become a successful pianist, and the future of his relationship with Ruth remains in doubt. The reader is left to ponder what desirable or likely options are available.

To challenge readers, a book should demand much of them. Baskin and Harris suggest that books for gifted children should require an imagination and a sense of humor, and assume some background either in reading or in experience. These students should have or be developing the ability to hold different levels of meaning in their minds simultaneously, and some of the books they read should give them experience in doing so.

Bloom's (1956) terminology helps to form a neat statement of the characteristics of books that offer intellectual challenge to gifted students: such books invite *analysis* of characters and events; *synthesis* of ideas from the book under discussion and from anywhere else in the reader's experience; and *evaluation* of the relationships, actions, consequences, alternatives, and possibilities found in the book and in the reader's interpretation of it.

One quick way of finding books that are intellectually demanding is to look for books from England or in translation from any of several foreign languages. Authors of children's books in many other countries assume more background and education on the part of the reader than many American children's authors do. There will probably be some colloquial terms unfamiliar to American readers, but the meaning of most can be determined from the context, and they add both to the challenge of the book and to its power for expanding the reader's knowledge of other cultures.

Again, it is obvious that no book will contain *all* characteristics listed for intellectually stimulating reading. However, if adults will keep the characteristics in mind while they read reviews and browse the shelves of young people's literature, they will gradually be able to gather a collection that will include these criteria in abundance — a collection that will be invaluable for the gifted children and young people who have access to it.

SUGGESTED BOOK LISTS

There are several good book selection guides available for parents and teachers looking for books to recommend.

Baskin, Barbara H and Karen H. Harris. *Books for the Gifted Child.* New York: Bowker, 1980.

Hearne, Betsy. *Choosing Books for Children: a Commonsense Guide.* New York: Dell, 1981.

Larrick, Nancy. *A Parent's Guide to Children's Reading.* 5th ed. New York: Bantam, 1982.

Polette, Nancy. *Picture Books for Gifted Programs.* Metuchen, N.J.: Scarecrow, 1981.

Waldhorn, Arthur, Olga S. Weber, and Arthur Zeiger. *Good Reading: a Guide for Serious Readers.* 22nd ed. New York: Bowker, 1985. (For senior high and older.)

REFERENCES

Baskin, Barbara H. and Karen H. Harris. *Books for the Gifted Child.* New York: Bowker, 1980.

Bloom, Benjamin S., ed. *Taxonomy of Educational Objectives.* New York: David McKay, 1956.

Freehill, Maurice. *Gifted Children: their Psychology and Education.* New York: Macmillan, 1961.

Polette, Nancy. *Picture Books for Gifted Programs.* Metuchen, N.J.: Scarecrow, 1981.

7

All the Wealth: Children's Literature

The comfortable phrase, "curling up with a good book," brings to mind the prospect of spending an evening with a thick novel — a romance or a mystery, perhaps an historical novel. Although we tend to think of fiction first, there is much more to reading than that, and adults should be prepared to introduce children to all of literature.

Within fiction there are several different types; there are also various categories of nonfiction. All of these are available to the child who wants to curl up with a good book — but only if he knows about them.

Four observations are particularly important to adults who use books for the guidance of gifted children:

1. Some children, especially as they grow older, resist reading fiction.
2. A lack of interest in this genre does not mean they must stop reading. There are many kinds of literature other than typical realistic fiction: nonfiction, biography, traditional literature, fantasy and science fiction, and poetry are all discussed in this chapter.
3. Gifted youngsters, like other children, must be introduced to the best in literature. They will not automatically find it on their own.
4. The different types of literature vary in their power to meet emotional and intellectual needs for gifted children, and their effect varies from one child to another.

> It is important that they be introduced to all kinds of literature, with enough exposure so that each child can decide which is most valuable for him or her.

Fiction will fall naturally into the hands of gifted elementary school children, but unless a planned effort is made to introduce young readers to other branches of literature, especially traditional literature and poetry, they may miss them altogether. Junior and senior high students need guidance, too, to become aware of the wealth of literature as they develop into adult readers. All literature is an important part of education — a key to histories, arts, and cultures, particularly for these youngsters who are more likely to draw information from many sources and integrate it in new ways.

Guiding the reading of gifted children, therefore, includes making them aware of the varieties of literature and helping them learn which kinds have most appeal for them. The resulting knowledge of books and of their own preferences is part of what makes a mature reader.

In elementary schools, the logical person to coordinate the introduction of literature through the grades is the librarian; not every elementary school, however, boasts a professional librarian with the time to plan and implement a program for introducing various types of literature at appropriate grade levels. Table 7-1, on page 133, summarizing an elementary literature curriculum used in the library of an independent school, may be useful. This chapter also offers background information for each literary type, as well as criteria for excellence in various genres. The children's librarian at the public library can suggest specific books in each category.

The information given here is presented with three questions in mind: What are the implications for work with gifted children? How should the literature be presented developmentally, as children grow from one stage to the next? How can adults who are just becoming familiar with children's literature most easily find the best?

In addition, for each type of literature there is brief background information. It is included to provide a quick

Table 7-1. K-6 Literature Curriculum

	Picture Books	Poetry	Traditional	Nonfiction	Fiction
Kindergarten	X	X	Folktales Fairy tales		Each genre is presented at the grade levels indicated by X or by the name of a type of literature
First grade	X	X	Folktales Fairy tales	X	
Second grade	X	X	Folktales Fairy tales	X	Realistic Fantasy
Third grade	X	X	Folktales Fairy tales Fables	X Biography	Realistic Fantasy
Fourth grade		X	Folktales Legends	X Biography	Realistic Fantasy High fantasy
Fifth grade		X	Legends Myths	X Biography	Realistic Fantasy High fantasy Historical
Sixth grade		X	Myths Epics	X Biography	Realistic Fantasy High fantasy Historical Science fiction

These are read aloud when classes come to the library.

These are introduced in the library through excerpts or booktalks.

summary, with the hope that readers will want to follow the suggestions for further reading at the end of the chapter.

Fiction

Fiction (called "realistic fiction" when fantasy is considered as a separate category) is the broadest body of literature, the earliest found by children exploring on their own, and the most easily judged by the traits given in the previous chapter. It comprises the bulk of the titles listed in the annotated bibliography in chapter 8, precisely because it is realistic — if well done, it portrays real life situations and characters who respond in ways that are true to the human spirit.

Since authors write about what they know, and many authors were gifted children, the characters in juvenile fiction are often gifted. Much less often is the giftedness pointed out; it is simply there to be recognized by child readers who see something of themselves in the story.

Types of Fiction

Realistic fiction can be divided into a number of subtypes: adventure, animal stories, mystery, sports stories, humor, romance, historical fiction, etc. Most of these can be thought of as one group, although historical fiction deserves special consideration.

How well each type suits the emotional or intellectual needs of gifted children depends largely on the author's point of view and on how well the books are written. Each kind, but some more than others, can be treated in ways that offer intellectual challenge or provide insights into emotional development.

Recognizing Good Fiction

Fiction that continues to appeal to new generations of young readers is that which speaks to their universal concerns, helps them explore themselves through the characters in books, and introduces them to life in other places and times. It does this by dealing honestly with the material and with its readers.

Honesty and accuracy are the two most important criteria for children's fiction. Settings must be described so that the reader can imagine them. Plots must relate something that could plausibly happen. Above all, people must react with understandable emotions and behavior; their speech must be true to their ages and experience and to the environment established for them in the story.

Beyond that, for fiction that has enough depth to engage the imagination of gifted children, something should happen within the characters during the course of the book. Even fiction for young children offers this: *Evan's Corner*, for example, is not just a story about a boy who needs a little privacy and is allowed to turn a corner of a room into his own space. It is also about Evan's getting everything he thought he wanted, and then realizing (the internal event) that it is not enough. He wants to share it, too.

Writers of historical fiction must walk a line between overburdening the plot with too much historical detail, and using so little historical background that the book amounts to a novel placed in an historical setting. The best writers base their books on serious research, and weave details gained thereby into the narrative to lend authenticity to plot and characterization.

For gifted readers, adults should recommend historical fiction that shows not only the culture and daily life of the period, but that also deals with some of the political and personal issues encountered by people of that age. An example is Esther Forbes's *Johnny Tremain*, in which Johnny, initially concerned with his burned hand, is gradually caught up in the political and military turmoil around him as the Revolutionary War begins.

Finding Good Fiction

Young children find a "good book" mostly by watching what their friends are reading. They may also be given recommendations by the school librarian or get ideas from what their teacher reads aloud. However, unless someone guides them to good books, their progress is haphazard at best.

Adults who want to recommend good literature have many more sources available, and can follow a more systematic procedure. Some of the sources are given in the references at the end of chapter 3 and under "Book Lists" in chapter 6.

Another rich source of information is the librarian's own reference collection. Here are found publications that list children's books by categories, often providing annotations or reviews for each. For most of these, inclusion equals recommendation; that is, they list only books that by some established standard merit recommendation to children. The public is usually welcome to use these references, but probably they cannot be checked out of the library.

Reference books for children's literature are useful in working with all of the kinds of literature mentioned in this chapter. Therefore, rather than giving specific titles here, a list of some of the best sources is provided at the end of the chapter.

Nonfiction

It may surprise some to know that at the end of a library story hour for primary grade children, when the children are free to find a book to check out, they are more likely to swarm to the nonfiction shelves than to the picture book shelves. No matter how attentively they have just listened to fiction or folklore, they appear to be hungry for fact in books they explore on their own. It may be that as nonreaders, they feel they can gather more information from the pictures of a fact book than they can from those in a picture book whose story they do not know.

Whatever the reason, it is obvious that even at that early age, nonfiction or "information" books are important to children, and this continues to be true as they grow older. With the introduction of new methods of teaching that require students to search for information beyond their textbooks, the number and quality of nonfiction books for young people have increased dramatically over the last three decades — a bonus of the educational reforms inspired by Sputnik. Gifted students in particular benefit from teaching practices that allow them to explore the views of different authors, in books that offer more information at a more challenging reading level than graded textbooks can.

For readers of any age, nonfiction written for children is a good introduction to a new field. If junior high students writing a report on continental drift, the human brain, economics, or another vaguely familiar topic can be persuaded to look first at books for children in the elementary grades, they will quickly grasp essential vocabulary and basic concepts. It will help them organize information gained later from more advanced books and articles. Some gifted students, particularly those whose enthusiasm for learning outweighs their adolescent self-consciousness, respond well to the suggestion that they return to the children's section in the public library for such a specific purpose.

Recognizing Good Nonfiction

It is not easy to write good nonfiction. Lacking a plot to maintain interest, the author must write with both a lucid style and a clear purpose. The author's attitude and reason for wishing to convey the information to young people become vital components of the book, providing a framework that may be nearly invisible but nevertheless gives shape to the contents. Furthermore, the simple appearance of the book, the format and the organization of the material, are important to attract and hold readers.

Beyond format, organization, and subtleties of style and attitude, there are the characteristics of good nonfiction — among them accuracy, readability, and especially for gifted readers, open-endedness.

Accuracy. Accuracy is absolutely essential in nonfiction. Several points should be considered in evaluating accuracy. The copyright date should be recent, especially if the book is in a field that is changing rapidly. The dust jacket or endpapers may provide biographical material on the author indicating his or her level of expertise. If possible, check the accuracy of a section of text that covers a familiar area of knowledge, or ask an expert to check it. Try to determine whether the author is writing from a biased point of view, keeping in mind that young children in particular are vulnerable: they are likely to ascribe authority to what they read simply because it is in print.

Look for accuracy in the graphic material, also. For illustrations in science books, a clear and precise line with correct labeling is needed. Photographs may be best for some social studies books, but they should be updated when the books are revised. Graphs and charts must be clear and current.

Readability. Since the appeal in nonfiction is to the intellect rather than to an emotional response, the author must be skilled in techniques that hold the reader's interest. Readability, the way in which the material is presented, is of paramount importance. Like a good teacher introducing a new subject by referring to related topics already familiar to the children, the author of a good nonfiction book will begin with an image or a setting that is familiar, then take the readers into new territory. A book for primary children on building barns, for example, might demonstrate stress factors with illustrations and text showing structures made of building blocks.

Nonfiction requires clear writing, logically and sequentially presented (the characteristics of left-brain thinking, according to current theories about brain function). In addition, writing for children requires some special techniques.

Because young children cannot yet think in abstractions, abstract concepts should be supported by concrete images, either in illustrations or by giving clear examples. A description of the structure of a bridge, for instance, should be accompanied by a drawing, preferably with the parts labeled. General statements must be followed by specific examples. Repetition is important for learning — authors should repeat key words throughout the book, and provide a summary at the end. The vocabulary should be accurate, reflecting the terms used by workers in the field discussed in the book. A glossary in books about specialized topics is always welcome. The writing style should flow comfortably, drawing the reader along.

Readability can be enhanced by the organization of the book. Maps, charts, graphs, drawings, and photographs increase readability and should be placed near the text they illustrate. An index helps readers to find their way around the book. And gifted readers should use some books that include bibliographies, to see what they are. They help as an introduction to the practice of documenting information.

Reading level — a book can be readable or not at any reading level — should also be considered. Often an assumed reading level is indicated either on the book or by its placement in a library or bookstore. However, gifted children with a strong interest in a topic will read beyond their grade level or even their measured reading level to learn as much as they can from a book that might otherwise be considered too advanced for them. They should, of course, have the freedom to select books for older readers along with those that are at a comfortable reading level.

Open-endedness. Finally, nonfiction for gifted readers should be open-ended. This may sound like a contradiction in terms for a fact book, but consider: Is the author clear about which statements are accepted facts and which are theories? Much of what we memorized as children — about space, genetics, paleontology, etc. — has been modified by newer discoveries. With their ability to delay closure, gifted children are receptive to lack of certainty and welcome the unknown as a challenge.

They should recognize the unanswered questions and methods used in current research and they should be stimulated to examine more deeply themselves. Does the author use an interdisciplinary approach, indicating points at which this subject leads into other, related topics? Is there some mention of the ethical questions that are being raised by new knowledge in the field?

Nonfiction and Gifted Readers

Gifted youngsters can and should learn to select nonfiction well so they can pursue their own interests through reading. It is a good idea to discuss with them the characteristics of good nonfiction books to help them make judgments about literature for themselves.

In some cases, gifted children may encounter obstacles in their search for books that match their interests. Adults who cannot believe that young children can really read so far beyond their age level may be reluctant to allow them to use such books, especially if they are expensive. Paul, for instance, discovered at the age of eight that his school library had purchased a new astronomical atlas. More than anything, Paul wanted to take that atlas home, even though he could hardly carry it. In addition to the question of a third-grader's reliability with a costly new book, the librarian had to consider that it was a reference book and could circulate only overnight. However, she knew Paul and understood his passion for science; arrangements were made. For months, he came to the library every Friday afternoon and checked the book out for the weekend, always returning it early Monday morning, always in perfect condition in spite of the winter weather. Paul certainly gained more from the atlas than the seniors for whom it had been ordered.

When librarians are not acquainted with children like Paul, parents or teachers may have to run interference, explaining why a child may need and merit special consideration. They may also help by coaching the child in how to respond to restricting rules.

Finding Good Nonfiction

Even armed with a list of characteristics to help select the best, a reader approaching the nonfiction section of a school or public library is likely to be overwhelmed by the sheer volume of material. It is worth the time to identify useful titles through reviews or booklists before turning to the card catalog. Reviews of nonfiction may be difficult to uncover because reviewing children's nonfiction is especially demanding — reviewers must be knowledgeable about the topic of the book as well as about good children's writing. Reviews and recommendations for nonfiction children's books can be found in the school library or the children's department of the public library. Reference books listed at the end of this chapter contain nonfiction sections or are entirely for nonfiction.

Lists of suggested nonfiction books are often found in periodicals, too. In fact, reviews for newly published books appear in periodicals first; it is usually at least a year before they appear in book form. The periodical *Booklist* presents nonfiction titles in its "Children's Books" section, in a separate nonfiction listing within the "Books for Young Adults" section, and in a third section, "Adult Nonfiction." In addition, journals for teachers often list a few new books for students among the book reviews.

Finding a review that makes a book sound ideally suited does not assure that the book will be on the library shelf. Readers should not be limited to books in the local school library or bookstore. Most titles can be ordered. With such a plethora of nonfiction available, some highly specialized, it is unreasonable to expect bookstores and libraries to stock enough for the varied needs of gifted readers. This increases the importance of finding and reading reviews.

Biography

Biography often becomes the favorite type of reading for gifted and mature readers as they grow older. Life stories of people who may also have been gifted can offer intellectually and emotionally rewarding reading for gifted adults.

Therefore, it is important that gifted children have a good introduction to biography. Like other forms of nonfiction, it is often assigned as part of a study unit, so most children are aware of biography as a separate kind of literature by the time they are in the upper elementary grades. The introduction can be made more interesting, however, by adults who know something of the various kinds of biographies and can teach the differences among them.

Types of Biographies

It is possible to classify biographies by placing them on a continuum with nonfiction at one end and fiction at the other. *Definitive biography* relies on historical evidence, containing nothing that cannot be documented. In the middle of the continuum is *fictionalized biography,* for which the author conducts extensive research and then invents dialogue or events that seem likely, based on the historical record. *Biographical fiction* is fiction based on the life of an historical person.

The characteristic that establishes biography most reliably on the continuum is dialogue. In a definitive biography, dialogue is rare, and occurs only when there is a written record of the discussion. For the most part, the characters "speak" only through their letters.

For fictionalized biography, the author is free to create scenes in which conversation furthers or dramatizes the action of the story. One library school professor described this type with a memorable example for a class in cataloging: "If there is a line like, 'After the last guest had left, Victoria dismissed the servants, retired to the royal suite, closed the door, turned to Albert, and said, ". . . .",' then you know you have a fictionalized biography."

In biographical fiction, on the other hand, conversation flows as freely as in any other kind of fiction, even between bit players for whose very existence there may be not historical record.

The type of biography children enjoy depends in large part on their age. For young children whose sense of history is not developed, biographies are stories that familiarize them with names such as Washington, Lincoln, or Martin Luther King. Older children enjoy both biographical fiction and fictionalized biography, and gifted senior high students should be encouraged to read some of the classic biographies such as Lytton Strachey's *Queen Victoria,* Marchette Chute's *Shakespeare of London,* or selections from Plutarch's *Lives.*

Recognizing Good Biography

Running the gamut from nonfiction to fiction, biography can be judged by some of the criteria used for each. As nonfiction, it must have accuracy and readability, with the added important element of objectivity.

Expectations of historical accuracy will depend on which type of biography the author has written. Even in biographical fiction, however, historical details should be authentic, as they should be in any good historical fiction.

A readable biography must bring an historical person to life, presenting characters as real people with human problems and responses. Small, intimate details make the biographee seem like a contemporary friend. Dialogue should flow as naturally as it does in a novel.

All nonfiction writers should approach their subjects with objectivity, but it is perhaps more difficult to be objective about people. Objectivity requires authors to maintain a balance between admiration and criticism for the biographee. Objective authors leave readers free to draw their own conclusions based on the facts; they do not suppress relevant but negative aspects of the principal character's life and place in history. Biography for children should show restraint and sensitivity in discussing character weaknesses, particularly when they are unrelated to the person's historical importance.

For gifted readers, one should look for human situations such as those in chapter 6 that meet emotional needs and for literary qualities given for books that meet intellectual needs. It is the blending of three strands of criteria — historical, personal, and literary — that determine quality in biography.

Finding Biographies

In libraries, biographies are usually shelved together in the nonfiction section, at the point where the number 921 would occur in the Dewey Decimal system. However, the call "number" is often a B followed by the last name of the biographee, so the books appear in alphabetical order by the person whose life they tell, not by the author.

The biography section may be astonishingly large in proportion to the rest of nonfiction. How to find the best? The sources suggested at the end of the chapter include sections on biography. Ask for the librarian's help, if necessary, to locate the biography sections in these listings.

Biography in Bibliotherapy with Gifted Students

The role of biography in bibliotherapy is a matter of some controversy. There are those who would recommend it as a way of presenting role models for young people. Others say that children cannot identify with adults until they reach adolescence; hence, biography could not be useful for bibliotherapy. There is the further objection that biography, like mythology, presents heroes of such dimensions that most readers are overwhelmed and left with no hope of emulating such a successful life (Groff, 1980).

While these arguments may be valid for young children, and perhaps for most children of any age, there are other considerations for gifted people in junior and senior high school. Biographies can be used with them with certain purposes in mind. These may outweigh any other objections.

One purpose is to demonstrate that many trials and failures often precede success. The biographies of scientists in deKruif's *The Microbe Hunters,* for example, provide evidence of the hours of preparation and even drudgery that must pay for the moment of discovery — and it is obvious that deKruif's scientists paid the price gladly, with lasting enthusiasm for their work. It is not difficult to imagine that this book might be informative, perhaps even inspiring reading for a gifted child who resists routine work.

Another purpose is to show the role of personal characteristics in achievement — characteristics that could be either evident or latent in the gifted child reading the book. *Carry On, Mr. Bowditch* is a good example, illustrating how Nathaniel Bowditch's inner drive, his energetic curiosity and thoroughness in inquiry helped him achieve far more than those who have so little opportunity for formal education usually accomplish.

In searching for appropriate biographies for gifted readers, one should look for this emphasis on the internal drives that propelled these individuals to become subjects of biographies. What is revealed about their motivation, moral imperative, intellectual curiosity, impulse to inquiry? What advantages did giftedness bring to them, and what problems? How did they turn their talents to their own advantage in coping with the problems? What evidence is there, if any, that they recognized their own gifts and consciously made use of them? What role did a sense of commitment, mission, or responsibility play in their achievements?

A third use of biographies with gifted adolescents is to provide them with examples of gifted people who experienced feelings of isolation and loneliness that readers can recognize. Gifted young people, especially if they sense their own giftedness, are quite likely to be able to identify with the aspirations and struggles of gifted adults — such as Marie Curie, studying alone in a Paris apartment so cold that one night she piled everything she could, including a chair, on top of her bed for warmth. Some gifted teenagers can understand that to Marie, the cold and the loneliness were incidental nuisances compared to the privilege of studying science at the Sorbonne. Rather than feeling overwhelmed, they can use such people as models without necessarily expecting themselves to achieve to the same degree.

Contemplating the potential grandeur of the wondering, reaching, striving human spirit is now rather out of fashion, but it is still necessary, especially for gifted people. Biography can be one of the most intellectually demanding forms of literature, but it can also be among the most inspiring. On both counts, it should be part of the reading program for gifted young people.

Traditional Literature

The literatures that have been passed from generation to generation from the beginnings of human culture include folk and fairy tales, fables, myths, legends, and epics. This rich heritage is now collected in many written versions, and modern children have it available to them in greater variety and from more different cultures than ever before. It is a vital part of the background of anyone who would hope to be truly educated. A knowledge of the Greek, Roman, and Norse myths (these especially for Westerners) will go far toward making young people feel at home with European and American art, literature, and history.

But at present it is an easily neglected part of our children's education. There is, sadly, little time for teaching literature in our elementary schools, apart from the excerpts that appear in reading texts, and even less time for traditional literature.

Most children will not find traditional literature on their own. When they swarm to the nonfiction shelves after the story hour, it is to science, technology, and craft books, not the mythology or folklore sections (which are also classified as nonfiction, strange as it may seem, because they are a way to learn about the cultures from which they come). Rare is the child who will ask where to find fairy tales or King Arthur stories, although they enjoy these stories when they are read to them. Traditional literature, therefore, must be actively introduced, or most children will grow up without adequate knowledge of it.

Introducing Traditional Literature at the Best Time

Presenting folklore, myths and epics effectively requires a knowledge of the ages when children are most likely to respond to them. Parents and nursery school teachers should begin by reading folklore, simple tales of the wisdom and foolishness of common people, to their three- and four-year-olds. Preschoolers love cumulative tales such as *The Three Little Pigs, The Gingerbread Boy,* and *The Little Red Hen.*

Fairy tales come next, appealing to children from about five to eight years old. Although the Grimm tales are the most familiar, there are many others in collections from different countries. Any concerns adults may have about violence in fairy tales can be allayed by reviewing the wide variety available — remembering Bettelheim's (1976) view that in their eagerness to see justice served and with their black-and-white view of the world, children are not nearly as alarmed by the violence as are adults.

By the time they are in fourth grade, gifted children should be introduced to some of the Greek and Roman myths. It may be difficult to believe that children can grow up without knowing these essential stories, but unless adults plan to prevent it, it will happen. The American Jack tales and other American folklore — Paul Bunyan, John Henry — are appropriate at this age, too.

Fifth and sixth graders are ready for Robin Hood and the Arthurian legends, as well as more Greek and Roman myths. Norse mythology can also be introduced at this age. Some sixth graders enjoy versions of the Odyssey and the Iliad, as well as legends from other countries such as Kate Seredy's *The White Stag,* the legend of the founding of Hungary — any of which could be read aloud in a classroom to enrich a history or social studies unit. These stories continue to interest some students through the early junior high years.

As American society continues to diversify, it becomes increasingly important to offer more than the familiar Greek and Roman myths. Norse mythology, Celtic legend, African tales, and Eastern European stories hold the cultural heritage of many children, some of it from so long ago that it is nearly forgotten. Books can give it back to them. Middle Eastern and Oriental traditional literatures represent the heritage of a growing number of children in American schools. A knowledge of these stories and others that appear in similar versions from different parts of the world help children understand their common humanity. In encouraging students to think of themselves as citizens of the world rather than having a provincial outlook, traditional literature is a valuable tool.

Recognizing Good Traditional Literature

By definition, traditional literature is the best of the ancient stories, those that have survived. In many tellings over the years, folk and fairy tales have been shaped and polished until when they have gathered and put into print during the last and current century. Myths and epics represent the highest literary achievements of their cultures. In a sense, the term "good traditional literature" appears to be a redundancy.

But this does not mean that every book on the shelves is a masterpiece. How to choose, especially for gifted children? Seek not one specific story or genre over another but *versions* written in the most demanding language, that can be characterized as most perceptive in delving into human character and into relationships among people and between human beings and their fate or their gods. The only way to judge is to read as widely as possible.

In choosing versions to share with children, one should pay foremost attention to the quality of the language. These tales, after all, represent the beginnings of our literary heritage, and the language should both respect and reflect the long history of refining these stories have undergone. Modern versions do not always serve them well; some of the wonder they stirred in their listeners centuries ago should linger in the present telling. Leon Garfield and Edward Blishen achieve this in *The God Beneath the Sea;* so do Rosemary Sutcliff in her version of *Beowulf* and Padraic Colum in his compilation of stories of the heroes who lived before the Trojan War, *The Golden Fleece.*

Illustrations, too, should convey a sense of the simple and eternal truths with which the stories are concerned. Banality and cuteness are too often found in children's books of fairy tales, but a little searching will yield books whose illustrations shine with dignity and grace. Examples of artists who illustrate traditional literature well are Kate Greenaway, Arthur Rackham, Barbara Cooney, and Adrienne Adams.

Finding Good Traditional Literature

Information about fine versions of traditional literature can be found in books about children's literature, which are typically published as textbooks for college courses in the subject. (See more on textbooks and a few suggested titles at the end of this chapter.) Local school or public libraries may have small collections of these. Traditional literature is also listed in the reference books on children's literature.

As with other "nonfiction," libraries usually carry much larger collections of traditional stories than bookstores do. In the nonfiction section of the children's collection, folk and fairy tales are found under sociology, Dewey Decimal number 398. Mythology may be shelved with religion in the 200s, since it was the religious literature of its culture, and epics in the 800s, with the literature of the country of origin. Each library may interpret the Dewey system slightly differently, however, so ask for help if necessary.

Many, many versions of the different tales are available. Here are a few examples that will appeal to gifted readers:

African	Aardema, Verna. *Tales from the Story Hat.* New York: Coward, 1960.
American	Chase, Richard. *The Jack Tales.* Boston: Houghton Mifflin, 1943.
	Harris, Christie. *Once upon a Totem.* New York: Atheneum, 1963.
Celtic	Sutcliff, Rosemary. *The Hound of Ulster.* New York: Dutton, 1963.
English	Picard, Barbara Leonie. *Stories of King Arthur and His Knights.* np: Walck, 1966.
	Pyle, Howard. *The Story of King Arthur and His Knights.* New York: Sharon, 1981.
	———. *The Merry Adventures of Robin Hood.* New York: Dover, 1968.
	Sutcliff, Rosemary. *Beowulf.* Magnolia, Mass.: Peter Smith, 1984.

Far East	Courlander, Harold. *The Tiger's Whisker and Other Tales and Legends from Asia and the Pacific.* New York: Harcourt, 1959.
Greek and Roman	Colum, Padraic. *The Golden Fleece.* New York: Macmillan, 1983.
	________. *The Children's Homer.* New York: Macmillan, 1982.
	Coolidge, Olivia. *Greek Myths.* Boston: Houghton Mifflin, 1949.
	Garfield, Leon and Edward Blishen. *The God Beneath the Sea.* New York: Pantheon, 1971.
	Picard, Barbara Leonie. *The Iliad of Homer.* New York: Oxford, 1960.
Norse	Colum, Padraic. *The Children of Odin.* Havertown, Pa.: Havertown Books, 1920.
	Coolidge, Olivia. *Legends of the North.* Boston: Houghton Mifflin, 1951.
	D'Aulaire, Ingri and Edgar Parin. *Norse Gods and Giants.* New York: Doubleday, 1967.
Russian	Ginsburg, Mirra. *Twelve Clever Brothers and Other Fools.* New York: Lippincott Junior Books, 1979.

This list is a mere beginning. There are many more collections and individual stories on the library shelves, giving evidence of the importance of traditional literature in portraying the human story. There is truly wealth in traditional literature. For some, it is the literary form most likely to move the spirit in the same mysterious way that art and music can do. Elizabeth Cook expressed this in *The Ordinary and the Fabulous* (1969):

> There is another door that can be opened by reading legends and fairy tales, and for some children, at the present time, there may be no other key to it. *Religio,* in one Latin sense of the word, implies a sense of the strange, the numinous, the totally Other, of what lies quite beyond human personality and cannot be found in any human relationships. This kind of "religion" is an indestructible part of the experience of many human minds, even though the temper of a secular society does not encourage it. . . . it may very well be in reading about a vision of the flashing-eyed Athene or the rosy-fingered Aphrodite that children first find a satisfying formulation of those queer prickings of delight, excitement and terror that they feel when they first walk by moonlight, or when it snows in May, or when, like the young Wordsworth, they have to touch a wall to make sure that it is really there. Magic is not the same as mysticism, but it may lead towards it; it is mystery "told to the children." (p. 5)

Fantasy and Science Fiction

For our older son's ninth birthday I went shopping, as usual, for a book. Browsing through the juvenile shelves of a favorite bookstore, I came upon a title that was then new to me: *The Book of Three.* Something about that title, something about the very feel of the book in my hand, told me that this was the book for David at this time and that there was something there for me, too, although that was not so clear.

The book was David's introduction to fantasy. He could not have had a better one. Later I learned that it was based on Lloyd Alexander's extensive knowledge of Welsh legend, part of my unknown heritage, and David's. Later still, after reading much more fantasy, mythology, and modern literature, David spent a summer studying Welsh at the University of Aberystwyth. His personal library now includes several titles in Welsh, and it will not surprise me if he returns to the study of that language in the future. All this might have happened in any case, but it is clear that *The Book of Three* reached David at just the right moment to catch his imagination, give it focus, and send it soaring.

Fantasy and science fiction can do this for some children. They discover it — and there is much of it for them — at just the age when they are entering their own personal quests for identity and beginning consciously to establish their personal values. The quest, and the attempt (sometimes failed) to live up to lofty ideals, are hallmarks of high fantasy. To judge from the avidity with which many young people read fantasy, it must be exactly what they need in the late elementary and junior high years.

Fantasy, Science Fiction, and Gifted Readers

Gifted readers are likely to read more fantasy and science fiction than average students; some children go through a stage lasting for several years, from the late elementary grades through junior high, when they read fantasy and science fiction almost entirely.

This becomes a source of concern for those parents and teachers who see it as escape literature and wonder whether the child will ever read "serious" literature again. It is an unnecessary worry; young people do move through this stage, and if they know how to distinguish good literature, they will continue with excellent choices in other areas. This is even more likely if they are reading *good* fantasy and science fiction.

Adults sometimes have more serious concerns that gifted children can become too engrossed in science fiction and live too much in a fantasy world. If a child is able to relate to others *only* through fantasy (only through games based on fantasy such as Dungeons and Dragons, for example), there is cause for concern. However, if this is only a part of his life and he has other ways of relating to friends, it should not be a serious worry.

The interest in fantasy should not be seen merely as a stage to be endured. What we are beginning to learn about right and left brain functioning may have intriguing implications here. It is too simplistic to say that rational, analytical, logical thinking is the function of the left brain, while intuitive, imaginative, mystical thinking originates in the right brain. However, this description of the brain at least provides a framework within which to consider how imaginative literature may promote intellectual development.

It appears that creativity has some basis in the ability of the individual to use both hemispheres of the brain, and in the flow of information from one hemisphere to the other (Clark, 1983). The productive use of acquired knowledge (left brain) apparently can be enhanced by our continuing ability to be imaginative (right brain). Undoubtedly, creativity is a product of integrating imagination and knowledge.

As children move through the grades in school and spend more and more time gaining factual knowledge, it is important that they also have opportunity to retain their imaginative functioning. Fantasy and science fiction provide such an opportunity. Perhaps this need to keep their imaginations alive is behind the voracious appetite some gifted young people display for this type of literature.

Introducing Fantasy and Science Fiction at the Best Time

For young children who have had a rich background in traditional literature in their preschool years, the introduction of fantasy may be barely noticeable. For adults who guide their reading, however, it is helpful to mark the inexact line between folklore and modern fantasy.

One way to clarify the difference is authorship. Traditional literature, true folklore, began as oral tradition and has no known author. The Grimm brothers did not write their tales, they collected them from those who were still telling them, in the oral tradition. Hans Christian Andersen, on the other hand, created his stories; they incorporate many elements of folklore but they are modern fantasy. Many authors since, such as MacDonald, Tolkien, Lewis, Alexander, Cooper, and LeGuin, whose works are mentioned here, have done the same, building a rich body of modern imaginative literature.

Fantasy. Elements of traditional literature linger in modern fantasy. Familiar characteristics of folklore and fairy tales blend over into fantasy in books such as A. A. Milne's *Winnie-the-Pooh,* in which animals talk, and P. L. Travers' *Mary Poppins,* in which the source of magic is not fairies but Mary Poppins herself. A child can move in easy stages from these early fantasies to modern fairy tales, fantasy based on time warps, high fantasy, and science fiction. With care, she can read excellent literature every step of the way.

For middle grade children, animal characters continue to appear in classic fantasies such as *The Wind in the Willows* and *Charlotte's Web,* echoing the talking animals of folklore. In George MacDonald's late nineteenth-century story, *At the Back of the North Wind,* the North Wind is a lady remarkably like a fairy godmother. Some fantasies written for this age group, such as Mary Norton's *The Borrowers,* feature characters who are miniature people, reminiscent of the elves and dwarfs of folklore.

The element of the time warp appears in Lucy M. Boston's *The Children of Green Knowe* and its sequels, and in Philippa Pearce's *Tom's Midnight Garden.* In these books, a contemporary child meets and plays or struggles with a child or children from the past.

There is much more fantasy for middle and upper elementary children than can be mentioned here. A few more titles will suggest the range: talking animals appear in Kipling's *Jungle Books,* Lawson's *Rabbit Hill,* O'Brien's *Mrs. Frisby and the Rats of NIMH* (which might also be classified as science fiction), and in Adams' *Watership Down,* an adult book that gifted children of this age enjoy hearing read aloud. Although these books are very different from fairy tales or magic, they are all fantasies.

For junior high readers another author worth knowing is Robin McKinley, whose retelling for older readers of "The Beauty and the Beast," called simply *Beauty,* is completely credible and compelling. The British authors Alan Garner *(The Owl Service)* and William Mayne *(Earthfasts)* also write fine fantasy for older readers.

High fantasy. By the fourth grade, many children have discovered C. S. Lewis's Narnia series, beginning with *The Lion, the Witch, and the Wardrobe.* There are seven books in this series, and as in most fantasy series, any one can be read independently of the others, although some children will want to read them in order. Written for middle-grade children, the Narnia series is the first experience with high fantasy for most.

It is in high fantasy that the protagonists are usually involved in a quest, drawn into it by forces beyond their control. They go willingly, but there is often some sacrifice involved and much learning; they grow up in the process of the quest. The theme is often no less than the epic and never-ending struggle between good and evil, the relationship between human beings and the gods, with ordinary human beings risking all, often alone, in their attempts to perform seemingly impossible tasks and to live up to high ideals. Authors of high fantasy typically spin out their tales in a series of books instead of a single volume because the theme and plot are so involved.

High fantasy is frequently based on mythology and legend, in particular Germanic and Norse mythology, the Welsh *Mabinogion,* and the Arthurian legends (which are Welsh in origin). This background gives it a mythical quality which heightens the effect of the quest theme and strengthens the potential for nobility and a kind of grandeur, even when humor is also present.

Both grandeur and humor are certainly present in the second example of high fantasy children are likely to meet: Lloyd Alexander's Prydain series, five titles beginning with *The Book of Three.* At this age (late elementary grades), they may also discover Ursula LeGuin's Earthsea Trilogy *(A Wizard of Earthsea, The Tombs of Atuan,* and *The Farthest Shore).*

Junior high readers enjoy Susan Cooper's series, which begins with *Over Sea, Under Stone.* They have probably already discovered Tolkien's *The Hobbit,* and some may attempt the trilogy that follows, *The Lord of the Rings,* although it is more difficult. McKinley's *The Blue Sword* and its prequel, *The Hero and the Crown,* for readers of junior high age and older, are also in the tradition of high fantasy.

Science fiction. At some time just before or during the

junior high years, students may shift from fantasy to science fiction. Or they may read science fiction without ever having read much fantasy. The line between the two is blurred.

One way to distinguish them is to remember that fantasy could not happen in the future because it includes imaginary creatures, while science fiction tells what might conceivably happen based on current scientific knowledge.

Science fiction, however, is evolving away from an emphasis on technological expertise to comment on what future societies might be like, based on present predictions regarding the environment, population density, and the likelihood of catastrophic war. It might be possible now to say that fantasy is concerned with the development of the

internal, intrapersonal world, and science fiction with that of the external, interpersonal world.

Science fiction is not often attempted for young children because the content is so complex. It is in fifth or sixth grade that students may begin reading John Christopher's trilogy, *The White Mountains,* and Madeleine L'Engle's *A Wrinkle in Time* and its sequels.

By junior high, gifted students will begin reading adult science fiction. Isaac Asimov's *Foundation* trilogy, Robert A. Heinlein's *Stranger in a Strange Land,* Ray Bradbury's *Martian Chronicles,* and Stephen Donaldson's *Chronicles of Thomas Covenant, the Unbeliever* (a series) are titles to recommend. There are many others.

Intensified concern for the quality of life will often prompt senior high gifted students more than others to become interested in reading utopian literature and also dystopian books, which are not about ideal societies but about society gone wrong. Aldous Huxley's *Brave New World* and George Orwell's *Animal Farm* and *1984* are examples of good literature in this category.

Recognizing Good Fantasy and Science Fiction

Good fantasy and science fiction are judged much like good fiction of other types. Plot, setting, literary style, and convincing characters are just as important. For gifted readers, the criteria for literature that meets emotional and intellectual needs listed in chapter 6 can be consulted.

One additional criterion, which may sound paradoxical, is that good fantasy and science fiction must be believable. The reader must be drawn into whatever world the author has created, and must believe in it; the created world must be consistent within itself. And the theme, the underlying thread that reveals the author's attitude toward the intrapersonal or the interpersonal world, must be based in truth.

Finding Good Fantasy and Science Fiction

As the preceding section indicates, there are excellent, prolific authors in both fields, and one way to find good fantasy or science fiction is to look for these and other books by the authors named.

To learn whether other authors are recommended, readers should consult the booklists suggested at the end of this chapter. Since not all of these references list fantasy and science fiction separately, a practical approach is to have an author's name in mind, and to search for that name in the fiction section of the reference book.

Usually, fantasy and science fiction are shelved with fiction on library shelves, but some libraries either shelve them in a special section or place stickers on the book spines with symbols identifying specific types of fiction.

Mythology, Fantasy, and Gifted Children

If this chapter has overemphasized traditional literature and fantasy, it is due to the belief that the former is neglected and the latter unfairly maligned, and that together they offer a vital mixture for the balanced development of gifted children.

Mythology and high fantasy in particular are accessible sources of a validation of the urge to strive for high ideals, to make commitments that cannot be justified on rational grounds, to find meaning outside of oneself. In our harsh world, it may be only in literature that some adolescents can find such affirmation. Especially for the gifted, with their emerging sense of the potential in themselves and the accompanying confusion about how or whether to reveal and use it, every possible source of affirmation must be recognized and encouraged.

Poetry

It is not difficult to introduce poetry to children, and the rewards are great; however, it does require a special approach. No matter how effectively they encourage children to explore other forms of literature, many adults may lose their enthusiasm when they consider introducing poetry. The result is that the children may also grow up feeling vaguely uneasy with poetry, not understanding it and not knowing how to approach it.

For any child, but especially for the gifted, this is a regrettable loss. For the very young child experimenting with sound and language, the stimulus of the rhythm and nonsense syllables of nursery rhymes is invaluable enrichment. Nursery rhymes may sound light and frivolous to adults, but they appeal to young children when they are at a critical point in their mastery of one of the most important tasks of early childhood: the acquisition of language.

The elastic mind of a child of four or five shows much more agility for learning foreign languages than does the more rigid mind of the adult. Adults who see little point in the repetition of Mother Goose rhymes may reconsider if they understand that a child's language ability is greater than their own, and the fascination with the sounds reflects the intelligence of the child working at the task of learning language.

The enjoyment of poetry as language may be reason enough to make the effort to use it with children. If more reason is needed, poetry can be considered in the same light as fantasy and science fiction: it helps to keep the imagination alive.

Poetry is one way to continue to stimulate mental processes such as intuition and imagery while the child learns to think more scientifically and literally. Music is another way, but children will be exposed to music in at least some forms whether or not adults make a conscious effort to introduce it. Unless someone deliberately shares poetry throughout the elementary years, most children will be left with a nursery school level of awareness of poetry — as serious a handicap, in its way, as it would be to enter junior high with "Three Blind Mice" as one's highest musical attainment.

Preparing to Introduce Poetry

Many children are offered nursery rhymes when they are preschoolers. From then on, however, their exposure to poetry may be limited to a few poems included in elementary school reading texts, or the poetry taught as part of secondary school literature courses. This is inadequate to develop the comfortable familiarity that springs from a love of poetry in an adult and turns into the same love in a child. For poetry more than for any other form of literature, adults must love it themselves or learn to love it in order to give it to children.

Adults who work with gifted children must realize that poetry has significant value for children in language development and imaginative thinking as well as in awareness of literature and pure enjoyment, but it must be continually kept in front of them as they grow older or they will lose it. They will surely discover books by Beverly Cleary, for example, in the second or third grade simply because Beverly Cleary is part of the culture of children of that age, but they are not likely to discover each new step in poetry for themselves.

Teachers know that they have to make an effort to find time in the day for poetry if it is important to them. It may be up to parents to keep poetry alive in their children if teachers cannot.

How can a teacher or parent achieve this, if poetry has not previously been part of her own life? She can go to the public or school library for books of poetry for children and books about children's literature. If children's poetry has never held much appeal for her, it is a good idea to read the poetry sections in the children's literature books first. One especially good book is *Literature for Thursday's Child* by Sam Leaton Sebasta and William J. Iverson (1975). Designed for teachers but adaptable by parents, it will surely send her back to the poetry books with energy and enthusiasm.

She can find poetry anthologies that she likes, both traditional and modern, take them home or to the classroom, and begin a pattern of reading a poem or two aloud, along with prose, at story time. A representative beginning would be Walter de la Mare's *Tom Tiddler's Ground,* Padraic Colum's *Roofs of Gold,* Nancy Larrick's *Crazy to Be Alive in Such a Strange World* and John Rowe Townsend's *Modern Poetry.* Inevitably she will develop favorites, and so will the children. When she finds herself or the children reciting lines spontaneously at appropriate moments, she will know that poetry is alive in her home or classroom.

Introducing Poetry

What is the different approach required for poetry? With other kinds of literature, teachers introduce examples to children as soon as they can read well enough to decode the language, and the children generally continue independently to find other examples if they are interested. However, until early adolescence, poetry is more accessible to children if they can hear it rather than read it silently, and they will need adult suggestions of poetry that will appeal to them. The different approach is to be more active in finding poetry to present, and to plan for time to read it aloud.

The teaching of poetry should begin with plenty of reading aloud until children have effortlessly learned a few poems "by heart." Gradually then, discussion can begin about the power of poetry. Rhythm, for instance, can be felt by the children when they are encouraged to sway with the lines of Stevenson's "The Swing," and they can hear how the words of David McCord's "The Pickety Fence" reproduce the stacatto sound of a stick being pulled along the top of a picket fence.

Generally it is thought that the teaching of poetry for young students should be imaginative (for example, through reading it aloud and then responding to it in movement or in drawing) rather than analytical (discussing such elements of poetry as meter and imagery), as it usually is for secondary students. Sebasta and Iverson (1975), however, give both arguments and methods for some analytical teaching of poetry to younger children. Other books about children's literature also suggest creative methods of introducing poetry.

Rather than teaching poetry, parents may be interested simply in reading poetry aloud, and teachers may wish to begin using poetry in the classroom by reading a poem each day. They need to know what kinds of poetry will hold the interest of children of different ages.

From Mother Goose rhymes in the preschool years, children in the primary grades grow to love humor and nonsense verses that play on words. Middle elementary children begin to enjoy ballads and other narrative poetry, and they prefer modern children's poems with ordinary, everyday language and content to traditional poetry. At all ages, humorous poetry is a great favorite — Shel Silverstein is always welcome. In order to explore the potential for emotional depth in poetry, lyric poetry should be presented as well. Junior and senior high students should take literature courses that introduce them to a variety of poets and types of poetry.

Recognizing Good Poetry

As the title of one book of children's poetry tells us, "It doesn't always have to rhyme." Poetry is not necessarily about rhyme; it *is* about rhythm, words, and the concise, even startling expression of thoughts and feelings.

The rhythms of poetry especially appeal to children, as they will demonstrate if they can clap their hands or bend their bodies to the movement of the lines. They should experience a variety of poetic meters and poetry with lines of varying length.

Words used in good poetry are vivid, evoking strong, clear images, like the opening line of Irene Rutherford McLeod's "Lone Dog":

> I'm a lean dog, a keen dog, a wild dog, and lone

that instantly creates a picture in the mind of the reader. They are also imaginative, perhaps made up for the occasion or used in a new context, like E. E. Cummings's words "Just-spring" and "mud-luscious" for his poem, "In Just-." For young children, Dr. Seuss books offer imaginative and creative uses of words.

Children, especially gifted children, respond well to poetry with unfamiliar words. There is little need to worry about a controlled vocabulary as long as the rhythm and the content of the poem carry the listener along.

The content of the poem — the humor, the narrative, the feeling expressed in lyric poetry — should use subject matter of interest to children: animals, friends, heroes, the stuff of their lives.

What is considered acceptable content for children's poetry has undergone a change in recent years, along with the change in fiction for young people. Contemporary poets are writing about city experiences and about the harsh realities of modern life, topics that would not have been considered appropriate for poetry, or for young people, thirty years ago.

There are advantages in this shift. Poetry thus becomes more accessible and immediate for modern young people, especially teenagers. The black experience as expressed in poetry has an added emotional appeal that may reach white adolescents in a way that no social studies class can.

Modern poetry also provides a vehicle of expression for the outraged idealism that is characteristic of gifted children and adolescents. It can provide a means of assuring gifted students that others share their moral concern, and a beginning point for discussion that will allow them to voice their own feelings.

Finding Good Poetry

As with every other type of literature mentioned here, recommendations for children's poetry books are found in the reference sources listed at the end of this chapter.

In the library, poetry is shelved in the Dewey Decimal 800's, the literature section; the 800's are subdivided by country, so that American poetry is 811, British poetry is 821, and so on. As with other types of literature, recommended books of poetry are listed in the booklists mentioned at the end of this chapter.

Many excellent anthologies and books by individual poets are available for children. A few are listed here:

Adoff, Arnold, compiler. *I Am the Darker Brother.* New York: Macmillan, 1968.

Aiken, Conrad. *Cats and Bats and Things with Wings.* New York: Atheneum, 1965.

Jones, Hettie, ed. *The Trees Stand Shining: Poetry of the North American Indians.* New York: Dial, 1971.

Larrick, Nancy, compiler. *Piping Down the Valleys Wild.* New York: Delacorte, 1968.

Lewis, Richard, ed. *The Moment of Wonder: A Collection of Chinese and Japanese Poetry.* New York: Dial, 1964.

Merriam, Eve. *It Doesn't Always Have to Rhyme.* New York: Atheneum, 1964.

Silverstein, Shel. *Where the Sidewalk Ends: The Poems and Drawings of Shel Silverstein.* New York: Harper & Row Junior Books, 1974.

Untermeyer, Louis, compiler. *A Golden Treasury of Poetry.* Racine, Wis.: Western, 1975.

Books about Children's Literature

The foregoing is only a brief introduction to the wealth of literature for children. As with the literature itself, there is plenty to read *about* children's literature.

Especially for Gifted Children

No attempt has been made in this chapter to suggest activities that introduce literature to children because there is plenty of material already available. Particularly helpful for work with gifted children is *Exploring Books with Gifted Children* by Nancy Polette and Marjorie Hamlin (1980).

Teachers who enjoy literature often have creative ideas for introducing it to gifted children. Many of these ideas are in print for local curricular use and some are published in pamphlet form to be shared with other teachers at conferences on gifted education.

Textbooks in Children's Literature

For parents who have never studied children's literature, for teachers who wish to refresh memories of their children's literature course, and for the many people who assist children in school libraries without the benefit of professional training, textbooks written for college courses in children's literature provide excellent background reading.

Textbooks offer much more information than is given here on the various kinds of literature, including plot summaries of hundreds of books and critical commentary. Many of them suggest activities for introducing literature to children in the classroom. Creative parents can adapt the ideas to home use.

Look for texts in the school or public library, or in the education library of a college if possible. Parents may wish to select a favorite for purchase, since they are really reference books; there is too much to absorb in one reading. The following texts provide a good introduction:

Donelson, Kenneth L. and Alleen Pace Nilsen. *Literature for Today's Young Adults.* Glenview, Ill.: Scott Foresman, 1980.

As the title implies, this book focuses on literature for young people "between the ages of 12 and 20."

Sebasta, Sam Leason and William J. Iverson. *Literature for Thursday's Child.* Chicago: Science Research Associates, 1975.

This book includes long sections on introducing nonfiction and fiction in the classroom.

Sutherland, Zena, and May Hill Arbuthnot. *Children and Books.* 7th ed. Glenview, Ill.: Scott Foresman, 1986.

This title has long been a classic in children's literature.

Essays on Children's Literature

Purely for inspirational reading, books written by authors and critics of children's literature are a delight, providing insight into the work of writing for children. Such books immeasurably heighten appreciation of the literature and reinforce the emerging recognition that literature for children is much more than mere child's play. Some recommended titles include:

Cameron, Eleanor. *The Green and Burning Tree: On the Writing and Enjoyment of Children's Books.* Boston: Little, Brown, 1969.

Cott, Jonathan. *Pipers at the Gates of Dawn: The Wisdom of Children's Literature.* New York: McGraw-Hill, 1985.

Egoff, Sheila, G. T. Stubbs, and L. F. Ashley. *Only Connect: Readings in Children's Literature.* Toronto: Oxford University Press, 1980.

Paterson, Katherine. *Gates of Excellence.* New York: Elsevier/Nelson, 1981.

Reference Books about Children's Literature

Here, at last, is the promised list of reference books about children's literature:

Adventuring with Books: a Booklist for Pre-K–Grade 6. Urbana, Ill.: National Council of Teachers of English, 1985.

A list of both fiction and nonfiction, this book gives annotations without reviews. Although it is published by the NCTE, it covers more than English or the humanities — there are sections on social studies, biographies, the sciences, the arts, and recreational activities.

The Best Science Books for Children. Washington, D.C.: American Association for the Advancement of Science, 1983.

Selected for children ages five through twelve, the books listed here are arranged by subject with brief annotations.

Children's Catalog, Junior High School Library Catalog, and *Senior High School Library Catalog.* New York: H. W. Wilson.

These three book lists are published every five years, with annual supplements. They classify nonfiction according to the Dewey Decimal system and provide both annotations and quotations from reviews. The Wilson catalogs may look daunting at first, but they are really quite easy to use and are very informative. Librarians will be happy to assist.

Children's Literature Review. Gerard J. Senick, ed. Detroit: Gale Research Co., 1976.

Now in 11 volumes, this reference offers excerpts from reviews, criticism, and commentary on books from preschool through high school. Each volume covers from 15 to 40 authors from all eras. Articles are long and include comments by the authors on their writing.

Cianciolo, Patricia Jean. *Picture Books for Children.* 2nd ed. Chicago: American Library Association, 1981.

Covering nursery school through junior high, this annotated list includes fiction, nonfiction, and poetry. There is also an essay on illustrations in children's books.

Gillespie, John T. and Christine B. Gilbert. *Best Books for Children: Preschool through the Middle Grades.* 3rd ed. New York: Bowker, 1985.

This listing of books that have been recommended in at least three respected sources of reviews of children's literature covers fiction and nonfiction for preschool through junior high. Biographies are especially easy to find here, with a separate section and an index.

National Association of Independent Schools. *Books for Secondary School Libraries.* 6th ed. New York, Bowker, 1981.

This is a book list arranged by subject, and offers titles of books to consider; however, no annotations or reviews are provided.

National Council of Teachers of English. *Your Reading: A Booklist for Junior High and Middle School Students.* New ed. Urbana, Ill.: NCTE, 1983.

Unusual in that the annotations are written for and to students, this listing includes fiction and nonfiction, with separate sections for humor, poetry, and other categories.

REFERENCES

Bettelheim, Bruno. *The Uses of Enchantment: The Meaning and Importance of Fairy Tales.* New York: Knopf, 1976.

Clark, Barbara. *Growing Up Gifted: Developing the Potential of Children at Home and at School.* 2d. ed. Columbus: Merrill, 1983.

Cook, Elizabeth. *The Ordinary and the Fabulous.* London: Cambridge UP, 1969.

Donelson, Kenneth L. and Alleen Pace Nilsen. *Literature for Today's Young Adults.* Glenview, Ill.: Scott, Foresman, 1980.

Groff, Patrick. "Biography: a Tool for Bibliotherapy?" *Top of the News*, Spring, 1980.

Polette, Nancy and Marjorie Hamlin. *Exploring Books with Gifted Children.* Littleton, Co.: Libraries Unlimited, 1980.

Sebasta, Sam Leason and William J. Iverson. *Literature for Thursday's Child.* Chicago: Science Research Associates, 1975.

Sutherland, Zena, Dianne L. Monson, and May Hill Arbuthnot. *Children and Books.* Glenview, Ill.: Scott, Foresman, 1981.

8

Annotated Bibliography

This bibliography is divided into five age groups: Preschool-Kindergarten, Early Elementary (Grades 1-3), Upper Elementary (Grades 4-6), Junior High (Grades 7-9), and Senior High (Grades 10-12).

Under each age grouping is a list of books in each of five categories:

1) Identity
2) Aloneness
3) Getting Along with Others
4) Developing Imagination (for younger children)
   Using Abilities (for older children)
5) Drive to Understand

The *Identity* sections list books that can be used to encourage gifted children to work toward a strong self-concept, accepting giftedness as a positive part of their identities. Remembering that they often feel different and somehow wrong, adults can use these books to help them be comfortable with their difference. This can occur even when giftedness is neither explicit nor even represented in a character in the book.

The *Aloneness* sections suggest books that can help gifted youngsters explore feelings of isolation. These books offer opportunities to assure them that requirements for time alone vary from one person to another, and that time alone can be both productive and necessary.

Under *Getting Along with Others* are books that facilitate discussion of interdependence, empathy, and respect for others with lesser or different abilities. In addition, some of these books promote an understanding of friendships and how they are formed.

For a number of reasons, gifted youngsters may not learn to use their full potential. In the sections for young children (Preschool-Kindergarten and Early Elementary) called *Developing Imagination,* books are listed that will stimulate thinking, observing, and questioning, keeping children in touch with the joy and power of using their imaginations. For older children and teenagers, the sections on *Using Abilities* offer books that raise questions about decision making, the responsibility gifted people have for their own talents, and the rewards that can follow the best use of those talents.

Drive to Understand is the most wide-ranging category, listing books that will challenge children intellectually and present them with ideas they may not otherwise encounter. The goal has been to suggest books that will both satisfy and whet the heightened curiosity of gifted children.

Many books, of course, can be included in two or more categories. For these, the annotations and comments are given under the dominant heading, but the books are also listed under other possible categories with discussion aids appropriate to each. Cross-indexing is provided. For example, a summary and comments for *Jacob Have I Loved* are found under Identity for grades 7-9, with questions relating to the search for identity. The reader is then referred to Getting Along with Others and Using Abilities. In these sections, he will find questions for the same book relating to those concerns.

Each annotation includes a brief plot summary, a few comments about the strengths and weaknesses and potential value of the book, and discussion aids. Discussion aids for preschoolers and kindergarteners (and in some cases for children in the early grades) are suggested themes that an adult will want to have in mind when talking casually about the book. For older children, specific questions are suggested to stimulate thinking.

The suggested questions are offered only as a starting point. In fact, for some books I have written questions for this bibliography with no particular child or group of children in mind, and then subsequently used the books with a discussion group — and found that with *those children* in mind, I have felt compelled to write an entirely different set of questions.

The questions suggested are the core or interpretive questions to be asked after children have warmed to discussion with some introductory questions. In planning a discussion, the leader can choose core questions that look promising and then plan appropriate introductory questions.

Finally, the decision whether a book is fit for eight-year-olds or ten-year-olds is always somewhat arbitrary. Many of these books can be enjoyed by children older and younger than the ages given.

Preschool-Kindergarten

Identity

Alexander, Martha. *Bobo's Dream.* Illustrated by the author. New York: Dial, 1970.

A wordless book in which Bobo, the dachshund, loses a bone to a larger dog. After the bone is retrieved by his master, a grateful Bobo dreams that he grows big enough to retrieve his master's football from a larger boy. When Bobo wakes up, the big dog returns. This time, bolstered by the new self-concept generated by his dream, Bobo stands up for his rights and the big dog shrinks away.

The child, not the adult, should tell the story from the pictures. This is a good book for a timid child (it is acceptable to stand up for one's rights) and for an aggressive one (a quiet assurance based on being in the right is enough).

Talk about how and why Bobo is different the second time the big dog comes, and why he doesn't have to fight to keep his bone. Has the child ever had an experience like this?

Charlip, Remy and Lilian Moore. *Hooray for Me!* Illustrated by Vera B. Williams. New York: Four Winds, 1975.

A joyful picture book celebrating the individual. The section on relationships with others can lead to discussion of how the child fits into his family and neighborhood. The section on identifying with things the child does ("I'm my dog's walker") is good for expanding from the book into the child's own life. No plot here, but wise use of the book will enhance the child's self-concept. Personalize the book, talking about your own family, your own neighborhood, and the child's place in it.

See also Getting Along with Others.

Heyward, DuBose. *The Country Bunny and the Little Gold Shoes.* Illustrated by Marjorie Flack. Boston: Houghton Mifflin, 1939.

The country bunny wants to be one of the five Easter Bunnies, but becomes a mother of 21 children instead. She teaches them to take care of the house and garden, and later she is selected to be an Easter Bunny because in rearing them she has proved herself to be wise, kind, fast, and clever. She also proves she is brave when she carries an egg to a sick boy on top of a mountain. The gold shoes are her reward.

This rather long and old-fashioned story still appeals to children. The special interest for gifted children is that Mother Bunny yearns to be more than the usual, and by attending to her daily tasks and performing them with excellence, she has her opportunity. It is tempting to turn this into a feminist story, but boys, too, can gain from attention to the routine and the unspectacular.

Discuss what is unusual about Mother Bunny, and ask if the child can name people who are like her. Consider whether she could be happy without being chosen to be an Easter Bunny, and why.

Hutchins, Pat. *Titch.* Illustrated by the author. New York: Macmillan, 1971.

Titch has an older sister and a bigger brother, and they have larger bicycles, noisier musical instruments, and higher-flying kites than Titch's. But more exciting than Pete's large spade and Mary's fat flowerpot is Titch's tiny seed, that "grew and grew and grew."

The lesson is clear: potential counts more than size, and young children who are constantly trying to keep up will be reminded of their own potential by this simple story.

What else grows besides seeds into plants? What will *you* be like when you get bigger?

See also Getting Along with Others.

Isadora, Rachel. *Willaby.* Illustrated by the author. New York: Macmillan, 1977.

Willaby likes to draw. She draws so much that she forgets to do her math, although she also likes math. She even draws on the playground during recess. When Miss Finney is sick, Willaby forgets to write a get-well card, even though she likes Miss Finney, and draws a fire engine instead. Then she worries that because she forgot to sign the picture, Miss Finney will think Willaby did not like her enough to send her a card — but of course, Miss Finney recognizes the drawing as Willaby's.

The child who becomes intensely interested in a favorite activity will understand Willaby, and discussion of this book may help both child and adult to put his interest in perspective. Questions to consider include why Willaby wants to draw more than most people, whether it is all right for her to draw so much, and the advantages and disadvantages of strong interests for people who have them.

See also Developing Imagination.

Keats, Ezra Jack. *Peter's Chair.* Illustrated by the author. New York: Harper & Row, 1967.

Peter is experiencing the pangs of sibling rivalry. His cradle and his crib have been painted pink for his new sister, and his father is painting his high chair even now. But his old chair has not been painted, and Peter decides to run away with a few treasures, including the chair and his dog Willie. Once everything is pleasingly arranged on the sidewalk outside his house, Peter tries to sit in his chair — and finds that he has outgrown it. Returning home, he offers to help his father paint the chair for Susie, too. Peter has learned that he is growing up.

Even if there is no new baby in the house, this story can lead to conversation about ways in which a child is growing up. What other signs indicate growing up, besides growing larger? How does *this* child know she is growing older?

Kraus, Robert. *Owliver.* Illustrated by Jose Aruego and Ariane Dewey. New York: Windmill Books, 1974.

Owliver wants to be an actor. His mother encourages him, but his father wants him to be a doctor or a lawyer. Owliver acts out all of these options, but in the end he becomes a fireman!

In a light humorous way, this book introduces a dilemma that is more familiar to the adult than the child, and will remind the adult of the futility of making a child's decision, as well as of the critical role of parental encouragement.

Point out how important it is for people to be what they want to be, to make their own decisions. Even among children, this is important. Is it important for the child to accept the decisions of playmates or siblings?

Lionni, Leo. *Pezzettino.* Illustrated by the author. New York: Pantheon, 1975.

Pezzettino ("little piece" in Italian) is so small that he is sure that he must be part of somebody else. In his search for the larger creature of which he must be a part, Pezzettino discovers that he too is made up of smaller pieces. He is not part of anyone else; he is complete in himself.

It is easy for a child to identify with Pezzettino, small and unsure of his place in the world. In addition, the child's imagination will be stimulated by Lionni's colorful, abstract illustrations.

Discuss what Pezzettino learns: that regardless of his size he is a whole person. List other examples (pets, plants). Why is it hard to be small for Pezzettino? For anyone? Discuss what Pezzettino means when he says "I am myself!" and why it makes him so happy.

Sendak, Maurice. *Outside Over There.* Illustrated by the author. New York: Harper & Row, 1981.

A fantasy told with pictures as much as with words, this is the story of Ida, who rescues her baby sister from the goblins, who turn out to be babies, too.

Ida is intuitive, resolute and brave, a girl of about six who knows her own mind and does what needs to be done.

The illustrations are full of details to be pored over and discussed.

The impact of this book is emotional rather than intellectual. The strengths in Ida's character may speak for themselves, but adults might wish to reinforce the child's awareness of the traits she represents by mentioning what is admirable about Ida, how her baby sister and father feel about her, and why. Perhaps a time can be recalled when the child showed some of Ida's qualities.

See also Developing Imagination.

Sharmat, Marjorie Weinman. *I'm Terrific.* Illustrated by Kay Charao. New York: Holiday House, 1977.

Jason Everett Bear tells himself and others how terrific he is, but this gains him no friends. So he changes his approach: instead of doing everything right, he does everything wrong, annoying others in the process. Finally he decides he is neither terrific nor terrible; he can be just Jason Everett Bear. His friends welcome Jason Everett Bear just as he is.

This is one of those books that provide catch-words that parent and child can use to identify different moods and behaviors long after the book is read. Develop the idea of being "terrific" (showing off) or "terrible," and how anyone can change from one to the other depending on what kind of day she is having. Be sure to talk about being just Jason Everett Bear — just yourself — and help the child identify when she is doing that so she can begin to recognize how it feels.

See also Getting Along with Others.

Sharmat, Marjorie Weinman. *The 329th Friend.* Illustrated by Cyndy Szekeres. New York: Scholastic, 1979.

Bored with himself, Emery Raccoon invites 328 friends to a picnic lunch, but they are all so busy talking to each other that no one talks to him. So Emery takes his lunch inside and converses with himself as he eats, finding that he is not so boring after all. When he goes back outside, his guests are looking for him, and the party ends successfully.

Emery has learned that he is a good friend for himself, and that makes it easier for him to feel that he is liked by the others — a double boost for his self-concept.

Talk about what Emery has learned about himself, and about the positive traits the child has, naming reasons other people like her and how she knows they do.

See also Aloneness, Getting Along with Others.

Viorst, Judith. *Alexander and the Terrible, Horrible, No Good, Very Bad Day.* Illustrated by Ray Cruz. New York: Atheneum, 1972.

The youngest of three brothers, Alexander goes through a day that includes finding nothing in his cereal box (his brothers find treasures in theirs), having the only cavity when they go to the dentist, and learning that the store has sold the last sneakers of the color he wants. The day goes from bad to worse, and the only solution seems to be to move to Australia. But, says his mother, some days are like that — even in Australia.

In spite of Alexander's awful day, when he rolls over to go to sleep the reader knows that tomorrow will be better. Some days are indeed like that, and even young children can learn that when they have a day like Alexander's, it does not mean something is wrong with them.

Parents can use this concept also to express to children when *they* are having a bad day. Recognizing the feeling and learning that tomorrow probably *will* be better is a step toward maturity.

Aloneness

Hill, Elizabeth Starr. *Evan's Corner.* Illustrated by Nancy Grossman. New York: Holt, Rinehart and Winston, 1967.

Living in a two-room apartment with a family of eight, Evan wants a space of his own. His mother suggests that he choose a corner for his own place, and Evan adds a picture, a plant, and a turtle. When his brother Adam asks why he wants a corner of his own, Evan says, "I want a chance to be lonely," and when Adam asks if he can come into Evan's corner, Evan helps him choose a corner for himself. But Evan is not entirely happy in his corner, and his mother understands why: "Maybe you need to step out now, and help somebody else."

Evan's story illustrates simply and beautifully the need to balance time alone and time with others, a lesson that gifted people must learn over and over. This book introduces the concept in terms a preschooler can understand.

Why does Evan want to have a chance to be lonely? What is good about being alone? How does he know when he has had enough time alone? What do you do when you need time alone? What do you do when you have had enough?

See also Getting Along with Others, Drive to Understand.

Lionni, Leo. *Frederick.* Illustrated by the author. New York: Random House, 1967.

Frederick is a field mouse who sits alone while the other mice store food for the winter. When they chide him for not working, Frederick responds that he *does* work: while they gather food, he is gathering sun rays, colors, and words. The others are reproachful, but in the winter when they are cold and hungry, Frederick is able to warm and nourish them with his words evoking the sun and the colorful flowers. Frederick is a poet, and the mice know that he offers more than food.

The torn-paper illustrations and the simple wisdom in the story make this book a favorite. Some children will empathize with Frederick's day-dreaming and his avoidance of tasks, but they may learn to value "alone time," which may very well be a new concept for them, needing reinforcement from an adult. Frederick's quiet acceptance of himself as he is, even though it sets him apart from the others, is a quality some gifted children have even at this age. For them, it is good to see the other mice learn to value Frederick's special contributions to the group.

What makes it all right for Frederick not to work with the others? Can the child tell you when she feels like Frederick, thereby identifying her own need for time to reflect?

Sarton, May. *A Walk through the Woods.* Illustrated by Kazue Mizumura. New York: Harper & Row, 1976.

The poet, her dog and her cat take a walk through a spring woods. Different moods are shown by the dog: "Speed . . . Speed is what I need!" and the cat: "A walk is a quiet thing. Don't wait for me. I'll be along, wild and alone, in my own good time." Each enjoys the walk in his or her own way, and while they stay separate, each also enjoys knowing the others are there.

Talk about what they see on their walks, what you and your child see on your walks (birds, flowers, rocks, insects), and about the joy of walking and observing which can be as much fun as running and shouting with friends.

Sharmat, Marjorie Weinman. *The 329th Friend.* (See Identity for full description.)

In discussion, reinforce Emery's discovery that he is not boring. How is Emery a good friend for himself? When are you a good friend for yourself?

See also Getting Along with Others.

Tresselt, Alvin. *Hide and Seek Fog.* Illustrated by Roger Duvoisin. New York: Lathrop, Lee and Shepard, 1965.

The fog approaches from the ocean and stays for three days, keeping the lobstermen and sailors off the water, and children inside by the driftwood fire.

The text and the illustrations by Roger Duvoisin blend beautifully to evoke the calmed, quiet, introspective mood induced by a heavy fog. If the book is read slowly, thoughtfully, liltingly, both child and adult will pick up the mood of cozy settledness.

Discussion can focus on the warm inside feel of a rainy or foggy day, the quiet pleasure of working alone on a favorite project, the contentment of playing alone but knowing there are people in the next room or coming home soon. The child who can appreciate such experiences is on the way to becoming a self- reliant person, capable of being at peace with himself.

Getting Along with Others

Charlip, Remy and Lilian Moore. *Hooray for Me!* (See Identity section for full description.)

Following up on the "I'm my dog's walker" theme, list with the child who she is to other people, developing her sense of place and importance in her world, however alone she may sometimes feel.

Clifton, Lucille. *Everett Anderson's Friend.* Illustrated by Ann Grifalconi. New York: Holt, Rinehart and Winston, 1976.

This is the story of how Everett Anderson finally admits that new neighbors can be a pleasant surprise even if the family does have all girls, including Maria who can beat him at races. Eventually, Maria is even welcome to play with Everett and Joe and Kirk.

Told in verse, the story has gaps which the child can fill with his own inferences.

Maria provides clear evidence that the way to have a friend is to be one. Preschoolers can understand her natural friendliness toward Everett in spite of his rejection of her — and the happy result.

Hill, Elizabeth Starr. *Evan's Corner.* (See Aloneness for full description.)

Why is Evan not completely happy in his corner? Will he want to go back there after he helps Adam decorate his corner? Why is it important to step out and help somebody else? How can someone who enjoys being alone also be a friend?

See also Drive to Understand.

Hoff, Syd. *Who Will Be My Friends?* Illustrated by the author. New York: Harper & Row, 1960.

Looking for friends in his new neighborhood, Freddy finds that the adults are friendly but busy, and the children ignore him. Undiscouraged, Freddy plays alone with his ball, throwing and catching it in full view of the other children. When they notice how well he handles the ball, they ask him to join them.

The obvious messages in this book are that it is easier to be accepted if we have something to offer to others, and that it is sometimes necessary to take the initiative in order to find friends. There are more subtle messages, however: Freddy does not force himself into the children's game; rather he quietly lets them see what his skills are. He seems to understand their reluctance to accept him immediately without being hurt by it.

For a young gifted child who feels rebuffed, this book can demonstrate that if we offer ourselves and our skills to others without being presumptuous, it is easier for them to accept us. Discussion about this will require a light approach, just a suggestion by the adult and then listening for response from the child, which will guide the duration and direction of any further dialogue.

Hutchins, Pat. *Titch.* (See Identity section for full description.)

How can big children help little children? Is there anyone smaller than you whom you can help/be kind to?

Sharmat, Marjorie Weinman. *I'm Terrific.* (See Identity section for full description.)

Can your child recognize when other children are being "terrific" (showing off), or "terrible" (behaving badly because they feel bad about themselves), or just being themselves? If he can begin to watch for this, it will be a big step toward understanding and empathizing with others.

Sharmat, Marjorie Weinman. *The 329th Friend.* (See Identity for full description.)

In talking about Emery's liking himself and being liked by others, help the child to see the link between the two. It might also be possible to discuss the link between being bored and being boring. When you are unhappy with yourself, how do you treat other people? Why is it easier to be a friend when you are pleased with yourself?

See also Aloneness.

Steptoe, John. *Stevie.* Illustrated by the author. New York: Harper & Row, 1969.

All the time Robert's mother is taking care of Stevie while his mother works, Robert resents Stevie. While Robert is in school, Stevie plays with his toys. After school, Stevie trails along after Robert like a little brother and disrupts his play with his friends. Only when Stevie's family suddenly moves away does Robert begin to focus on the good times he had with Stevie.

Discussion should bring out the fact that we all have strong and weak points, and it's best to look for the good in others — while we can still be friends with them.

Wilt, Joy. *A Kid's Guide to Making Friends: A Children's Book about Social Skills.* Illustrated by Ernie Hergenroeder. Waco, Tex.: Word, 1979.

This book introduces concepts that can be useful for children who feel awkward with other children or who do not make friends naturally. In three chapters (What Is a Friend?, How to Make a Friend, How to Keep a Friend), it offers specific attitudes and behaviors that foster friendship. Interspersed are questions relating each point to the reader and his own potential friends.

Introductory pages indicate a religious orientation that is not mentioned in the body of the book, so parents and teachers can use it or ignore it. The text will seem plodding to a gifted child, and adults may choose to use the book freely rather than page by page. It is recommended as a good summary of concepts relating to friendship.

The points made are numbered and repeated for clarity. Once they enter the vocabulary of a family or a classroom they can be recalled whenever pertinent.

Developing Imagination

Carroll, Lewis. *Jabberwocky.* Illustrated by Kate Buckley. Niles, Ill.: Albert Whitman, 1985.

Kate Buckley illustrates Lewis Carroll's famous nonsense poem from *Through the Looking Glass* as the story of a boy who bravely slays a fearsome beast and returns home to a joyful reception from his father, who has warned him about just such creatures. The simple story line will appeal to preschoolers, as will the words of Carroll's poem, which sound as though they ought to make sense but don't quite.

The illustrations suit the words. Buckley's creatures look almost but not quite like recognizable animals. The slithy toves, gyring and gimbling in the wabe, are especially endearing. The final illustration shows boy-hero and father headed toward home against an evening sky, leaving the mome raths outgrabing still — a return from imaginative adventure to secure reality.

To avoid confusion, using this poem with a preschooler may require clarifying the fact that both words and animals are imaginary, just for fun. This is a thoroughly delightful book; enjoy it.

Cole, Brock. *The King at the Door.* Illustrated by the author. Garden City, N.Y.: Doubleday, 1979.

Little Baggit believes the stranger who appears at the inn and says he is the king, so in spite of the landlord's skepticism, Baggit gives the stranger food, drink, warm clothing, and his own donkey to ride home. Little Baggit even believes when the stranger says he will return the next day to take Baggit to live at the palace — and to the landlord's chagrin, he does!

The story is told with delightful repetition, even to the steadily decreasing subtlety in the sarcasm of the landlord.

The gifted child can enjoy his comments each time Baggit gives something more away, which at first are compliments and then only *sound* like compliments at first hearing: "You're sharper than a frog's tooth."

This book is verbally stimulating, worth reading for the sheer fun of it and for the sly wit of the landlord.

Crews, Donald. *Carousel.* Illustrated by the author. New York: Greenwillow, 1982.

With pictures of a carousel and a calliope created as collages and then photographed by a moving camera, Crews gives the impression of the movement and sound of a carousel in this brief but memorable book.

The book invites children to relate their memories of riding or seeing a carousel to the feelings triggered by the pictures, a synthesis of visual imagery and physical experience.

Crews, Donald. *Freight Train.* Illustrated by the author. New York: Greenwillow, 1978.

The only words in this book identify the kinds of cars in a freight train and their colors, and then where the train goes. The impact is produced visually by means of the illustrations, and the effect is amazingly emotional for such an austere format. The illustrations give the sense of a train slowly gathering speed and then racing through tunnels, past cities, over trestles until it is gone.

Reading it aloud, an adult will hear speed and volume increasing in her voice, and will almost hear the whistle. The child will have an experience in visual and sensory imagery.

Hutchins, Pat. *Rosie's Walk.* Illustrated by the author. New York: Macmillan, 1968.

"Rosie the hen went for a walk . . . and got back in time for dinner." The text is deliberately commonplace; the real story is told in the illustrations. The child watches in suspense as the fox nearly catches Rosie over and over again, landing in positions of ever greater indignity as the story goes on. Rosie is blissfully unaware of all this, giving the child the opportunity to be in on a secret as she tells the full story to an adult.

Although this is not a wordless book, it offers the same advantage of encouraging children to "read" the pictures and tell the story in their own words, and to laugh at the understated humor of it all.

Isadora, Rachel. *Willaby.* (See Identity for full description.)

Discussion about the importance of developing one's imagination might include considering how much time people who excel in a particular activity should spend on it. What does the child like to do so much that people don't understand how much time she spends on it? What could help them understand?

LeGuin, Ursula. *Leese Webster.* Illustrated by James Brunsman. New York: Atheneum, 1979.

Soon after spinning her first web and admiring the traditional, practical design, Leese asks herself, "I wonder why a web can't be a little different now and then?" She experiments with new patterns, taking ideas from the old carpet and paintings in the ruined castle that is her home. Other spiders scorn her creations, but Leese does not mind. When the castle is renovated to become a museum, cleaning women find the webs, which are assumed to be tapestries and are displayed behind glass. Leese is thrown outside where she continues to spin, enchanted by the additional beauty of dew on her webs in the morning sun.

Leese's question, why can't it be different, is one gifted preschoolers should be encouraged to ask. Leese not only models independent thinking, she carries through, making the best of meager resources — the designs in the room which are her inspiration. She can be used as an example when adults wish to stimulate divergent thinking.

Mayer, Mercer. *A Boy, a Dog, and a Frog.* Illustrated by the author. New York: Dial, 1967.

Pictures tell the story of a boy and his dog who fail so spectacularly to catch the frog that they go home in disgust. The frog watches them go and, disappointed, he follows their soggy footprints all the way home, up the stairs — and with great joy joins both boy and dog in the bathtub.

This wordless story offers humor on every page, in the situations and in the facial expressions, especially the frog's. A delightful story for a preschooler to read and tell.

Sendak, Maurice. *Chicken Soup with Rice.* Illustrated by the author. New York: Harper & Row, 1962.

For each month of the year, Sendak's cheerful child has a sound reason or an exotic place for enjoying chicken soup with rice, and he tells it all in memorable verse. There is no story here, but rhyme, rhythm, and the fun of the ridiculous.

Sendak's imagination and intuitive sense for childhood make his books especially appropriate for gifted preschoolers. Adults are sometimes startled by Sendak's ideas, but his books stand the test of time, perhaps because of his inherent respect for (and lack of fear of) the imagination of the child. This book can be used for the sheer fun of it. The poems are easily memorized and could be the subject of a car game in which family members recite the poems for each month in turn.

Sendak, Maurice. *Outside Over There.* (See Identity for a full description.)

With its fairy-tale quality, this book is recommended for its potential to stir the child's imagination, both visually and verbally.

Sendak, Maurice. *The Sign on Rosie's Door.* Illustrated by the author. New York: Harper & Row, 1960.

In the long summer days before every family had a television set, children had to amuse themselves by using their own imagination. In this skill, Rosie is the neighborhood leader. She is so inspiring at imaginative play that she brightens the lives of the other children too.

For the child with a vivid imagination, Rosie is a role model. She wants to be the center of attention, but she is a good sport when attention shifts. She puts her imagination to good use for herself and others, and she is valued for it.

Sendak's illustrations show a variety of emotions on the children's faces. What do they think of Rosie at various points in the story? How is Rosie feeling as the story moves along? When is she a good sport, even though it would be difficult to do so? How does she use her imagination to bring fun to a potentially dull day? To turn aside disappointment? How does the child do the same? How could she?

Drive to Understand

Anno, Mitsumasa. *Anno's Alphabet: An Adventure in Imagination.* Illustrated by the author. New York: Crowell, 1974.

A wordless alphabet book that invites looking and looking again, like all of Anno's books. Each left-hand page has a letter of the alphabet, painted as if cut out of wood, often with a twist that catches the mind and requires analysis. The right-hand pages show pictures of objects that can be named, discussed, and observed. The borders offer insects, birds, and plants whose names also begin with the letter being considered. The back of the book offers a guide identifying some of the objects in the borders, which will challenge adult readers to find them. Invite the child to join you in the search.

Anno, Mitsumasa. *Anno's Counting Book.* Illustrated by the author. New York: Crowell, 1977.

This wordless book begins with a snowy landscape for zero. The "one" page shows one adult, one child, one tree, one building, then two of each, progressing to 12. In the meantime the seasons change, the clock tower shows the time for each number, a tower of blocks counts by tens, and the trees, buildings, and people offer enough variety for many discussions with much observing, identifying, and counting. There is always something more to see in Anno's illustrations, and the child will enjoy looking with an adult and then alone.

Anno, Mitsumasa. *Topsy-Turvies.* Illustrated by the author. New York: Walker-Weatherhill, 1970.

This is another of Anno's visually rich, wordless books, full of double-page spreads of optical illusions, mathematical impossibilities, and incongruities to tease and expand the imagination. Children will need time to look — silently. Adult input will be to reinforce the wonder, the open-minded approach required, and an appreciation of the variety of possibilities Anno presents.

Hill, Elizabeth Starr. *Evan's Corner.* (See Aloneness for full description.)

Especially for children not familiar with cities, the illustrations in this book reveal the profusion of inner city life in details of home, streets, shops, and playgrounds. Evan is able to cope with it, and he is part of a stable, loving family.

See also Getting Along with Others.

McDermott, Gerald. *Anansi the Spider: A Tale from the Ashanti.* Illustrated by the author. New York: Holt, Rinehart, and Winston, 1972.

Anansi the Spider is a folk hero to the Ashanti people, a rogue who escapes trouble through his wits, rather like Br'er Rabbit. This colorfully illustrated Anansi tale tells of how his sons, each with a special talent, come to his rescue when Anansi is lost and swallowed by a fish. An argument ensues over which son should have the reward for the rescue: a shining white ball. Since the spiders cannot reach a decision, Nyame, the God of All Things, takes the ball into the sky where it shines forever as the moon.

The illustrations are characteristic of McDermott's work, brilliantly colored geometric shapes creating distinctive images. Children love the story and will ask for it again and again. *Anansi* is a good introduction to non-European folklore for preschoolers.

MacDonald, Golden. *The Little Island.* Illustrated by Leonard Weisgard. Garden City, N.Y.: Doubleday, 1946.

Life on the little island in the ocean includes spiders and chuckleberries, lobsters and seals, kingfishers and gulls — and a kitten who comes to the island one day and learns the secret of how an island is really a part of the land.

The rhythmic prose and award-winning illustrations make this book a delightful way for children to learn what an island is. The kitten reflects the child's sense of wonder, imagining what she cannot see: the island connected to all the land underneath the sea.

Scarry, Richard. *Richard Scarry's Best Counting Book Ever.* Illustrated by the author. New York: Random, 1975.

Because Willy Bunny has nothing to do, Father suggests that he count whatever he sees during the day and report to Father in the evening. Willy and his friend Sally count up to ten watermelons and then review before going on to the teens. After they count 19 pigs having a picnic, the counting goes on by tens to 100 fireflies that evening. Each page shows the correct numbers of items for child or adult to count, and the items themselves beg to be examined for identification, small visual stories, and humor.

Discussion of this book provides familiarity with the sounds of number words and the order of counting, as well as the opportunity to see objects in manageable groupings. Ninety carrots are shown five on each plate, for example, and there are enough plates in the double-page picture to see exactly how many carrots it takes to make 90.

Preschoolers will not necessarily count to 100 independently because of this book, but better than that, they will be introduced to mind-stretching numbers concepts.

Scarry, Richard. *Richard Scarry's Best First Book Ever.* Illustrated by the author. New York: Random, 1979.

Each page of Scarry's book is filled with pictures for discussion with labels to promote vocabulary building. A very slight story line carries the Cat family through a day that allows Scarry to touch on colors, counting, letters, and shapes as well as everyday events such as housework, school, shopping, trips to the doctor's office and a farm, and more. The book presents a wide range of information for discussion and plenty of detail for sharp eyes to search out, with an adult asking questions to guide the search. Children can then spend time alone with the book, looking for more.

Spier, Peter. *Peter Spier's Christmas!* Illustrated by the author. Garden City, N.Y.: Doubleday, 1983.

This wordless picture book documents the Christmas season, showing a family of five shopping, gift-wrapping, baking, decorating — all the rituals that make up the anticipation of Christmas. The three children (and the dog and cat) star in nearly every picture, but the parents' role in creating Christmas is clear. Grandparents and elderly neighbors are included, too.

Spier's 90-plus pictures are full of details and mini-stories told by facial expressions or enacted by the pets. Each illustration provides conversation material, plenty of opportunity to spot details, tell stories, name familiar objects, compare this family's Christmas traditions with the reader's, and identify small kindnesses people show one another at Christmas time.

Adults are likely to be caught by nostalgia with this one. Highly recommended as an antidote to the bustle of Christmas is a series of rocking chair sessions with a preschooler and this book, looking and talking.

Early Elementary: Grades 1-3

Identity

Aliki. *Feelings.* Illustrated by the author. New York: Greenwillow, 1984.

This is not a story, but a book showing on each page a different familiar childhood event — a birthday party, a space capsule created of wood blocks and then destroyed, getting lost in a store, being bored — with the characters commenting on their positive and negative feelings.

A calm, objective discussion of both good and bad feelings based on the book can help a child recognize and accept her own feelings later, when emotions may run so strong that rational discussion is not possible: How would you feel if this happened? Why? What would you do? Are there other times when you feel the same way? How do you act when you feel that way? Is it all right to feel that way? Do other people ever feel the same way you do?

See also Aloneness, Getting Along with Others.

Burningham, John. *Time to Get Out of the Bath, Shirley.* (See Developing Imagination for full description.)

Daydreaming like Shirley's is a normal experience for children, sometimes difficult for task-oriented adults to tolerate. In discussion, the adult should be accepting not only of the daydreaming, but also of Shirley's need — and right — to tune out her mother's mundane monologue.

See also Aloneness.

Drescher, Joan. *Your Family, My Family.* Illustrated by the author. New York: Walker, 1980.

Not a story, this book presents the great variety of family constellations we have today: adopted children, fathers keeping house, single-parent families, commune arrangements, foster homes, grandparents as parents. The book will reassure a child in a nontraditional home and will broaden the definition of family for children from traditional homes.

In discussion, reinforce ideas that a family is people living together, sharing chores, and caring for one another, and the child's own role in making it work.

See also Getting Along with Others.

Galbraith, Judy. *The Gifted Kids Survival Guide for Ages 10 and Under.* Illustrated by Priscilla Kiedrowski. Minneapolis: Free Spirit, 1984.

Written to help students understand what the label "gifted" means, this book explains what giftedness is and how it relates to some of the frustrations that gifted children experience in school, with peers, and at home. It includes reassuring information and practical help for making friends and fighting boredom.

The book is written to children in a comfortable conversational tone. One of its major values is the assurance that being gifted is positive and that gifted children, though different from many of their classmates, are not alone.

For young children, adults may wish to select sections of the book that seem especially pertinent. It may also be wise to give some thought to whether group or individual discussion would be best. Five sections of the book cover various issues of identity for gifted children.

See also Getting Along with Others.

Kuskin, Karla. *Dogs and Dragons, Trees and Dreams: A Collection of Poems.* (See Developing Imagination for full description.)

This book can be used to help foster a child's awareness of his own feelings, a very important step in developing a sense of identity. Use it as a springboard to encourage the child to talk about how he feels in similar situations.

Simon, Norma. *All Kinds of Families.* Illustrated by Joe Lasker. Chicago: Whitman, 1976.

This picture book shows nuclear families and extended families, emphasizing that even when people don't live together, they are still part of a family. Divorce is not mentioned, and adoption is mentioned just once, but the concepts are implicit in the definition: "A family can be a mother, a father, and children who are growing up. A family can be a mother and her children, living, loving, working and sharing. A family can be a father and his children, living, loving, working and sharing. People in a family help each other and take care of each other."

This book and discussions based on it will give a child a warm feeling of belonging to his own family, and a sense that, whatever his family constellation, it fits nicely into the whole human family.

Which pictures remind you of our family? Why? (These questions are better asked by family members than by teachers or librarians. If this book is being used at school, it would be better to discuss it in very general terms with a group of students.)

See also Getting Along with Others.

Aloneness

Aliki. *Feelings.* (See Identity for full description.)

Identify lonely or alone situations in the book (such as boredom). What do you do when you feel like that? What else could you do?

See also Getting Along with Others.

Burningham, John. *Time to Get Out of the Bath, Shirley.* (See Developing Imagination for full description.)

Shirley uses her imagination to provide herself with some alone time, even with her mother in the room. Why does she do this? Do you ever want to be alone? What are things you can do best alone?

See also Identity.

George, Jean Craighead. *All Upon a Stone.* (See Drive to Understand for full description.)

Although the mole cricket is an example of contentment with being alone, a better use of this book would be to develop (in connection with the discussion questions suggested under Drive to Understand) the recognition that quiet time alone can be very rewarding, and for some things it is necessary.

Gripe, Maria. *Hugo and Josephine.* Translated from the Swedish by Paul Britten Austin; illustrated by Harald Gripe. New York,: Delacorte, 1962.

Shy and timid, Josephine is teased at school because her father is the vicar and she has made the mistake of carrying her books unfashionably in a knapsack. School is easy, but social life is hard until Hugo Anderson joins the class. Hugo is quietly, rationally, imperturbably independent, always out of step, always polite, and always making perfect, if unexpected, sense. He finds it odd, for example, that the teacher talks and the children speak only to answer her questions: "There's no sense in our answering, when we don't know anything. We're the ones who ought to ask questions." When he realizes how distressed the teacher is because he has not followed his reading lessons, Hugo teaches himself to read in a weekend.

Hugo befriends Josephine and gives her confidence, but when he is suddenly absent for an extended time her timidity returns and the teasing resumes. He finally returns with a sensible, unapologetic explanation for his absence, and helps Josephine in her efforts to be accepted.

Many gifted children will recognize the discomfort of feeling out of place and different as Josephine does. Hugo's personality is the strength of the book. He accepts everyone, including himself, and presents a self-contained maturity that commands the respect of all. In addition, the book offers the opportunity to compare school life in Sweden to that in the United States.

Hugo represents the kind of aloneness called Being Alone and Different in chapter 1. He stands alone quite naturally and with such integrity that it brings him respect rather than loneliness. To help the child articulate Hugo's strengths, ask him to describe Hugo. Do you know anyone who is like him in any way? Think of a problem you or your class is having — what would Hugo think of it?

See also Getting Along with Others.

Ward, Lynd. *The Silver Pony.* Illustrated by the author. Boston: Houghton Mifflin, 1973.

In 80 pictures, this wordless book tells the story of a lonely midwestern farm boy who escapes to the wider world via his imagination. A winged pony takes him on flying rides, and on each trip they find some other lonely child living his or her particular life: fishing through the ice, struck by a devastating flood, keeping pigeons on a city rooftop, shepherding in the West. Each child originates from a different ethnic group. The bond the farm boy has with them is loneliness, and his ability to give something to them on his imaginary flights.

This book would best be used by a child looking through it alone first, and then telling an adult the story portrayed by the pictures. The adult can bring out themes of the common experience of loneliness, the similarities between the children, and the fact that the lonely farm boy has something to give. Each child will tell a slightly different story, revealing her or his own feelings, and discussion can arise from that story rather than from a preconceived list of questions.

It is important to spend time with this book. If the reader yields to the temptation to go through it once quickly, much will be lost.

The Silver Pony is listed also in the Upper Elementary section. A knowledge of the child or children with whom the book will be used can determine whether this book should be presented now or later.

Getting Along with Others

Aliki. *Feelings.* (See Identity for full description.)

This book can be used to help children focus on how other people feel as well as on how they themselves feel. How can you tell what these people are feeling? How can you tell when your friends feel angry, lonely, happy? What do you do then?

See also Aloneness.

Clifton, Lucille. *My Friend Jacob.* Illustrated by Thomas di Grazia. New York: Dutton, 1980.

Sam tells the story, explaining that Jacob is his best friend. Jacob helps Sam shoot baskets and carry things at the grocery store, and he writes a birthday card for Sam all by himself. Sam teaches Jacob a new skill: to knock before entering.

Sam is eight and black; Jacob is seventeen, white, and mentally handicapped. This is a gentle story which implies but does not preach acceptance and empathy. Friendship is based on giving and receiving, not necessarily on similarity, and both Sam and Jacob are able to give and receive.

How do you know that Jacob is Sam's best friend? How do you know how Jacob feels about Sam? Do you have a friend who is very different from you in some way? How do you show that person that you are his or her friend?

Drescher, Joan. *Your Family, My Family.* (See Identity for full description.)

To help children understand and accept family arrangements that are different from theirs, this book is a good introduction to the various kinds of families in our culture. Which family is most like your own? Which ones are like families of friends of yours? How do families help people get along with each other?

Galbraith, Judy. *The Gifted Kids Survival Guide for Ages 10 and Under.* (See Identity for full description.)

This book includes sections on friends, coping with teasing, and "gifted grief at home."

Gripe, Maria. *Hugo and Josephine.* (See Aloneness for full description.)

Although Hugo and Josephine are both bright, there is a striking difference in their ability to get along with people. How can Huge be so comfortable with being so very different, while Josephine is teased if she is only a little different from the other children?

Simon, Norma. *All Kinds of Families.* (See Identity for full description.)

This book can be used to help children accept family patterns that are different from their own as well as understand the difficulties all families experience. Thus it can help them better understand how their friends may feel about their families. Problems of family life are gently portrayed in the illustrations, and much discussion could be based on them: What do you think is happening? Why? How do these people feel? Why?

More questions will arise from the children's responses.

Viorst, Judith. *Rosie and Michael.* Illustrated by Lorna Tomei. New York: Atheneum, 1974.

Michael tells why Rosie is his friend, and Rosie, in parallel terms, tells why Michael is hers. There is no plot here, but a lot of understanding of what friendship is: tolerating imperfection, plotting (and accepting) friendly pranks, sharing fears and sorrows, keeping secrets, forgiving mistakes, accepting idiosyncracies.

For a gifted child who feels rebuffed and is puzzled about how to be a friend, discussion could grow out of each page of this book. What exactly are Rosie and Michael doing for each other here? The analytical power of the intellectually gifted youngster should help her to generalize, or to follow adult generalizations, from the situations Viorst presents.

Do you know any friends who treat each other this way? Does anyone do this for you? When did you last do this for someone else? Can you plan to do this for someone tomorrow? Tell me how it turns out.

Wilt, Joy. *A Kid's Guide to Making Friends: A Children's Book about Social Skills.* Illustrated by Ernie Hergenroeder. Waco, Tex.: Word, 1979.

This book is fully described in the Getting Along with Others section for preschool and kindergarten. It could also be used with early elementary children, with more examples of each concept from the children's experience to enrich the discussion. Even if the children have used the book before, repetition of the ideas in more depth can be beneficial.

Zolotow, Charlotte. *A Tiger Called Thomas.* Illustrated by Kurt Werth. New York: Lothrop, Lee, and Shepard, 1963.

When Thomas moves to a new neighborhood, he decides people might not like him, so he does not try to make friends. At Halloween, in his tiger costume, he is surprised to find that neighbors, adults and children, call him by name and invite him to come back. He decides maybe they do like him — and he likes them.

This is a good book for a shy child, or one who does not take the initiative in building friendships because he or she feels unaccepted. Thomas does nothing toward friendship. He is quite passive, yet he is accepted by people who are clearly willing to be his friends.

Why does Thomas think his new neighbors might not like him? (There is no answer in the book, so this question asks for the child's perception of how Thomas feels.) What could he have done to make friends earlier? Do you know anyone like Thomas? How can you be a friend to him or her?

Developing Imagination

Aiken, Conrad. *Cats and Bats and Things with Wings.* Illustrated by Milton Glaser. New York: Atheneum, 1965.

This collection of poems about animals is appropriate for young gifted children whose reading interests still include animals but who can benefit from Aiken's fresh, sophisticated perception. Glaser's illustrations contribute to the book's power to evoke a variety of moods.

For children whose experience with animal poems is limited to those that depict animals as soft and cute, Aiken's poetry may be an acquired taste. Help them make the transition by considering with them what characteristics of the animals might have caused Aiken to write as he did. Encouraging them to write their own animal poems after reading Aiken will reinforce the imaginative impact of the book.

Burningham, John. *Time to Get Out of the Bath, Shirley.* Illustrated by the author. New York, Crowell, 1978.

While Shirley's mother carries on a typical maternal nagging monologue about neatness and cleanliness on the left-hand page, Shirley, who is taking a bath on the right-hand page, imagines herself riding her rubber duck out of the bathtub drain and into a wonderful world of castles and kings. After she unseats the king himself in a joust on inflated rubber animals in the river flowing by the castle, Shirley is ready to return to the real world and the bath.

The book is a celebration of the imagination of the child as well as of the value of imagination in dealing with humdrum daily routines and concerns. How does Shirley make her trip? Where can you go in your imagination? Can you make up stories? When do you find time to do this?

See also Identity, Aloneness.

de la Mare, Walter. *Peacock Pie.* Illustrated by Barbara Cooney. New York: Alfred A. Knopf, illustrations copyright 1961.

This collection contains over 80 poems from a poet who hoped to give "the rarest kind of best" to children. It is recommended for gifted youngsters because it includes a variety of types and moods of poetry, including narrative and lyric poems and ballads. Some are immediately appealing and others are more difficult, perhaps requiring a few hearings before the child develops a clear response.

Many of de la Mare's poems are open-ended, leaving the reader wondering about questions hinted at but not answered, a stimulus for the child's imagination. Read aloud from the book until favorites emerge, but continue reading the less familiar poems, too. This is a book for a child's personal library.

Fritz, Jean. *Where Do You Think You're Going, Christopher Columbus?* Illustrated by Margot Tomes. New York: Putnam, 1980.

This lively biography tells much more than that Columbus discovered America in 1492. Fritz follows Columbus on all four of his voyages, describing his bravado and stubbornness, his successes and failures, and providing along the way glimpses of the late 15th-century European view of the world.

The contrasts are instructive. Columbus was a good seaman but a poor governor. He returned to Spain from his first voyage to a royal welcome, but from 1493 to the end of his life he faced one disappointment after another. Although he was clearly intelligent, the qualities that carried him through difficulties were persistence and faith in what he was doing. This book offers a way of demonstrating the importance of these characteristics to gifted students who may be relying on native intelligence alone.

This book is best for children in the middle grades. Third or fourth graders can discuss questions such as: What words would you use to describe Columbus' character? What qualities made him a good explorer? A poor governor? Do you know people who have some of Columbus' traits? Why do we hear only of his successes? Do you know of other famous people who had to undergo failure? What characteristic was most important to Columbus' success? Are you like him in any way? What are the advantages? Disadvantages? How can you enhance the advantages and overcome the disadvantages?

Gardner, Beau. *The Look Again . . . and Again, and Again, and Again Book.* Illustrated by the author. New York: Lothrop, Lee and Shepard, 1984.

A graphic designer, Beau Gardner has created a series of designs each of which can be viewed from all four sides (or from a bird's-eye view) and be seen as at least four different objects. As the child turns each picture around and his perception of the design changes from one object to another, he will almost be able to feel his mind stretching.

Just these continuing changes can be discussed. How does the design change from a teddy bear's foot to a pipe bowl? What actually changes? How does the child's mind do that? What other things can his mind do?

Hodges, Margaret. *The Hatching of Joshua Cobb.* Illustrated by W. T. Mars. New York: Farrar, Straus and Giroux, 1967.

It is Joshua's first summer at camp, and after a rough beginning with an impatient and neglectful counselor, he improves steadily at swimming and makes friends as well. The high point of the two-week session is a talk with Dusty, his new counselor, who reveals that he is an orphan. Dusty encourages Josh, whose father is dead, to grow into the "man of the house." As camp ends, Josh wants to win a race for Dusty, but comes in second in all four of the races he enters. Disappointed, he learns that his four seconds total the highest score for the track meet, and Dusty tells Josh that he is a consistent performer.

The warmth of the relationship between Dusty and Josh make this a book worth reading, especially for boys. It is listed for early elementary grades because of its reading and interest level, even though it does not relate to Developing Imagination as well as it does to Using Abilities, the category for older readers. The race results offer an opportunity to introduce the idea of perfectionism — second place is not all bad.

How do you feel when you come in second? Is it better to be a consistent performer or to be first? Why? In what areas can you be a consistent performer?

Kuskin, Karla. *Dogs and Dragons, Trees and Dreams: A Collection of Poems.* Illustrated by the author. New York: Harper & Row, 1980.

Through this book, Kuskin introduces poetry to children (or keeps them involved in poetry as they leave nursery rhymes behind) with a light personal touch, so they will feel that someone real is speaking to them — a real person who understands something of children, something of cats, and certainly something of humor.

As with Aiken's *Cats and Bats and Things with Wings*, read the poems aloud until the child knows her favorites, and continue occasionally reading from the rest of the poems.

See also Identity.

Lear, Edward. *The Scroobious Pip.* Completed by Ogden Nash. Illustrated by Nancy Ekholm Burkert. New York: Harper & Row, 1968.

As might be imagined, the combined talents of Edward Lear and Ogden Nash produce a poem with strong rhythms and words newly coined for the occasion, telling a nonsense story with a humor sure to hold the interest of children. The illustrations are true to life even though they are of imaginary creatures; wonderfully inventive, they create a thoroughly charming world for the reader to enter.

The illustrations invite careful examination and the words must be read aloud. Gifted children, especially artists, will gain appreciation for the illustrations from the notes by Nancy Ekholm Burkert that precede the poem.

Lobel, Arnold. *On Market Street.* Illustrated by Anita Lobel. New York: Greenwillow, 1981.

Like the Anno books, this one is to be pored over for the detail in the illustrations. In content, it is simply an alphabet book with such commodities as apples, books, clocks, and doughnuts for sale on Market Street, but each page presents a picture of a person made up of gloves, hats, ice cream, and so on.

The drawings and the rich colors may prove inspirational. Give the child some time with this book, and then ask what he could draw for Market Street.

McCloskey, Robert. *Time of Wonder.* Illustrated by the author. New York: Viking, 1957.

McCloskey's book evokes in words and pictures a child's experience of late summer in Maine. Weather is a factor to be reckoned with, and the children in the story pick up the adults' apprehension about the approaching hurricane, but also their knowledgeable preparation for it and their sturdy survival of the storm. Coziness and family security are the themes. Awareness and enjoyment of nature pervade the book, along with respect for its power and wonder at its mysteries. Where *do* hummingbirds go in a hurricane?

Although it is full of action, the book is also quiet and thoughtful, acknowledging the moods of children at play in the sunshine and singing to cover fear in a storm, then experiencing a bittersweet farewell as they leave for another school year.

What are special places for the child, like the coast of Maine for the children in the book? How does it feel to know you are standing where Indian children stood hundreds of years ago? Or to wonder over the age of a fossil? What other places or events or objects have aroused wonder in you? What do you find to wonder about on a simple walk near your house?

Willard, Nancy. *A Visit to William Blake's Inn: Poems for Innocent and Experienced Travelers.* Illustrated by Alice and Martin Provenson. San Diego: Harcourt Brace Jovanovich, 1981.

This collection of poems about a visit to an inn hosted by poet William Blake is enhanced by pictures of the inn's interior, with one wall cut away like a dollhouse so readers see everything on several floors and the roof. Each poem creates an imaginative world of its own, but all are tied together by the mystical spirit of William Blake and the poetry he wrote 200 years ago.

Willard's poems should be read aloud and enjoyed. Some lines could be memorized for the sheer pleasure of knowing them by heart. The illustrations can be examined for the unexpected surprises on every page. A few poems written by Blake could be read aloud, too. Willard has used some of Blake's rhythms, and children will enjoy comparing them.

Yolen, Jane. *The Seeing Stick.* Illustrated by Remy Charlip and Demetra Maraslis. New York: Crowell, 1977.

Hwei Ming, the emperor's daughter, is blind, and when the emperor sends a message over the land asking for help in curing her, an old man from the south comes with his seeing stick. As he travels he whittles the story of his journey on the seeing stick, and after he tells Hwei Ming about his journey he helps her to "see" the carvings on the stick with her fingertips. He continues to teach her to see through her fingers, and she teaches other blind children to see as she does, to "grow eyes on the tips of [their] fingers" like the blind old man.

Yolen's story is told as a folktale and does not mention until the last page that the old man who takes such a long journey and carves with such skill is also blind. The story provides inspiration for finding ways around difficulties that cannot be changed, as well as an example of the power of imagination.

More than discussion, an appropriate response to this book might be to encourage children to try growing eyes on the tips of their fingers. What can they sense by feeling faces, flowers, pets, fabrics, surfaces of all kinds? If they had never *seen* what they are feeling, how would they perceive them by touch?

Drive to Understand

Anno, Mitsumasa. *Anno's Journey.* Illustrated by the author. New York: Putnam, 1981 [c1977].

This wordless book shows a man journeying on horseback through a medieval European landscape. The reader who looks carefully can identify a fair, a duel, a foot race, a ping-pong game, visual jokes — the book is full of details to observe and discuss.

A child can pore over this book for hours, still finding something new. An adult can enrich the experience by questioning. What are they doing? Tell me a story about this. What do you think this is?

Ceserani, Gian Paolo. *Marco Polo.* Illustrated by Piero Ventura. New York: Putnam, 1977.

This is a visually arresting account of Polo's life, his visit to China, and his friendship with Kublai Khan. The story will appeal especially to a gifted child since both Marco Polo and Kublai Khan were able to pursue their intellectual curiosity in particularly spectacular ways. Their relationship is an example of a friendship based on a "meeting of the minds."

Marco Polo is a good book to read and discuss methodically, with a globe available. Describe how difficult it was to travel across the desert and around India by sea, when there were few or no other travelers, and comment on the courage required to explore the unknown as Marco Polo did.

What was most important to Marco Polo; what did he value? How was he able to accomplish so much? What did he give up to achieve what he did?

George, Jean Craighead. *All Upon a Stone.* Illustrated by Alan Bolognese. New York: Crowell, 1971.

Nature's activity around, on, and under one large stone is told by following a mole cricket through its day, the one day this normally solitary species seeks contact with other mole crickets. Each illustration is a detail of the double page illustration at the end, which rounds out the concept of the variety of life forms and activities in a small space.

This book is useful for developing appreciation for how much can be discovered in an ordinary spot by those who learn to watch quietly and with patience.

How do you suppose the author and the illustrator knew what the mole cricket is and what it does? Are there things that you enjoy just watching quietly when you are alone? If you mark off a small patch of lawn and sit still and watch, what will you see happening there? What do you think about while you watch?

See also Aloneness.

Godden, Rumer. *The Mousewife.* Illustrated by Heidi Holder. New York: Viking, 1982.

A house mouse yearns to know more than hunting for food, and steals time to gaze out of the window at the garden, the fields, and the woods. A newly-captured dove in a cage tells her of wind, corn, clouds. She frees the dove and, seeing him fly away, is saddened by the thought that he will tell her no more. But now she can see the stars for herself; she no longer needs the dove's help. She remains a mousewife, but with a difference.

Some gifted children will be able to identify with the mousewife's yearning to know, to learn what is beyond her horizon, and also with the sadness of recognizing the limitations placed upon her by circumstances she cannot control. To some, it may be simply a story. The leader can ask for a general response to the book, and give her own to initiate discussion, then base further discussion on what she learns about the children's responses.

Will the mousewife be happier now that she has talked with the dove, or less so? Would it have been better if she had never met him? Is it worth learning new things if you can't use what you learn? Why or why not?

Godden, Rumer. *The Story of Holly and Ivy.* Illustrated by Barbara Cooney. New York: Viking Kestrel, 1985.

Ivy is an orphan who goes looking for an imaginary grandmother at Christmas. Holly is a doll in a toyshop who wishes for a girl to own her. Mrs. Jones wants to celebrate Christmas so much that she decorates a Christmas tree for the first time, and Mr. Jones is the policeman to whom Peter, who works at the toyshop, turns when he discovers that he has lost the key. Because of Peter, Holly, Ivy, and Mrs. Jones are united on Christmas Day, and each wish is granted.

This story is told from three alternating points of view — Holly's, Ivy's, and Mrs. Jones' — so the reader must hold three separate stories in mind until they merge. In addition to this intellectual challenge, this is a heartwarming story with an implied appreciation for home and family.

Hall, Donald. *Ox-Cart Man.* Illustrated by Barbara Cooney Porter. New York: Viking, 1979.

The ox-cart man lives in New England at a time when embroidery needles still come on ships from England. In October, he and his family load all of the produce of their farm that they can sell onto the ox-cart and he walks ten days to Portsmouth. There he sells everything, even the cart and the ox. He buys a few necessities for his family, and walks back home, where he and his family begin preparing for next October's trip. While the ox-cart man carves a new yoke and builds a new cart, his wife spins flax into linen, his daughter embroiders the linens, and his son makes brooms.

The story is about the self-sufficiency of the farm family, with everyone sharing in the work that sustains them. The illustrations carry much of the story, providing details for discussion as well as evoking the New England seasons and the well-regulated, productive life that results from the family's work.

The family makes use of everything available to them. Some of it will be new to contemporary readers. For example, what does the farmer actually do when he splits shingles to sell? What does the child know about spinning flax into linen, making maple syrup, and shearing sheep?

The book can also be enjoyed simply by examining the pictures and discussing the many details that tell of their hardworking life.

Langstaff, John. *Hot Cross Buns and Other Old Street Cries.* Illustrated by Nancy Winslow Parker. New York: Atheneum, 1978.

Do children who sing "Hot Cross Buns" realize that it is a forerunner of the tunes they hear with television commercials? Originally it was cried in the streets of English cities and towns by bakers selling their wares. Collected here are similar cries for other goods sold in the marketplace, such as milk, strawberries, baskets, walnuts, even sand, as well as services offered there such as mending chairs, grinding scissors and knives, and repairing barrels. Tunes are provided, and Langstaff points out those cries which can be sung as rounds and those that can be sung together.

This book can be used as a starting point for better understanding of history, advertising, occupations, and music. And as Langstaff suggests, the cries can be used by characters in plays about old England.

Ness, Evaline, illustrator. *Tom Tit Tot.* New York: Scribner's, 1965.

The text of this English variation on the Rumpelstiltskin story is from Joseph Jacobs' *English Folk and Fairy Tales,* and it sounds as authentic as it is — which is to say it includes plenty of new words and expressions for children to interpret from context. Ness' caricature-like drawings suit the homespun language of the English version, a pleasing combination of illustration and text.

Tom Tit Tot offers an opportunity to discuss some of the elements of folktales: the spare, descriptive language the original storytellers would have used, the magic number three (visits from Tom Tit Tot), and the familiar Rumpelstiltskin theme in another version. The freshness of the language also recommends it for gifted children.

Norris, Louanne and Howard E. Smith. *An Oak Tree Dies and a Journey Begins.* Illustrated by Allen Davis. New York: Crown, 1979.

The old oak is uprooted during a storm and falls along a river bank. Spring flooding carries it downstream, where it lodges against the bank. Animals, insects, fish, and mushrooms all make use of the dead tree until it is again carried downstream, this time to the open sea, where birds, barnacles, oysters, seaweed and fish find their own ways to use it. A storm reduces it to a log which is washed onto a beach, where more animals and insects live in and from it. Finally a boy finds a part of the old oak, now a piece of driftwood that causes him to wonder what it came from and what its story is.

For children who have seen many of the stages this book traces — dead trees standing and fallen, logs on the beach, driftwood — this book helps to pull all of them together into a connected story. In addition, the examples of the dead oak's continuing contribution to the environment offer material for discussion.

Sobol, Donald. *Encyclopedia Brown, Boy Detective.* Illustrated by Leonard Shortall. New York: Nelson, 1963. (1st of a series)

Leroy Brown is called Encyclopedia because he knows so much from his constant reading. He is a boy detective who helps his father, the Chief of Police, solve crimes. They do not reveal that Encyclopedia is helping because, as explained at the beginning of each volume, he doesn't want to seem different from other fifth graders. There are ten cases in each book, with the clues Encyclopedia used to solve them given at the end.

Beginning readers love this series. Encyclopedia has no problems he can't solve; he out-thinks every adult he meets, and everyone — with the possible exception of Bugs Meany — loves him for it.

There is no deep meaning here, only a bright ten-year-old who enjoys and uses his brain and is valued for it. Don't try to discuss these books (other than perhaps asking why Encyclopedia doesn't want to be different). Introduce them and let children enjoy them in their own way. They are a bridge from beginning readers to "chapter books," one which gifted readers cross rapidly.

Spier, Peter. *Tin Lizzie.* Illustrated by the author. Garden City, N.Y.: Doubleday, 1975.

Spier traces the history of a Model T touring car from the factory in 1909 through three owners to its retirement behind a barn in 1945 and eventual purchase and restoration in the early 1970's. The car is called Lizzie but not otherwise personified, lending integrity to the history for readers who are no longer interested in machines with faces and personalities.

The story is told through the eyes of her owners, and especially through the many detailed illustrations, which faithfully depict changes in fashion, cars, roads, towns and farms over 65 years of American history. The book includes carefully drawn diagams of the Model T with over 50 parts precisely labelled.

Upper Elementary: Grades 4-6

Identity

Conford, Ellen. *And This is Laura.* Boston: Little, Brown, 1977.

Everyone in Laura's family has a special talent except Laura. Even when she learns that she is psychic and gives a credible performance as the second lead in a school play on short notice, her feeling of being ordinary and unworthy persist. When she finally expresses her sense of inadequacy to her parents, they point out that she is an all-A student. They both explain that she is valuable to them as a person, not for her gifts. Her gifts are for her to enjoy, not for them to be proud of.

Laura is an example of a sibling unsure of where she fits in a gifted family. As a gifted child who does not recognize or appreciate her own gifts until circumstances or other people point them out, she is like many gifted girls who minimize the quality and importance of their own abilities, limiting what they accomplish because of a low self-concept.

In what different ways does Laura recognize each of her gifts? What difference will it make to her to have recognized them? What difference will it make to others? If you were Laura, would you be convinced by her parents' reasons for loving her? Why or why not? Why is it especially difficult for people who have a lot of talent to know why other people like them?

Danziger, Paula. *The Cat Ate My Gymsuit.* New York: Dell, 1974.

Shy, overweight Marcy Lewis is propelled into the small group of student leaders when a favorite teacher is dismissed and Marcy proves her ability and willingness to speak out in the effort to have the teacher reinstated. To her amazement, Marcy finds that Joel, the smartest, most self-assured boy in the class, likes her — and that Joel's family life, like hers, is not entirely happy. As the students work together they come into conflict with some of the adult community, including Marcy's father, but Marcy's self-confidence grows.

It may be worth while to point out the copyright date and give some background on Marcy's mother's discomfort with speaking her own mind, since she may not seem credible to some readers, but that will not be a major problem for students. The characters line up so clearly on one side or other of the issue of firing the teacher that it is easy to discuss the real theme of the book: standing up for one's own beliefs against following the majority, a good theme for upper elementary students to consider.

What makes shy Marcy speak up when Mr. Stone announces Ms. Finney's leaving? Why is Joel so self-assured? What does he mean when he says that when he grows up he wants to be Joel Anderson? How does one decide when to be part of the majority, and when to be different? Is it worthwhile to be different? For Marcy? For you? Under what circumstances?

See also Getting Along with Others.

Galbraith. Judy. *The Gifted Kids Survival Guide for Ages 10 and Under.* Minneapolis: Free Spirit, 1984.

Written to help students understand what the label "gifted" means, this book explains what giftedness is and how it relates to some of the frustrations that gifted children experience in school, with peers, and at home. It includes reassuring information and practical help for making friends and fighting boredom.

The format makes extensive use of graphics to add impact, and the writing style is informal. Children respond well to both, so they are able to make use of the information and suggestions; however, the dominant value of the book may well be the assurance it offers to gifted children that they are not alone.

For specific discussion relating to identity and self-concept, use the five sections that deal with what giftedness is.

See also Getting Along with Others, Using Abilities.

Greene, Constance C. *A Girl Called Al.* (See Getting Along with Others for full description.)

Why is it important to Al to think of herself as a nonconformist? How does her nonconformity increase her problems? How does it help her with them? How does her intelligence help her to cope? How do you know she is lonely, even though she never says so?

Heller, Sherri Z. *What Makes You So Special?* (See Using Abilities for full description.)

The section that discusses how children are chosen for gifted programs would be useful in helping children accept and integrate the concept of giftedness into their self-image.

See also Getting Along with Others.

Konigsburg, E. L. *From the Mixed-up Files of Mrs. Basil E. Frankweiler.* Illustrated by the author. New York: Atheneum, 1967.

Claudia Kincaid persuades her brother Jamie, who has enough money to finance the project, to join her in running away. Following Claudia's careful plans, they hide in New York's Metropolitan Museum of Art for a week. At first Claudia's reasons for running away are unclear even to her, but as she becomes fascinated by the mystery of a statue the museum has purchased, she realizes what she wants to accomplish before she returns home.

Written with a light touch, this is nevertheless not a frivolous book. It gives much useful information for children who do not live in New York about the city, the Metropolitan Museum, and art. In addition, it portrays inquisitive children who have had superb educational opportunities and are appealing models for lively intellectual curiosity.

Why did Claudia want to run away at first? What is her reason by the end of the book? Why does she want to be different? What are some advantages to being different? How could someone like Claudia accomplish the same thing without running away? What does Mrs. Frankweiler mean when she talks about having some days when rather than learning new facts, it's good to "allow what is already in you to swell up until it touches everything"?

Konigsburg, E. L. *(George)*. Illustrated by the author. New York: Dell, 1970.

Ben Carr is a very bright sixth grader who has an imaginary friend, George, living inside him. George is both Ben's worse self and his better self. He makes the outrageous comments Ben would never dare say, and he sees long before Ben is willing to recognize it that William, the senior Ben admires so much, is leading Ben into trouble. George becomes Ben's conscience, but Ben does not want to listen, and for a while Ben is totally out of touch with George — until Ben himself sees trouble and begins to change.

This is a humorous book with a serious message: it is important to stay in touch with our inner selves. As he grows older, Ben's voice "becomes indistinguishable from George's." It is sometimes easier for gifted children to accept themselves as they get older; Ben has integrated George into his own personality.

How did being gifted cause a predicament for Ben? How did it help him cope? Are you ever in difficult situations with people older than you? How do you feel about it? What abilities do you use to cope? What are differences between George and Ben? Which do you like better? Why? Is there sometimes a difference between what you think inside and the "you" that other people see? What are the advantages and disadvantages of that?

See also Aloneness, Using Abilities.

Konigsburg, E. L. *Jennifer, Hecate, Macbeth, William McKinley and Me, Elizabeth.* (See Aloneness for full description.)

Why does it not seem to bother Jennifer that she is not popular at school? Do you think she is happy just as she is? Why or why not? How do you know when Elizabeth begins to do more thinking for herself? Why does this happen?

See also Getting Along with Others.

Krumgold, Joseph. *Henry 3.* Illustrated by Alvin Smith. New York: Atheneum, 1967.

After years of striving, Henry's father finally becomes vice-president of his company and the family moves to Crestview, a suburb within sight of the towers of New York City. Henry hopes he can hide his handicap, an IQ of 154, here as he has elsewhere, but Fletcher Larkin learns the truth. In a community of corporate conformers, Fletcher is the outcast — his family owned the potato fields on which Crestview is built. Fletcher pledges silence, and Henry and his family are accepted in Crestview until, as a result of his father's job, a bomb shelter is placed in their yard. All the hostilities surrounding bomb shelters emerge, and the family's standing in the community is seriously threatened until a hurricane draws everyone together. During the hurricane people drop their masks and Henry realizes that they are all hiding parts of themselves as he hides his IQ. He realizes, too, that he is most honest when he is with Fletcher.

The story is clearly set in the mid-sixties, and the view of corporate striving is painful. The substance of the book begins around page 100. It is worth the wait. Henry's parents are not entirely stereotypical; his mother and

Fletcher's grandfather are both well-drawn characters. The issue of Henry's IQ is a minor theme, lightly handled. The real issue is the deeper one of being oneself.

Do you agree with Henry that we hide the best in ourselves? Do you agree with his mother that not living up to your best is not dishonest? How honest are you about what is your best?

See also Aloneness, Getting Along with Others.

L'Engle, Madeleine. *A Wrinkle in Time.* New York: Farrar, Straus and Giroux, 1962.

Fourteen-year-old Meg Murry, her younger brother, Charles Wallace, and Calvin O'Keefe travel through time and space in search of Mr. Murry, a scientist who disappeared while experimenting with a tesseract, a wrinkle in time. When they find him, they must use all their strength to free him and themselves from the force of evil.

Almost all of the characters in this story are gifted, and the three children respond in different ways to the difficulties this causes them in relating to others. L'Engle creates a world in which it is psychologically safe to be gifted, in which the characters care for and challenge one another.

How are the children different from their schoolmates? How does each feel about being different? How do we show that we do or do not value differences among people?

See also Drive to Understand.

LeShan, Eda. *What Makes Me Feel This Way? Growing Up with Human Emotions.* Illustrated by Lisl Wiel. New York: Macmillan, 1972.

This book about feelings is written as a conversation with a child. Psychologically sound, it covers typical feelings of children, parents, and teachers, and the behaviors that display or hide the feelings. LeShan discusses the responses of different people to the same feelings, and the importance of recognizing, understanding, and paying attention to our own feelings.

While the concepts presented apply to every child, some are especially apt for gifted children. Among these are preferring study to athletics, showing early concern for world problems, and understanding the importance of using interests and abilities and being oneself.

A good way to use the book would be for adult and child to read one chapter at a time, noting ideas they would like to discuss with each other. The adult might prefer to be the first reader, to be prepared for questions a child might ask while reading it. (The chapter on "Feelings about Being a Boy or a Girl" mentions masturbation in a low-key, easily discussable way.) A general question to begin discussion would be: Have you ever felt this way? Adults should be ready to reveal times when they have felt this way, too.

See also Aloneness, Getting Along with Others.

Lowry, Lois. *Anastasia Krupnik.* Boston: Houghton Mifflin, 1979.

In her green notebook, ten-year-old Anastasia records her favorite words, important private information, and a list of "Things I Love!" and "Things I Hate!" When she learns that her mother will have a baby boy in March, she adds "my parents" and "babies" to the hate list, but stops short of running away when her father suggests that she give the new baby whatever name she chooses. Anastasia writes a horrible name in the green notebook. Over the next few months, she considers becoming a Catholic and changing her name, learns how to listen to her 92-year-old grandmother, falls in and out of love, decides she likes her name — and records all of this in the green notebook, occasionally moving an item from the Hate list to the Love list. Eventually even "babies" appears on the love side of the ledger.

Anastasia is a bright, inquisitive, sensitive girl who is doing her best to make sense of the world and the process of growing up. She vaguely dislikes her teacher, without knowing the reason. The reason is clear to the reader when the teacher rejects a poem Anastasia has written that does not rhyme. Later her teacher makes a special effort to be kind, and Anastasia moves her name to the Love list. Anastasia's parents are models of support and understanding for a gifted child. There are no major issues here, only Anastasia becoming more aware of herself through her own efforts and with her parents' help.

How do *people* get moved from the Hate to the Love list? What do all have in common? Describe the difference between the college students' attitude and Anastasia's attitude toward Wordsworth. Do you know people who have the students' attitude? What are the consequences? (If it seems appropriate, discussion leaders may want to add questions related to Anastasia's knowledge of and attitude toward her own giftedness.)

North, Sterling. *The Wolfling.* New York: Dutton, 1969.

Growing up in rural Wisconsin in the 1870s, Robbie Trent leads a rigorous life, lightened by the companionship of his pet, a wolf cub, and by the friendship of his teacher, Hannah Hitchcock, and his neighbor, the Swedish-American naturalist Thure Kumlien. His hard-working and demanding father expects Robbie to end his education at the eighth grade and work for him until he is 21. Robbie must buy his time from his father if he hopes to continue his education, and he is encouraged by others to do so. He needs this encouragement, because it is difficult for him to see a way out of the obligation imposed by his father.

The story is based on the life of the author's father with the historical accuracy documented in a separate section. It is particularly useful for discussing the difference in values between parents and children, and the need for children to be encouraged by other caring adults. Robbie's father is not uncaring, and is sympathetically depicted as careworn with the shortsightedness that often goes with a daily struggle for a livelihood.

How does Robbie feel about his father? What causes his father to feel as he does about Robbie's education? Why is it important for Robbie to continue his education? What traits does Robbie need to develop in order to do so? Do you think he will succeed? What traits does he already have that will help him? If you were in Robbie's situation, what person do you know who would help you as Thure Kumlien and Hannah Hitchcock helped Robbie?

Paterson, Katherine. *A Bridge to Terabithia.* Illustrated by Donna Diamond. New York: Crowell, 1977.

Sensitive and interested in art, Jess is a misfit in his family and in school. When Leslie moves to his rural area of Virginia and joins his class, she frees Jess to play and learn in the country of their imagination, Terabithia. When Leslie is killed in a flooded stream, Jess must face her death and his aloneness. Although he is still different from others, he realizes that he has gained strength from the friendship and can be himself now.

Katherine Paterson wrote this book after the death of a special friend of her own son, and it rings with the truth of the relationship between two sensitive people who find strength and validation in their friendship. Gifted children respond to that truth whether or not they themselves have such a relationship, and this book is highly recommended for upper elementary gifted readers.

How is Leslie different from the other students at Jess's school? How is Jess different? How does each one feel about being different? What would happen if they tried to change in order to fit in better? If you could meet them, would you like them better as they are, or if they changed in some way? Do you know anyone who seems different from the group, but who is pretty good at being who he or she is?

See also Aloneness, Getting Along with Others, Using Abilities, and Drive to Understand.

Paterson, Katherine. *Come Sing, Jimmy Jo.* New York: Dutton, 1985.

Eleven-year-old James Johnson belongs to a family of singers of country music. When their new agent hears James sing, he urges him to join the Family on stage. His feeling for the music helps James overcome his initial fear, but it is not so easy to become comfortable with the new identity that goes with performing. He does not want to become

"Jimmy Jo" instead of James, does not want school friends to know that he appears on television each Friday night, and he is not happy about the rivalry his popularity sets up between him and other members of the Family.

The stability in James' life comes from his grandmother and his father. Family relationships and tolerance of difficult personalities are well portrayed. Grandma encourages James to sing, saying "You got the gift. . . . It ain't fittin' to run from it. . . . The Lord don't give private presents." James' challenge is to use his gift and remain himself.

Why is it so important to James to remain James? Why does it not bother his mother to change herself for the sake of publicity? How would you feel? Why? Why does James feel that he betrayed Grandma? Do you agree that he did? What could you say to help him feel better about that?

See also Using Abilities.

Paterson, Katherine. *The Master Puppeteer.* Illustrated by Haru Wells. New York: Avon, 1975.

Growing up in a time of famine in medieval Japan, Jiro becomes an apprentice under Yoshida, master of the puppet theater, in order to free his parents of the burden of feeding him. The famine causes unrest, and a mysterious bandit steals from the rich to give to the poor. It is a dangerous time in the streets of Osaka, and Jiro finds himself, his new friends, his parents, and the master puppeteer involved in a network that he only slowly comes to understand.

The book is well-written and suspenseful, as well as full of information about old Japan. Different moral views come into conflict here and Jiro must decide where he stands, even as he watches the people who are most important to him make their decisions. Therefore, the book provides good discussion material for young people who are working to establish their own values, especially for gifted children concerned with their response to injustice and world turmoil.

Is Saburo right or wrong to steal rice? Why does Kinshi join the night rovers? Would you have done so? Why or why not? What was Jiro's father's reason for deceiving Jiro's mother? Do you agree with him? How can an individual decide how he or she should behave in times as tumultuous as Jiro's?

See also Aloneness.

Peck, Robert Newton. *A Day No Pigs Would Die.* New York: Dell, 1972.

Robbie tells of his 13th year growing up in a Shaker family in Vermont, and especially of his father, who was both illiterate and wise. Rather than a plot, Peck offers a series of vignettes that reveal the daily concerns of a rural community in which a Shaker family is even more traditional than most.

Rob grows up knowing he is different and valuing his own family even as he sees the disadvantages of their way of life. Rob is different because of his religion, not because of giftedness, but the principle is the same: to recognize and value the strengths of his family and himself, to be able to accept both himself and his father in spite of their differentness.

How is growing up Shaker an advantage to Rob? How is it a disadvantage? Will he overcome the disadvantages? How? What does Rob admire in his father? What do you admire in Rob? In his place, what would you have done differently? Would you have rebelled? When? Why? Was Rob wrong not to? What factors help Rob accept his and his family's difference? Is this story outdated, or is it relevant today? How? Generalize: What are the advantages and disadvantages of being different? How can people decide how and when to accept being different?

Sebestyen, Ouida. *Words by Heart.* Boston: Little, Brown, 1968.

Lena's papa has high hopes for his daughter, so he moves his family from the post-Reconstruction South to the more open West where a black family may have a better chance. But papa's willingness to work brings resentment from Mr. Haney, whose job is given to him, and Lena learns that not everyone rejoices with her when she wins the scripture-reciting contest. It is clear that prejudice here is only more subtle than in the South, and the family will still need extraordinary fortitude to survive.

Racial prejudice is the theme of this book, with Lena's giftedness adding emphasis to the need of blacks for opportunities to grow and develop. Gifted blacks can see a version of their own struggle in Lena's story, and gifted whites will recognize Lena's and her father's acceptance of the responsibility to use one's gift even against difficult odds.

What does Papa teach Lena that will help her to survive? What else do you think she will need to get through the next few years? If you were in her position, do you think you could make it? What would be your greatest asset? Your greatest liability?

See also Using Abilities.

Sperry, Armstrong. *Call It Courage.* New York: Collier, 1971 [c1968].

When Mafatu was three, his mother was killed at sea. Mafatu survived, but his childhood experience left him afraid of the sea, a coward in the Polynesian world where courage is everything. Rejected by all, Mafatu finally leaves Hikueru, his home island, and sails to a deserted island where he must depend only on himself for survival. While providing food and shelter and building a new canoe, he also kills a shark, a wild boar, and an octopus. Finally he must flee the island, pursued by a band of men from a nearby island. Having so abundantly proven his courage to himself, Mafatu returns home to the welcome of his people.

This fast-paced adventure will hold children's attention and give them a vivid picture of life in another part of the world. Mafatu's journey is the classic quest story, and he sets for himself tasks that correspond to the rites of passage marking the beginning of manhood in many societies. Although younger gifted children can read *Call It Courage* with enjoyment, those in the upper elementary grades are at a more appropriate age to respond to the story of Mafatu's search for identity.

Why did Mafatu leave Hikueru? Why did he explore the island he found, even though he suspected it might be one of the dark islands? Why did he go to the plateau instead of leaving the island when he heard the drums? Describe Mafatu's character. What traits helped him survive psychologically (survive the teasing and rejection of his people)? Physically (survive the dangers of sea and island)? Do young people in the United States face challenges in growing up that these traits will answer? How can you use the traits Mafatu had or developed?

Tolan, Stephanie S. *A Time to Fly Free.* (See Aloneness for full description.)

Why is Josh so comfortable with Rafferty and his parents, but not with classmates? Does this bother him? What will he be like when he is grown up?

See also Using Abilities.

Voigt, Cynthia. *Building Blocks.* (See Getting Along with Others for full description.)

How are Brann and Kevin different? What strengths of Kevin does Brann discover? What caused Kevin to become the person he is now? Choose one of Kevin's traits and discuss how it can look like a weakness from one angle, a strength from another. Do you know anyone like Kevin, with a characteristic that can be both bad and good? Do you have any such traits?

Wojciechowska, Maia. *Shadow of a Bull.* Illustrated by Alvin Smith. New York, Atheneum, 1964.

Manolo's father had been the greatest bullfighter in Spain, and everyone expects Manolo to be like him. When he is almost 12, the age when his father first fought a bull, a group of men begin training Manolo to become a toreador. Manolo is not sure that he wants to be a bullfighter, and he assumes that his fear means that he lacks courage. He sets for himself the task of learning to be brave. Two people help clarify his hopes for the future: Juan, who passionately longs to become a bullfighter, and the doctor who has spent his life repairing bodies broken in the bullring.

Manolo is trapped by the expectations of others and confused by his own definition of courage. The decision he eventually makes reflects both self-knowledge and moral courage. This well- written story conveys the historical tradition behind bullfighting with respect and raises the inevitable questions without giving a definitive answer. Manolo's answer, as it should be, is only for himself.

How does Manolo feel about himself? How would you describe him to someone else? How does Manolo define courage? How does he show it? How would you have defined it before reading the book? Now? Do you see examples of moral courage in others? In yourself?

See also Using Abilities.

Aloneness

Gripe, Maria. *In the Time of the Bells.* New York: Delacorte, 1965.

Arvid, the 17-year-old king, is a dreamer, no less unhappy on the throne than his people have been to have him as their monarch since his father abdicated to study astrology. To improve Arvid's attentiveness to matters of state, his parents bring to the castle Helge, the son of the executioner, to serve as whipping boy, and Elisif, Arvid's cousin, to become his wife. At the first public whipping ceremony, an unusual bond develops between Arvid and Helge. Arvid continues, even more strongly, to insist on his need for privacy, and Helge and Elisif are drawn to each other. At last, Arvid names Helge king for a day for the midsummer festival, and a resolution works itself out as he had hoped.

Arvid is a good example of an individualist thinker who needs more time alone than most people. His introspection and self-analysis will strike a chord with gifted people who do not fit the social expectations of their peers. The personalities of Arvid, Helge, Elisif, and her sister Engelke are clearly differentiated without a trace of judgmentalism, each valued for what they are and what they can contribute.

Arvid thinks that he is insensitive and does not like people. Do you agree? How does his response to the whipping show sensitivity to others? How can one express love for humanity if one does not love people? How does Arvid do this? Is anyone you know like this? Arvid knows he is a difficult person to understand. How does he accept that? What advantages are there in being such a person? Could he change it? How?

Jarrell, Randall. *The Bat-poet.* Illustrated by Maurice Sendak. New York: Macmillan, 1963.

The bat stays awake during the daytime and wants the other bats to do so, too, to see all the wonders he sees. They will not, so he makes up poems to tell them about the day. They do not understand. He tells his poem to the mockingbird, who comments on the rhyme scheme and the meter, but misses the feeling altogether. Only the chipmunk will listen. The bat makes more poems, finally one about bats that he wants to share with the other bats. But when he goes to the barn to find them, they have gone to sleep for the winter.

Older elementary children will appreciate the story line which parallels Plato's story of the man who left the security of the cave, and when he returned could not make the others understand his descriptions of the wider world. Both stories can be used to help gifted children understand the uniquenesses of their perceptions, and why they are not always shared by others.

The bat-poet never found another bat to listen. How did he feel about that? What did he do about it? Have you ever felt that you wanted to say something no one else could understand? How did you find someone to listen? If you couldn't find anyone, what did you do instead?

Konigsburg, E. L. *(George).* (See Identity for full description.)

What role does George play in Ben's life? Why has Ben developed George? Why has George stayed so long? (Adults may wish to reassure children that many gifted children have imaginary playmates; usually they disappear when the children begin school.) Why does George leave, or stop talking to Ben? Did you want him to come back, even though the psychiatrist said it was good that he had gone? Why? Why does he come back? What does this sentence mean: "Ben's own voice had deepened by then, and it had become indistinguishable from George's"? How do you listen to your conscience or your inner self? Do you have any particular way or place or time for doing that? How could you develop one?

See also Using Abilities.

Konigsburg, E. L. *Jennifer, Hecate, Macbeth, William McKinley, and Me, Elizabeth.* Illustrated by the author. New York: Atheneum, 1967.

Jennifer and Elizabeth become friends on Halloween of Elizabeth's first year at William McKinley School. Jennifer says she is a witch, and she does some mysterious things that make it seem possible that she is. Elizabeth becomes an apprentice witch, and all winter the girls meet at the library on Saturdays to study witchcraft, planning to make a magic potion that will enable them to fly.

Elizabeth is lonely at first in the new school. Jennifer, being gifted and black, is different and is not included in the school's social life, but she seems unconcerned about it. A subtheme is Elizabeth's gradual separation from Jennifer's influence, with Jennifer's help, so that the friendship becomes more equal than the original follower/leader relationship.

Why doesn't it bother Jennifer that she is not included in school parties? Do you think Jennifer is lonely? Why or why not?

See also Identity, Getting Along with Others.

Krumgold, Joseph. *Henry 3.* (See Identity for full description.)

Discuss Fletcher's grandfather's opinion that "lonely is something you're going to be anyway."

LeShan, Eda. *What Makes Me Feel This Way? Growing Up with Human Emotions.* (See Identity for full description.)

Adults using this book with children they know well will understand which sections to choose for discussion. The book is useful for talking about the need to have time alone to work on issues that are bothering them, as well as the need to do so in conversation with others.

See also Getting Along with Others.

Paterson, Katherine. *A Bridge to Terebithia.* (See Identity for full description.)

Why do Jess and Leslie enjoy Terebithia so much? What other places could serve the same purpose? Do you have such a place? Would you like one? How would you find it? When would you go there? What would you do there? Would you go alone or with someone else?

See also Getting Along with Others, Using Abilities, Drive to Understand.

Paterson, Katherine. *The Master Puppeteer.* (See Identity for full description.)

Jiro must work out his problems without much help from anyone else. How is he able to do this? If you were in his situation, how would you reach a decision? (Not what would your decision be, but how would you reach it?)

Speare, Elizabeth George. *The Witch of Blackbird Pond.* Boston: Houghton Mifflin, 1958.

Kit Tyler grew up with her grandfather in Barbados, but he dies when she was 16, and she sails to Connecticut to live with an aunt whom she has never met. Kit does not fit in the Puritan Connecticut of 1687, but she finds a few kindred spirits: Nat, first mate of the ship in which she sailed; Prudence, a downtrodden child hungry to learn; and Hannah, the outcast Quaker who lives by Blackbird Pond and is thought to be a witch. Kit's friendship with Hannah leads to the accusation that she herself is a witch.

Characterization is excellent in this book. Kit is accepted if not understood by her Puritan relatives, and comes to respect especially her stern uncle's fairness and sense of justice. Several characters — Kit, her uncle, Hannah, Nat, the young minister-in-training, and even Prudence — provide examples of standing alone for their own beliefs and the consequences (both difficulties and rewards) of doing so. The book also offers examples of ways in which we need and support each other.

Consider each of the people who take a stand for their beliefs. What characteristics do they have that put them in this position? How do they find the strength or courage they need — what sustains them?

See also Getting Along with Others.

Tolan, Stephanie. *A Time to Fly Free.* New York: Scribner, 1983.

By the time he is in fifth grade, Joshua Taylor has developed a defensive wall to keep from being hurt by the cruelty of other students to animals, to weaker students, and to himself. But this year, the wall no longer protects him. His teacher is unimaginative and humorless and school is unbearably boring. One day, Josh simply walks out. His parents agree to a temporary leave of absence while his mother looks for a new school, and Josh begins to work with Rafferty, a retired man who cares for injured birds. Even here, Josh cannot escape the fact of cruelty, and begins to face his own responsibility to accept it and go on in spite of it.

Tolan writes with perception of the feelings of a highly gifted child who does not fit, describing both his stress and the reactions and concern of the adults around him. This book will invite discussion of sensitivity in people and sensitivity to the environment. It will give parents and teachers insight into the feelings of children like Josh that may surprise them.

Why does Josh leave school? Do you understand how he felt? Have you ever known anyone else you think might have felt that way? What clues do you have that make you think so? If such a person cannot leave school, how else can he or she deal with the situation? Is it all right that Josh does not have close friends of his own age? Describe Josh as you think he will be when he is an adult.

See also Identity, Using Abilities.

Ward, Lynd. *The Silver Pony.* (See Aloneness in the Early Elementary section for full description.)

This book can be used with older elementary children, too. The stories they tell should be more detailed than those of younger children. Discussion can focus on the loneliness of each child the boy visits and what compensations they may have. Children of this age can develop an appreciation of the fact that there are other people like them in the world, even though they may not live nearby. As they grow older, they will have opportunites to meet more people like them.

Wier, Ester. *The Loner.* Illustrated by Christine Hilda Price. New York: David McKay, 1963.

The loner is a migrant boy who does not know how old he is or who his parents were. He does not have a name. He follows the crops, hitching rides with other migrant workers until the one person who has befriended him is killed because she ignores the only code the loner knows: look out for yourself and forget the rest. He flees, and is found by another loner, Boss, a middle-aged woman herding sheep alone this season so she can watch for the bear that killed her son. Choosing the name David, the loner tries to learn to work with dogs and sheep. As he learns from his mistakes, he also learns to care for animals and then for people, and he must re-examine his code. Eventually he learns to care for others even at great risk to himself.

An adventure book that will appeal especially to boys, *The Loner* gives a vivid picture of sheep ranching, evoking respect and sympathy for this demanding life. The few people at the ranch accept David without asking questions and respect his aloneness, at the same time expecting him to pull his weight as a contributing member of the ranch community. They are each loners themselves, but comfortably so, without the defensiveness that David has developed.

What advantages are there to the loner's code? Drawbacks? How do people show that code in situations familiar to you, for example, in a classroom? What are the advantages and disadvantages in that situation? Should loners change? Why or why not? Can a person be a loner and still be friendly?

See also Getting Along with Others.

Getting Along with Others

Byars, Betsy. *Summer of the Swans.* Illustrated by Ted CoConis. New York: Viking, 1970.

Since their parents' divorce, Sara and her older sister Wanda and younger brother Charlie have lived with Aunt Willie. Charlie has been mentally handicapped since he was ill at three and Sara is fiercely protective of him. At fourteen, she is also concerned about her moods, her appearance, the size of her feet, and Joe Melby, who seems to have taken Charlie's watch. Then Charlie gets lost and in the search for him, which Joe joins, Sara develops a new perspective.

The characters are especially well drawn in this book, and Sara and Joe in particular will stand as models of empathic and caring behavior in situations where impatience might be expected. Byars' descriptions of Charlie's thinking can help children who have been ignorant or afraid of the mentally handicapped to develop a sympathetic understanding. This understanding can be generalized, with sensitive guidance, to a tolerance and valuing of all others who are not so quick as a gifted child.

How do the different characters treat Charlie? (Include negative treatment.) How did you feel about the different ways he was treated? Can you understand those who tease? How and why does Sara help Charlie? Why is she able to understand how he feels so well? Is there someone you know who needs your help? Are you the kind of person who offers help when it is needed? Why or why not?

Danziger, Paula. *The Cat Ate My Gymsuit.* (See Identity for full description.)

Marcy finds herself in a situation that gives her a chance to know other students better and gives them a chance to know her. How does that happen? What role does Marcy play in making it happen? In your own situation, what could you do to make it happen if you needed to? What are the rewards?

Fitzhugh, Louise. *Harriet the Spy.* Illustrated by the author. New York: Harper & Row, 1964.

Harriet spends her after-school time spying on neighbors. She keeps a notebook filled with comments, not always flattering, on them and on her classmates. Shortly after Harriet's nurse, Ole Golly, leaves the family to get married, the other sixth graders discover Harriet's notebook and form a plan to get revenge. The loss of Ole Golly and her two best friends cause Harriet to respond with the sturdy independence that got her into trouble in the first place. Her parents and teachers help her use her keen powers of observation and her writing ability in positive ways. Gradually, Harriet softens enough to apologize, and her friends return.

Harriet is a prickly person who comes to realize at the end of the book that she is intelligent. She has never known what to do with her precocious insights, and has used her ability in negative ways. The problem is really only pointed out, not solved, in this book.

Why is Harriet's notebook so important to her? Why does she write so many stinging comments? How does her intelligence get her into trouble? How can it help her get out of it? If you were writing a sequel to this book, what would you have Harriet do to make and keep friends, but still be herself? When is it all right not to be popular?

See also Using Abilities.

Galbraith, Judy. T*he Gifted Kids Survival Guide for Ages 10 and Under.* (See Identity for full description.)

Getting along with others is discussed in sections on making friends, coping with teasing, and getting along at home.

See also Using Abilities.

Greene, Constance C. *A Girl Called Al.* Illustrated by Byron Barton. New York: Viking, 1969.

Al(exandra) has an extraordinary IQ, but she doesn't work to capacity and is a nonconformist. She explains all this when she meets the narrator (a girl of Al's age who is never named) shortly after she moves into the same apartment building. Al is also lonely and well-defended regarding her weight and her parents' neglect. The narrator introduces her to Mr. Richards, the building janitor, and he very gently works to help Al lose weight and to relieve her loneliness.

Giftedness is mentioned just once, but is clear in Al's conversation and insights. The emphasis of the book is on the gradual development of sensitivity to the feelings of others, on the common courage of people facing loneliness, and on the way in which friendship can compensate for lost family ties. This book is better used with fourth graders than with older gifted children.

Al is a very strong character, clearly the leader in the girls' relationship. Discussion can begin with this relationship: What do the two girls have to offer each other in spite of their differences? What sets Al apart and contributes to her loneliness? What does she offer to the narrator and her family and Mr. Richards? What does the narrator offer Al? How will Al become less lonely over time? What does she need from other people? Would you be willing to give it to her? What would make it difficult for you to do so?

See also Identity.

Heller, Sherri Z. *What Makes You So Special?* (See Using Abilities for full description.)

The section of the book about relating to friends who were not chosen for a gifted program will help to identify and develop attitudes that promote successful interpersonal relationships.

See also Identity.

Hunt, Irene. *Across Five Aprils.* (See Using Abilities for full description.)

For what reasons do some people in this book criticize others? What is your own response to the criticisms, at the beginning of the book and at the end? In real life, what are your reasons for sometimes looking down on other people? What can you do to develop your own tolerance for people who are different from you? Is it worth the effort? Why or why not?

Hunt, Irene. *The Lottery Rose.* New York: Scribner's, 1976.

When seven-year-old Georgie wins a rosebush in a grocery store lottery, it brings to life the beautiful gardens in books, which represent to Georgie a safe haven from his alcoholic mother and Steve's beatings. Finally the neighbors call the police to stop a beating, and then Georgie is sent to a residential school. Georgie knows that a lovely garden across the street is the perfect home for his rosebush, but when he plants it there without permission, Mrs. Harper is so angry that he continues to fear and hate her, even after he learns to love her father, Mr. Collier, and her mentally handicapped son, Robin. Georgie's old school file labels him "retarded," "destructive," and "incorrigible," but in the accepting environment of the new school with Mr. Collier teaching him to read and Robin looking up to him as a friend, Georgie begins to relax and give as well as receive love and trust. Eventually, Georgie learns to trust Mrs. Harper, and then a tragedy brings them even closer.

With a background in psychology, Hunt writes with knowledge and sensitivity about the strong and conflicting feelings of a victim of child abuse. Robin is depicted with love and respect, and Mrs. Harper's anger and grief are shown in ways that young readers can understand. No one in the book enjoys a perfect life, but the story shows how interdependence can lift people above the limitations of circumstance.

What does Georgie need from other people? What does he give to them? Ask the same questions for Robin and Mrs. Harper. Why is it hard to ask for what we need from others? Who in the story gives without being asked? Do you know someone who does this? Do you know what you need from other people? What you give to others?

See also Using Abilities.

Konigsburg, E. L. *Jennifer, Hecate, Macbeth, William McKinley and Me, Elizabeth.* (See Aloneness for full description.)

Why is Elizabeth uncomfortable at the birthday party? Do you agree with her behavior? Why is she more comfortable with Jennifer? Why does Elizabeth finally pull away from Jennifer? How does this affect their friendship? What does each girl offer to the other?

See also Identity.

Krumgold, Joseph. *Henry 3.* (See Identity for full description.)

Explore the friendship between Henry and Fletcher. If Henry is so much brighter than Fletcher, why do they get along so well? Try to relate Fletcher's comments or actions that would cause you to like him if you were Henry. Do you have friends who offer you what Fletcher offers Henry?

LeShan, Eda. *What Makes Me Feel This Way? Growing Up with Human Emotions.* (See Identity for full description.)

Find sections that discuss issues related to getting along with others and ask the child for his response. What personal experiences does the book bring to mind? He may remember past events that he is now ready to discuss. The book can promote discussion of how he feels about his relationships with classmates and how he is presently coping with situations that bother him. Adults should consider whether this book is better used with groups or with individual children.

See also Aloneness.

Paterson, Katherine. *A Bridge to Terabithia.* (See Identity for full description.)

How do Jess and Leslie recognize each other as potential friends? What does Leslie offer to Jess? What does Jess offer to Leslie to build a friendship? What do you offer to and gain from special friends?

See also Aloneness, Using Abilities, Drive to Understand.

Speare, Elizabeth George. *The Witch of Blackbird Pond.* (See Aloneness for full description.)

Consider instances in which one person supports another even without agreeing with what that person is doing. Have you ever seen someone offer that kind of support to another? Why do people do this? Have you ever done it yourself? Can you think of an opportunity to do so? What would be the consequences, both positive and negative?

Voigt, Cynthia. *Building Blocks.* New York: Atheneum, 1984.

Brann Connell has grown up believing that his father is weak, indecisive, and ineffectual. In a time-warp experience, he spends a day with his father as a boy, seeing his father's childhood home and family and watching how ten-year-old Kevin coped with a situation too difficult for Brann's comprehension. He returns to his own time with a better understanding not only of his father, but also of his father's traits which represent a strength Brann lacks.

Voigt reveals a sensitivity to different personality styles that can help gifted children recognize, even look for, something of value in people they have not been able to understand. This book suggests that there is much to know about others for those who look below the surface and are open to another's experience.

How will Brann's experience change his future relationship with his father? Can you choose someone you have difficulty understanding or with whom you are impatient and imagine a story like this told about that person? How does it change your feeling about him or her? How does the experience help Brann understand himself better?

See also Identity.

Wier, Ester. *The Loner.* (See Aloneness for full description.)

What events cause David to change? How do people help to cause the change? What did David do to bring about the change in himself? In your classroom, what would make it difficult for a loner to make friends? How could you help them? What would a loner at school have to do to make that happen?

Using Abilities

Fitzhugh, Louise. *Harriet the Spy.* (See Getting Along with Others for full description.)

Harriet has been using her special ability in ways that have given other people good reason to dislike her. Do you know anyone who does this? Why do people behave that way? What are the disadvantages? What do they need from others to help them change? What can they do for themselves to change? What will enable Harriet to use her ability more positively?

Fritz, Jean. *Where Do You Think You're Going, Christopher Columbus?* (See Developing Imagination in the Early Elementary section for full description.)

This biography is best suited for the middle elementary years. Fourth graders who have not read it yet should be introduced to it now.

Galbraith, Judy. *The Gifted Kids Survival Guide for Ages 10 and Under.* (See Identity for full description.)

The sections on boredom and perfectionism will be helpful in discussing ways of using one's potential.

See also Getting Along with Others.

Heller, Sherri Z. *What Makes You So Special?.* Illustrated by Jon Enten. Phoenix: Thinking Caps, 1979.

Addressed to students who have been assigned to a gifted program at school, this book briefly defines giftedness (the ability to become a good thinker) and then discusses such issues as risk taking and how to relate to friends who were not chosen for the program. The remainder of the book offers constructive ways of coping with boredom in class so that children use rather than waste ability. The suggestions encourage children to use their creativity to make assignments more interesting, promoting self-motivation and the value of challenging oneself.

Parents or teachers can read this book along with children soon after they have been selected for a school gifted program, discussing and answering questions that arise from each page. It would be ideal if both parents and teachers knew the content of the book, so they could reinforce the ideas in working with the child on school assignments.

See also Identity, Getting Along with Others.

Hunt, Irene. *Across Five Aprils.* Illustrated by Albert John Pucci. Chicago: Follett, 1964.

Following a southern Illinois family across the five Aprils of the Civil War, this book depicts the pain of families and communities divided by loyalties to North and South. Jethro Creighton is nine when the war begins, and within a year has the responsibility of managing the farm that feeds the family members still at home. Through letters, they follow the sons at war while at home, they face danger and hatred because one son has joined the Confederate Army.

A minor theme is the growth of Jethro, whom his unlettered mother recognizes as having special talent. Encouraged by the schoolteacher before he goes off to war, and by the newspaper editor in a nearby town, Jeth follows the war through newspapers and atlases and works to improve his crude country speech. He will be the first of the family to go to college.

The book has many possibilities for discussion. When discussing giftedness, include the distinction between intelligence and education, the need to look behind poor speech patterns for a good mind, and the value of an education where it cannot be taken for granted.

What does Matt mean when he says the replacement teacher has a "mean and pinched-in mind"? How does Shad encourage Jethro to learn without school? Give examples of people who have expansive minds. How can you cultivate that for yourself?

Hunt, Irene. *The Lottery Rose.* (See Getting Along with Others for full description.)

Why does Georgie think he will never be able to read? Why can he learn so much more easily at his new school than at the old one? What factors affect how well children do in school other than their intelligence? (For broader understanding, encourage children to name more than those in this story.) Do you know anyone who is not doing as well in school as he or she could? What do they need to be able to do their best?

Kelly, Eric P. *The Trumpeter of Krakow.* New York: Macmillan, 1966 [c1928].

Joseph Charnetski is 15 in 1461 when his father's house and fields are destroyed and he flees with his parents to the busy medieval city of Krakow. Here they meet the alchemist and scholar, Kreutz, and his niece Elzbietka. Kreutz finds lodging for the family and work for Joseph's father as a trumpeter in the church tower. But those who destroyed the Charnetskis' home have followed them to Krakow, seeking the Tarnov Crystal which has been the responsibility of the Charnetski family for generations. Kreutz, too, is in danger. One of his students is systematically hypnotizing him to gain the secret of turning base metals into gold.

The setting of this book is one of its strengths, giving a picture of Krakow as a medieval center and of the 15th century as a time of transition from superstition to science. The story is suspenseful, and the subplot raises questions about the moral uses of knowledge.

How valid are the arguments Tring uses to persuade Kreutz to do the experiments Tring wants him to do? In Kreutz's position, what would have been your attitude toward the general interest in making gold from base metals? Are there situations now in which scientists are asked to work for gain rather than for knowledge? What is the responsibility to society of anyone with unusual knowledge, ability, intelligence?

Konigsburg, E. L. *(George).* (See Identity for full description.)

Read aloud the section about using skills to "collect attention" and "buy friends" (page 52 in the edition noted). Why is it tempting for Ben to do this? How can people who do this learn not to? What help do they need from others? Read about "not-knowing gracefully" (page 53 in the same edition). What does George mean by this? What do you not-know gracefully? What does Ben learn about using his intelligence well?

See also Aloneness.

Paterson, Katherine. *A Bridge to Terebithia.* (See Identity for full description.)

Why is it so difficult for Jess to develop his artistic talent? What will he have to do to be able to use his talent? What traits will help him? If you were in his situation, what traits do you have that would help you? What talent do you have that you can develop? Is it harder or easier for you than for Jess? Why?

See also Aloneness, Getting Along with Others, Drive to Understand.

Paterson, Katherine. *Come Sing, Jimmy Jo.* (See Identity for full description.)

How is James' gift a "burden" to him? ("Sometimes the gift seems more like a burden.") What are his rewards for singing? Are they worth the sacrifices? Identify a gift or talent of yours. What would be the sacrifices and rewards of developing it fully? Do you want to? How? Discuss Grandma's statement that "The Lord don't give private presents." To what extent do gifted people have a responsibility to use their gifts? If you think there is no responsibility, what other reasons are there to use gifts?

Rodgers, Mary. *Freaky Friday.* Illustrated by the author. New York: Harper & Row, 1972.

Annabel Andrews and her mother trade places, so Annabel goes through the day in her mother's body and sees herself as others speak to her "mother" about her. She learns that her brother loves her despite her impatience with him, that the housekeeper will not clean her room because it is so messy, that the boy she admires thinks she is ugly and awful, and that her teachers are frustrated with her underachievement.

The book is sometimes hilarious as the reader follows Annabel's thoughts and reactions. The high point is her mother's interview with her teachers, in which Annabel learns that she has a high IQ and that her teachers are concerned about her lack of achievement. When she and her mother resume their own bodies, she finds that her mother has had her braces removed, her hair cut, and has bought Annabel a new wardrobe. Instant transformation from an ugly duckling to a budding beauty — what every adolescent girl would love to have!

What is it about the interview with her teachers that makes Annabel want to change? How would Annabel describe herself at the beginning of the book? How would you describe her at the end? What *inner* changes take place? Why? Do you know anyone like Annabel? What do you think he or she is like inside?

Sebestyen, Ouida. *Words By Heart.* (See Identity for full description.)

What did Papa teach Lena, both by what he said and by the way he lived? Is there anything in it that could be useful to you? If your own life is easier than Lena's, how might that make it more of a challenge for you to grow up to be a productive person, making full use of the abilities you have? How are you doing so far?

Tolan, Stephanie S. *A Time to Fly Free.* (See Aloneness for full description.)

What effect will dropping out of school have on Josh's ability to make good use of his intelligence? What responsibility (if any) does a bright person have to use his or her intelligence? Who determines what is a "good" use of intelligence? In making that decision for yourself, what factors would you consider?

Wojciechowska, Maia. *Shadow of a Bull.* (See Identity for full description.)

What advice would you give Manolo? Manolo's mother says that what his father did was "for himself, most of all for himself." Is that all right, or is it selfish? Why? What does Manolo do for himself? Is it selfish? What do you do for yourself that is not selfish?

Drive to Understand

Anno, Mitsumasa. *Anno's Medieval World.* Illustrated by the author. New York: Philomel, 1979.

With text and pictures, Anno presents the religious beliefs and superstitions that made up the medieval world-view. The infant sciences of the time were not understood by many people, and their message was frightening — nothing less than the rejection of age-old convictions about how the world was structured. Anno mentions the burning at the stake of Bruno, who espoused Copernicus' theory of the universe, and the recanting of Galileo. The book ends with adventurers sailing off to learn whether the world is indeed round.

This book could be used as the basis for discussion not only of the medieval world, the Ptolemaic and Copernican theories, and the blend of science and culture, but also of how it feels to know, as Galileo did, a truth that others cannot yet recognize. In an author's note, Anno speaks of our ability (or lack of it) to feel what Bruno or Galileo felt, having knowledge and unable to convince others of its truth. ". . . it troubles me," Anno says, "to hear it said, lightly and without any feeling, 'The world is round and it moves.'" Through discussions of this book, children can gain appreciation of how hard-won that knowledge is, as Anno hoped.

How would it feel to live in a world where it is dangerous to have or seek scientific knowledge? Knowledge of any kind? Why is it important for scholars to be able to speak about what they learn, even if it is not popular?

As a picture book, this appears to be for young children but the ideas can profitably be explored by students in the upper elementary grades or in junior high.

Cresswell, Helen. *Ordinary Jack.* New York: Macmillan, 1977.

Jack is the only ordinary member of the extraordinary Bagthorpe family. Father writes scripts for BBC, Mother writes an advice column, and siblings William, Tess, and Rosie all have several "strings to their bows," a circumstance which is highly valued in the Bagthorpe clan. With Grandma (irascible), Grandpa (selectively deaf), Uncle Parker and Aunt Celia (poet and potter) and their daughter Daisy (arsonist), life is always interesting if not chaotic. Jack's only claim to fame is his hapless dog, Zero. Uncle Parker decides that Jack will become known as a Prophet and helps him set this up, advising Jack to stage Mysterious Impressions and Visions, building to Rosie's birthday party, when the vision of the red and white bubble and the Great Brown Bear comes true.

The zany humor is sure to appeal to gifted readers. In addition to good characterization and dialogue, *Ordinary Jack* provides some insights into the quirks — good and bad — of creative people.

This book is for sheer fun. It would be difficult, and probably inappropriate, to try to base a serious discussion on it, but gifted readers should have the experience of participating in the antics of this bright and unusual family.

Dickinson, Peter. *The Weathermonger.* Boston: Little, Brown, 1969.

Set five years in the future, this science fiction story tells of an England propelled back to the Middle Ages by the Changes, unexplained forces that cause the people to reject machinery and rely on magic and superstition. Geoffrey, the Weymouth weathermonger, is to be drowned with his sister, Sally, because he has maintained the motorboat they had before the Changes. They escape to France in the boat and are sent back to England to find the source of the Changes. Their search leads them to a medieval forest near the Welsh border where they confront a reawakened Merlin and learn how the Changes originated.

This well-written book is a good introduction to science fiction and fantasy, containing elements of each. It is clearly a "boys' book," combining adventure and love of machinery. More seriously, it raises questions about the environmental impact of machinery. What are the relative advantages and disadvantages of the Middle Ages and the present? Can we manage to have the best of both?

Latham, Jean Lee. *Carry On, Mr. Bowditch.* Illustrated by John O'Hara Cosgrave. Boston: Houghton Mifflin, 1955.

Nathaniel Bowditch grew up in Salem in the age of sailing ships. He had a quick mind, especially in math, and it was clear that he should go to Harvard. But there was no money, so instead he was indentured for nine years.

People who recognized his brilliance offered the use of their libraries, and Nat never stopped learning. He taught himself languages, mathematics, and astronomy, and when he went to sea he learned navigation. Soon he was teaching others, and before he was 30 he had written a book on navigation which is still a standard text.

This biography is a story of both physical and intellectual adventure. In addition, it includes several themes related to giftedness: Nat's thirst for learning and the necessity of persistence; the eagerness of uneducated sailors to learn and Nat's commitment to teaching them; and his commitment to accuracy and the importance of risking a new approach, trusting new knowledge rather than traditional methods. Nat's example of zest for learning and disregard for obstacles shines throughout the book.

People think of Nat as a "brain." What is your response to that? Have you ever felt as though you are "stumbling on other people's dumbness. And — you want to kick something."? What traits does Nat have that enable him to overcome that while continuing to use his brain? What can you learn from Nat?

L'Engle, Madeleine. *A Wrinkle in Time.* (See Identity for full description.)

Like many of L'Engle's books, *A Wrinkle in Time* features an entire cast of gifted characters. They exhibit the drive to understand, as a gifted reader will easily recognize. What is more, they show that it adds meaning and purpose to living. The book is intellectually satisfying to gifted children because of frequent references to math, science, literature, and music. Challenging discussions based on the book could begin with the question, "What do you think about life on Camazotz?"

Paterson, Katherine. *A Bridge to Terebithia.* (See Identity for full description.)

Describe the difference in background between Jess and Leslie. Why is the trip to Washington, D.C. so important to Jess? Have you had any such experience?

Phelps, Ethel Johnston. *The Maid of the North: Feminist Folk Tales from Around the World.* Illustrated by Lloyd Bloom. New York: Holt, Rinehart and Winston, 1981.

Phelps has gathered folk tales from Europe, Africa, the Far East, Asia, and North America, the common thread being that the main character in each is a woman who is spirited, clever, or brave — a heroine instead of a hero.

The feminism is not belabored. These are simply good tales, little-known and therefore fresh and spritely, in the authentic folklore form. They are good reading for gifted children, both boys and girls.

Rawls, Wilson. *Where the Red Fern Grows.* Toronto,: Bantam Pathfinder, 1974 [c1961].

Billy works for three years to save the money to buy Old Dan and Little Ann, the coon hounds he so ardently wants. Old Dan is strong and tenacious, Little Ann is smart and quick, and Billy trains them until they hunt with skill and precision, a well-matched pair. Rivalry with a neighbor and his hound and a championship hunt add both adventure and tragedy.

Where the Red Fern Grows offers unforgettable images of a life few boys know: coon hunting in the Cherokee country of the Ozarks. Rawls vividly describes the country, the hunt, and the dogs. The relationship between Billy and his family, especially his grandfather, is convincing and moving. Most memorable, however, is the bond between Old Dan and Little Ann, and the love between Billy and his dogs.

Junior High: Grades 7-9

Identity

Galbraith, Judy. *The Gifted Kids Survival Guide for Ages 11 to 18.* Minneapolis: Free Spirit, 1983.

Written for gifted students from ages 11 to 18, this book speaks directly to junior and senior high school students.

Compiling contributions from over 300 gifted teenagers, the author describes the frustrations of growing up gifted and offers suggestions for dealing with them: What to do when bored in class, tips for making friends, steps to improve educational opportunities, how to handle stress, and techniques for setting goals. With extensive use of eye-catching graphics and a fast-paced breezy style, the book speaks directly to junior and senior high students.

There is a wealth of material for discussion. One approach would be to choose a paragraph of particular relevance and ask general questions: What do you think of this? Is this a problem for you? Have you tried this? How did it work?

For discussions to clarify self-concept, the first five sections of the book will be useful since they all deal with identification of the gifted.

See also Getting Along with Others, Using Abilities.

Gardam, Jane. *Bilgewater.* New York: Willow Books, 1977.

Marigold, nicknamed Bilgewater, grows up in an isolated environment — the English boys' boarding school where her widowed father is a master. Her best friends are the other masters — who are her father's friends — and Paula, the matron who is a substitute mother for her. Dyslexia adds to her isolation and masks her intelligence for years. By the time she is 17, she has overcome it and is suddenly encouraged to take the entrance exams for Oxford and Cambridge. At the same time a childhood friend returns and draws her into a social life, and two of the boarding school boys begin to notice her, with mixed results. All of this plays a significant role in her slowly growing self-confidence. Marigold, her father, and Paula are memorable individuals, and the surprise ending contributes to a book well worth reading.

The many British terms add to the challenge and interest without being a barrier to good readers. Characters and setting are well drawn, and Marigold's intelligence and wit come through plainly — to the reader, if not to her.

How does Marigold's self-concept affect her behavior? How accurate is it? Does she like herself? Do you like her? Why/why not? What do Terrapin and Boakes see in her? How does her appearance affect the kind of person she becomes? How does our appearance, or our perception of it, affect the kind of people we all become? How do all of these questions apply to you?

See also Aloneness, Getting Along with Others.

Konigsburg, E. L. *Father's Arcane Daughter.* New York: Atheneum, 1976. (See Using Abilities for full description.)

Why was it important for Heidi to know that she was gifted? What was more important to Heidi's and Winston's adult success than their intelligence?

LeGuin, Ursula K. *Very Far Away from Anywhere Else.* New York: Atheneum, 1976.

Owen Griffiths tells his story, of being "a bright little jerk" and how he deals with being different. When he was in junior high, he tried conforming but now that he is 16, he knows that conforming for the sake of conformity will not work for him, although he is still not comfortable being himself. Natalie Fields is. She is also a gifted musician, self-sufficient and self-directed. Owen learns from Natalie, and when the friendship shows signs of turning into love he learns even more, especially about taking charge of his own future.

This book shows several facets of being alone and different because of being gifted, and how two people cope with it, although they are also different from each other.

How does Owen feel about himself when he says he was a bright little jerk? Have you ever tried to conform, as Owen did, and found it not right for you? What will happen to Owen's and Natalie's sense of being different as they grow older? Describe how you think of them as adults. What are they doing now that will cause them to grow into the kind of people you describe? Describe yourself as an adult. What characteristics do you have that will bring about the person you describe?

See Aloneness, Using Abilities.

Oneal, Zibby. *The Language of Goldfish.* New York: Viking, 1980.

For someone who resists change, adolescence can be frightening. Carrie Stokes is frightened, but she doesn't know why. She is most comfortable on Saturday mornings in her art teacher's home, but when confronted with symbols of growing up like junior dancing class, she has brief spells of dizziness. Finally she loses touch with reality enough to need a psychiatrist. The combination of her talks with him and her art work, plus her acceptance of an unexpected change in her art teacher, bring Carrie to an acceptance of change in herself.

Gifted in math as well as in art, Carrie has the advantage of being in the advanced math class; nevertheless she feels out of step. The critical times come when she is forced to do something she is not ready for by people who expect her to act 13 before she is ready to do so. She must be herself, and have some control over her own rate of growth.

The book offers insight into the pressures placed on young people to grow up at the rate society dictates, into the necessity of being oneself despite external pressures, and into the experience of psychotherapy — something about which young people probably need more information than they have at present. It also brings out how different individuals respond to the same situation in different ways, for entirely legitimate reasons.

Why did Carrie respond the way she did to the pressures of growing up? Can Carrie's story help you to be more tolerant of responses you may not understand in people around you? In yourself? What does Carrie learn about herself? What does she do to help herself to get better? What are her strengths to help her cope with being different? Your strengths?

See also Aloneness, Getting Along with Others.

Paterson, Katherine. *Jacob Have I Loved.* New York: Crowell, 1980.

Growing up on an island in Chesapeake Bay, Louise is convinced that everyone despises her and loves Caroline, her beautiful, musically talented twin sister. Not until she is 17 does Louise recognize that she is gifted intellectually and capable of doing anything she chooses. Others are willing to help, but she must make the choice.

A Newbery winner, this complex book has several themes other than giftedness, and a thoughtful teenager will find much here to think about: sibling rivalry, responsibility for one's own decisions, tradition breaking and respect for tradition, going one's own way despite being and feeling different.

How do Caroline's and Louise's picture of themselves affect their behavior? Their decisions? How accurate are their pictures of themselves? How does being gifted affect each girl's childhood? What difference does it make (in personal happiness, in career choice, in the way you treat other people) to know you are gifted?

See also Getting Along with Others, Using Abilities.

Peck, Richard. *Remembering the Good Times.* New York: Delacorte, 1985.

At 16, Buck Mendenhall looks back over the last four years to tell the story of his friendship with Kate Lucas and Trav Kirby. Coming from different backgrounds, they are brought together by the transformation of their rural area into an affluent suburb. Together they face the stresses of adolescence in a too-rapidly changing world. It is Trav, the brilliant and wealthy one, who finally cannot cope with the combination of pressure at home and mediocrity and neglect in the new school.

This book is rich in characters, relationships, and issues for discussion, but paramount is the suicide of bright, intense, sensitive Trav. Discussion of suicide is difficult but worth the effort. Leaders should be prepared with their personal answers to the questions they ask, however incomplete those answers may be.

Trav and Kate both have talent. What are the differences that make Kate stronger? Do you agree with Kate: "I'll never trust anything again. I'll never believe in anything or anybody. You can count on that"?

See also Using Ability.

Peyton, K. M. *The Beethoven Medal.* New York: Crowell, 1971.

In this second Pennington book, following *Pennington's Last Term,* Patrick Pennington is studying piano on a scholarship and working as a bakery delivery boy when Ruth Hollis meets him. Ruth is puzzled by the gulf between Pat's working class background, his aggressive, rough manners, his jail record, and the other world he enters as a potential concert pianist. The two sides of Pat are not resolved by the end of the book, and the relationship between him and Ruth seems likely to continue, at least for a while.

The book presents a strong portrait of the lengths to which a gifted person may have to go to develop a gift. Pat is an example of one who has made a firm commitment to his talent, but is still tormented by the negative aspects of some of the very characteristics that, put to constructive use, could make him a concert pianist. A complex person, Pat is not entirely explained in this book, nor is Ruth, whose relationship to Pat seems to be rather slavish without sufficient reason given for that. The book can nevertheless be useful for discussion. It is demanding reading, partly because of British slang. The toughness of Pat and his friends may make the book appealing to some readers.

There are two very clear sides to Pat. Which do you think is real? What reasons do you have for your answer? What factors will determine which side of himself Pat develops? What responsibility does he himself have in the determination?

See also Using Abilities.

Platt, Kin. *The Boy Who Could Make Himself Disappear.* New York: Dell, 1968.

Roger Baxter's parents have just divorced, and Roger and his mother have moved to New York City. Roger has a speech impediment (he cannot say "R", so he cannot pronounce his own name correctly) caused by a childhood injury and exacerbated by anxiety. His parents ignore Roger; only his speech therapists really care for him. He is sensitive but cannot express his feelings because he has learned that his parents will not listen and because he tries to avoid R-words. The stress of his parents' divorce and his relocation finally drive Roger into a schizophrenic state — the reader can see him gradually fade out of touch with reality and "disappear." The book ends with some hope as Roger begins to make contact with a man who will care for him.

The book makes demands on the reader through flashbacks and by presenting past events in fragments as Roger remembers them, so that the reader only gradually is able to build up the entire memory. It provides a description of how it feels to be different seen from the inside, and a view of how much can be going on inside a person who seems merely quiet to most outsiders.

How does the Roger you would know if you went to school with him differ from the Roger you know from reading the book? How do you differ from the way people know you at school?

See also Getting Along with Others.

Rand, Ayn. *Anthem.* New York: New American Library, 1946.

In a future collectivist society, Equality 7-2521 is out of place because he is more intelligent than most. Assigned to be a Street Sweeper, he discovers a tunnel which becomes a hiding place where he writes and experiments, eventually discovering electricity. When he presents his discovery to the Scholars, they reject him and he flees to the Uncharted Forest, finding there an abandoned house from the Unmentionable Times (the 20th Century). Here he finds manuscripts and reads in them his heritage, including the forbidden, lost word: ego, I. Recognizing the possibilities of individualism, he resolves to begin a new life and a new political order.

This novel was written for the purpose of extolling individualism over collectivism. Gifted junior high students are enthusiastic about it. They understand the political message, see a need for balance between the individual and the community, and identify with Equality's urge to know and his frustration at being repressed.

Does anything like the Scholars' rejection of Equality's idea ever happen to students in school or to teenagers in their families? How do they react? How can people who are different cope in our society without leaving, as Equality did?

See also Getting Along with Others, Using Abilities.

Rhue, Morton. *The Wave.* (See Aloneness for full description.)

Different characters respond in different ways to The Wave. Why does Robert become so deeply involved so easily? What is happening to the teacher in the course of the experiment? How is Laurie different from the others in the book, causing her response to be different from theirs? How does all this relate to a sense of identity?

See also Using Abilities.

Tolan, Stephanie S. *No Safe Harbors.* New York: Fawcett Juniper, 1981.

Amanda Sterling is the 16-year-old daughter of the wealthy mayor of a town on the Ohio River. Her ten-year-old brother, Doug, is a precocious loner, intent on rock-hunting, and her mother represents the proper mayor's wife, an activist in correct causes. Amanda has just met Joe Schmidt, who is working at the marina because his father refused to sign the college financial forms when Joe insisted on studying English rather than something practical. When Amanda learns that her father is guilty of accepting a bribe, her problem of rejecting her father is comparable to Joe's problem of rejecting his.

Both Doug and Joe are gifted, and some of the problems of giftedness are explored through them. They cope in different ways. Doug has given up on having friends his own age; Joe tries to learn to like rock music. Amanda's difference from her friends is in terms of values. Her friends assume and accept her father's guilt. Amanda eventually accepts him, but not what he did.

What are the advantages of Doug's way of coping with being different? The disadvantages? Reread the discussion about dealing with feeling different (beginning on page 64 in the noted edition). What would you add to that? What does it say that you have not considered before?

See also Using Abilities.

Aloneness

Cunningham, Julia. *Dorp Dead.* New York: Pantheon, 1965.

Gilly Ground is a ten-year-old orphan when his grandmother dies. He spends a year in an orphanage, hiding his intelligence so he can use it as a weapon of defense if necessary, and not allowing himself to become emotionally involved with anyone. His single pleasure is to go to a crumbling tower on a hill near town. One day he meets a man there who identifies himself only as The Hunter. On that day, Gilly is expelled for leaving the orphanage without permission, and he is sent to live with Mr. Kobalt, the ladder-maker and a recluse. Gilly welcomes the change and the quiet, warm, regulated life at first, and befriends the spiritless dog, Mash. He is horrified when Mr. Kobalt whips Mash, explaining that the dog must prepare to die because the animal is getting old and will soon have to be replaced. Gilly realizes that he is as expendable as the dog to Mr. Kobalt and when he discovers that Mr. Kobalt is secretly building a cage for Gilly, he knows he must escape. Eventually he and Mash do so and become the family of The Hunter.

Tension builds slowly and evenly, and the reader realizes along with Gilly that the safety he sought, the protective shell, is actually threatening his life. The book should be discussed with this symbolism in mind: seeking safety, not taking risks, can ultimately threaten the potential one has for life.

Why does Gilly not make friends? Why does he welcome Mr. Kobalt's routine? What is the real danger at Mr. Kobalt's? What strengths does Gilly have that help him handle the situation?

See also Using Abilities.

Gardam, Jane. *Bilgewater.* (See Identity for full description.)

Marigold had more time alone as she was growing up than most children have. How was this an advantage to her? What would she have said if you had asked her this question when she was 15 or 16? What would she say now?

See also Getting Along with Others.

Hunter, Mollie. *A Sound of Chariots.* (See Using Abilities for full description.)

Bridie makes friends at the Wishart school by giving up time for herself and by stifling her leadership qualities. Why would these choices be difficult for some people? Why are they possible for Bridie? How does she compensate for the loss? Have you made similar sacrifices? How do you compensate?

See also Getting Along with Others.

LeGuin, Ursula K. *Very Far Away from Anywhere Else.* (See Identity for full description.)

What is the difference between Owen's kind of aloneness, and Natalie's kind? Natalie likes herself better than Owen does. How has she learned to do that? What difference does it make in her life? Does it make her less alone?

See also Using Abilities.

Moser, Don. *A Heart to the Hawks.* (See Getting Along with Others for full description.)

Is Mike too much of a loner? Why or why not?

See also Using Abilities.

Oneal, Zibby. *The Language of Goldfish.* (See Identity for full description.)

Why does Carrie withdraw from friends at school? How does she spend the time by herself that she gains by withdrawing? Is withdrawing or the wish to be alone good for her? What are you reasons for your answer?

See also Getting Along with Others.

Rhue, Morton. *The Wave.* New York: Delacorte, 1981.

Based on a real incident in a California high school, this is the story of a teacher's attempt to demonstrate to a history class how it felt to live in Germany under Nazism. Within a short time, the students and even the teacher are caught up in The Wave, their experimental totalitarian organization. It spreads to include students outside the history class until the teacher realizes that it has gained a momentum of its own, and he must stop it somehow. It is clear that this will hurt some of the students, especially Robert, an underachiever who is rebelling against his brother's success, for whom The Wave is a born-again experience. The story is told largely form the point of view of Laurie, an A student and editor of the student paper, who questions the group and finally writes an editorial exposing its dangers.

Rhue does well at presenting The Wave from various points of view so that the reader begins to understand how such a group can be attractive, and to whom. The saving grace is Laurie's insistence on thinking for herself, and her mother's support as she stands alone for what she sees as right.

Why does Laurie take the Hitler film "too seriously?" How does she keep fighting, even after David and Amy desert her? What qualities does that take? Do you have them? How can one develop them? Why and how do good people like David become involved in such a group? How could that be avoided?

See also Identity, Using Abilities.

Rimm, Sylvia B. "It's Dumb to Be Smart." In G/C/T, March/April, 1981.

Published in a magazine about gifted, creative, and talented children, this short story is about Jennie, a junior high student who feels unpopular because she is too smart. She decides it is not dumb to be smart, as her friend Christi says, but it is lonely. Her school counselor arranges a talk between Jennie and Bob, two bright students who respond very differently to their loneliness. Jennie recognizes that she is not lonely when she is reading or thinking; then it feels good to be alone. In contrast to Bob, she sees also that she has benefited from being alone.

Since it is a short story, "It's Dumb to Be Smart" can be read aloud and discussed in one session — or in two, one on aloneness and one on using abilities.

Discuss the differences between Bob and Jennie. What do you think causes them? Do you know anyone like Bob? Like Jennie? What activities can you do alone without being lonely?

See also Using Abilities.

Getting Along with Others

Galbraith, Judy. *The Gifted Kids Survival Guide for Ages 11 to 18.* (See Identity for full description.)

To build discussion of getting along with others, use the two sections on friends, the one on teasing and the one on getting along with parents.

See also Using Abilities.

Gardam, Jane. *Bilgewater.* (See Identity for full description.)

How did Marigold make it difficult for other people to know her? How do we all do that? What are the consequences? What are some remedies?

See also Aloneness.

Hamilton, Virginia. *The Planet of Junior Brown.* New York: Dell, 1971.

Junior Brown is obese, an artist and a musician. The adults in his life are his mother (who wants Junior to be cultured but is not able to understand his art or listen to his music), his piano teacher (who is demented, but Junior cannot afford to recognize that), his absent father, and Mr. Pool, the school janitor. There is also Buddy, a fellow student who has no family and who is part of an underground network that helps homeless boys to survive in New York City. Buddy and Mr. Pool watch Junior slip toward insanity, and they are able to begin to help him back to reality.

This well-written book offers challenging reading and at least two themes that would be useful for gifted students to discuss: the frustration of Junior's talent, symbolized by the silent pianos; and the challenge of getting along with others, exemplified by Buddy, a leader who progresses from teaching his boys to live for themselves to teaching them to live for others. In spite of his strength, it is clear that Buddy also needs help — a reminder that we are interdependent, not self-sufficient.

Why does Junior need Buddy? What does he offer to Buddy? How do Nightman and Franklin help each other? Identify a leader whom you follow. What do you offer to that person?

See also Using Abilities.

Hipp, Earl. *Fighting Invisible Tigers: A Student Guide to Life in "The Jungle."* (See Using Abilities for full description.)

The section on weaving a safety net offers ideas that junior high students will find especially useful for building supportive relationships.

Hunter, Mollie. *A Sound of Chariots.* (See Using Abilities for full description.)

Bridie develops into "two separate people," one a chatterbox and one an observer, and then she is lonely. Is this a good way to handle the problem Mr. Purves describes as grownups not liking her insight? How else could she have done it?

See also Aloneness.

Moser, Don. *A Heart to the Hawks.* New York: Atheneum, 1975.

At 14, Mike Harrington is an amateur biologist, a collector of small wild creatures, and a sophisticated student of the pond near his home. But in this summer of 1947, the post-war building boom is reaching his pond and he is powerless to stop it. He tries various means to save the pond and woodland, and then resorts to violence in what he knows will be a futile gesture.

This book should appeal to boys, even those who are scientists first and readers of literature second. They will relate to the friendship between Mike and Corcoran, to their unpolished curiosity about girls, and to Mike's high idealism, his imaginary episodes of life as a lone naturalist, and his need to achieve some measure of acceptance of what he cannot change. The reader believes that as Mike grows older, he will learn more effective ways of bringing about change.

Mike says he hates "stupid people." What ways have you found to deal with people who don't understand you or your interests? What effective ways have you seen others use? What do you think will happen in Mike's relationship with Angelina? How will Mike have to change in order to become effective in protecting the environment?

See also Aloneness, Using Abilities.

Oneal, Zibby. *The Language of Goldfish.* (See Identity for full description.)

How do other people help Carrie to get better? What does Carrie do to allow them to help her? Have you ever been in a situation in which others could help you if you would allow it? What makes it difficult to do that? What are the rewards for people who can do it?

See also Aloneness.

Paterson, Katherine. *Jacob Have I Loved.* (See Identity for full description.)

Louise has what might be called a "prickly" personality. What makes her that way? How does her personality complicate her life? What role does her giftedness play? What can happen to people like this as they become adults? What keeps Louise from turning into a prickly adult? If you could talk to Louise as a teenager, what advice would you give her?

See also Using Abilities.

Platt, Kin. *The Boy Who Could Make Himself Disappear.* (See Identity for full description.)

Few people know the *real* Roger. How could Roger do better at letting others know him? How could they do better? How could you do better at knowing who your classmates really are, and letting them know you?

Rand, Ayn. *Anthem.* (See Identity for full description.)

Do you agree with Equality that "we have no need of our brothers"? Under what conditions might Equality recognize the need for other people? How can people like Equality who are different from or brighter than others manage to be themselves and fit into a community at the same time?

See also Using Abilities.

Using Abilities

Adderholdt-Elliott, Miriam. *Perfectionism: What's Bad about Being Too Good?* Illustrated by Caroline Price. Minneapolis: Free Spirit, 1987.

Many gifted teenagers are victims of perfectionism, harboring so strong a desire to do everything perfectly that they consider second place or a B a failure. Some go so far as to avoid risking failure by refusing to accept a new challenge or to take an advanced course.

Perfectionism speaks to these students, describing its effects on mind, body, and relationships and then prescribing practical steps toward becoming more realistic about expectations. Counselors, teachers, and librarians will find the book a useful tool for school-based discussions on giftedness, and parents can use it effectively at home. The insights it offers are as important for adults working with gifted youngsters as for the students themselves.

Barrett, Susan L. *It's All in Your Head: A Guide to Understanding Your Brain and Boosting Your Brain Power.* Minneapolis: Free Spirit, 1985.

Most gifted students will be fascinated by this informative book on the capacity of the human brain. Barrett gives facts about the physical structure and functioning of the brain, and then goes on to discuss ways of working with it, including different kinds of thinking, developing good memory skills, and enhancing creativity.

The sections about using the brain provide a challenge to students who enjoy mental activities, and create appreciation for the untapped powers that we all have. This book can be used simply to focus on the joys of having a good mind and the potential our minds give us to lead interesting and productive lives.

Clapp, Patricia. *I'm Deborah Sampson, a Soldier in the War of the Revolution.* New York: Lathrop, Lee and Shepard, 1977.

It is an historical fact that Deborah Sampson Gannett, 1760-1827, enlisted in the Continental Army under the name of Robert Shurtlieff. Patricia Clapp uses what little is known about Deborah and adds her own ideas to create a largely hypothetical story of Deborah's life. When Deborah was five, her mother gave her to a cousin to raise because her sailor father could not provide enough for all the children. At ten Deborah is bound out to a family of ten boys. When the Revolution begins, the boys go off to join the army. By then, Deborah and Robbie are in love. Five years after he leaves for the army he is killed. Deborah decides that the one service she can offer him is to live out his wish to serve for the duration of the war. The story goes on with her army service and her marriage to Ben Gannett after the war.

Deborah is a strong character, willing to face discomfort and hardship to accomplish her goals. Her spirit of adventure, willingness to risk, and commitment to her goals make the book useful for considering making full use of one's abilities.

What traits do you most like in Deborah? How are they helpful to her? Do you have any of them yourself? If so, how have you found them to be useful?

Cunningham, Julia. *Dorp Dead.* (See Aloneness for full description.)

Why does Gilly hide his intelligence? Can you give a better explanation than he does? When Gilly changes, how does he do so? Why does he want to use his intelligence at the school he attends after he becomes The Hunter's family? Is it just because of The Hunter, or has something happened in Gilly?

DeKruif, Paul. *Microbe Hunters.* New York: Harcourt, Brace and World, 1926.

This exuberant book is a collection of biographies of the scientists (Pasteur, Koch, Bruce, Reed, Ehrlich et al.) who worked to discover causes and cures of diseases such as anthrax, malaria, diphtheria, hydrophobia, yellow fever, and syphilis. Written in 1926, it is recommended with reservations because of stereotypical comments about women and various ethnic groups, and its careless attitude toward experimenting with animals and human beings.

Despite these drawbacks, the book can be useful. If adults review it before using it with students and discuss these problems with them frankly, they can then focus on what DeKruif intended to convey: a contagious enthusiasm for scientific search, and the role of patient, persistent, routine, dull work — and luck — in bringing about exciting discoveries. These men were gifted, courageous, fallible, devoted, and above all hard- working. The stories of their searching are still an inspiration for young scientists.

What questions does the book raise about medical ethics? What made these people work so hard? Is there any cause which would inspire such devotion in you? Would you like to find one?

Galbraith, Judy. *The Gifted Kids Survival Guide for Ages 11 to 18.* (See Identity for full description.)

Sections of the book relating to using one's potential are those on how to make school more challenging, perfectionism, stress, and goal setting.

See also Getting Along with Others.

Garner, Alan. *The Stone Book.* London: Collins, 1976.

Mary takes a lunch to her stonemason father, climbing to the pinnacle of a church steeple to give it to him. Unable to attend school, she has not learned to read, but she asks him for a book. That evening, her father takes her to a mine, leading her into the hill and directing her to follow a path too narrow for him, as his father had directed him when he was still small enough to go. There Mary learns from markings on the rock something of her own heritage. Then he carves her a book of stone in which her imagination can roam free. Although Mary cannot read, it is clear that her mind is open to wonder, as is her father's, in spite of the narrowness of their existence.

The first of four books about four generations of a family living near Manchester, England, this is a good introduction to the atmosphere and literary style of Garner's books. Tension and mood build quickly through spare, precise language. Much is felt and suggested but left unsaid between the characters and for the reader.

This is a book to ponder more than to discuss. Mary climbs to height and depth. It is in depth and silence that she learns the most. What is the relationship between imagination, creativity, the spirit of wonder — and formal education? What has her father given to Mary? What experience of yours compares?

Hamilton, Virginia. *The Planet of Junior Brown.* (See Getting Along with Others for full description.)

What does Junior need in order to be able to use his artistic and musical talent? What does Buddy need?

Hipp, Earl. *Fighting Invisible Tigers: A Student Guide to Life in "The Jungle."* Illustrated by Troy Acker. Minneapolis: Free Spirit, 1985.

This manual on stress management for 11- to 18-year-olds covers the basics of what stress is, and then provides the fundamentals of stress management, including the distinction between merely coping and true management. The roles of fitness, food, and relaxation in stress management are covered, as well as the importance of "weaving a safety net," consciously working to build relationships with others that will be supportive and stress-reducing.

Teenagers will find that the book speaks to them and offers suggestions that can be applied to their lives. Although it does not claim to be written specifically for the gifted, it is aimed at them, pointing out that "being bright, talented, creative, motivated, smart, ambitious, and even good-looking can add to the stress in your life," and "academic success and drive aren't enough to make life manageable."

Sections relating especially to making good use of one's ability are on assertiveness, taking charge of one's life, risktaking, and perfectionism. (Also available: *A Teacher's Guide to Fighting Invisible Tigers* by Connie Schmitz with Earl Hipp. Minneapolis: Free Spirit, 1987.)

See also Getting Along with Others.

Hunter, Mollie. *A Sound of Chariots.* New York: Harper & Row, 1972.

This is the story of Bridie McShane's growth from her father's death when she is nine until she leaves home and school to go to work at 14. The first half is a flashback that establishes the close relationship between Bridie and her father and develops his character. He was an Irish socialist, intelligent but uneducated. Bridie is like him in appearance, in love of learning and language, and in passion for life. The second part, telling of her adjustment to his death, is almost surrealistic in its evocation of her new awareness of symbols of death and her realization that she, too, will die. She develops a heightened sensitivity to life and begins to write poetry. She also learns to hide her strong feelings and her precocious powers of observation and analysis in order to avoid censure.

Hunter's writing style is challenging and the imagery is beautiful. This along with the subject matter make it an excellent choice for gifted readers.

Bridie is told, "Creativeness, my child, is all out-going." Do you agree? What examples of your own creativity are out-going? Bridie's mother says, "Don't be proud of any gifts you have, dearie. Be grateful for them, remembering they are a trust from God that you must render back some day." How do you feel about the responsibility gifted people have because of their gifts? How does this apply to you?

See also Aloneness, Getting Along with Others.

Konigsburg, E. L. *Father's Arcane Daughter.* New York: Atheneum, 1976.

Winston Carmichael has grown up taking care of his younger handicapped sister, Heidi, but now Caroline has returned. Their father's daughter from a previous marriage, Caroline had been kidnapped and was presumed dead. Through her efforts, both children develop in ways that would not have been possible without her, but the question always remains: Is this really Caroline?

This is a sophisticated mystery with a challenging structure of flashbacks featuring unidentified speakers. Caroline's role as change agent can lead to discussion of ways in which we are all potential change agents for others.

Why was Caroline so important to both children? Winston says that Heidi has the makings of a brave soul but not the focus. What does he mean? What happens when people are unable to fulfill their potential? What characters in the book had special gifts? What gifts? What else did they need if they were to be able to use their gifts?

See also Identity.

Langone, John. *Thorny Issues: How Ethics and Morality Affect the Way We Live.* Boston: Little, Brown, 1981.

In a book for the teenaged reader, Langone explores ethics in several pertinent areas: medicine, war, capital punishment, business and government, science and technology, the press, and human rights. In each case he presents the issues and abiding questions, only occasionally giving clues as to the "right" answer. He makes it clear that far from being a matter for philosophers only, ethics and morality should be concerns for everyone who wishes to live responsibly.

Both the book and related discussion will help to focus the thinking of gifted adolescents who are already debating these issues internally. The book makes clear, and discussion can affirm, the responsibility we all have to think these issues through and to make what impact we can on decisions regarding them. Idealistic and sometimes cynical gifted young people need to hear the assertion that we *can* do something about these problems, and that they can and must contribute.

Questions abound in the book. Each chapter will provide material for several discussions. The leader might consider covering one chapter at a time, rather than hoping to discuss the entire book in one session. Some sections, especially those on medical ethics and war, may be depressing for idealistic young adults, and discussion should confront the depression or discouragement. The adult leader would do well to have thought through his or her own answers before discussing the book with a teenager.

LeGuin, Ursula K. *Very Far Away From Anywhere Else.* (See Identity for full description.)

How does Natalie make decisions about her future? And Owen? What changes does Owen make in this book? What has he learned?

See also Aloneness.

L'Engle, Madeleine. *The Arm of the Starfish.* New York: Ariel Books, 1965.

Adam Eddington has been hired to work in the island laboratory of Dr. O'Keefe the summer after high school, and he finds himself caught in an international struggle for the information from Dr. O'Keefe's experiments. Each side seeks to enlist Adam, and he must decide for himself which group to support.

In one of her warm and loving large-family settings, L'Engle raises the issue of the moral use of information as well as of one's intelligence. The plot is tightly written and suspenseful, and will lead to discussions of good and bad use of intelligence and knowledge, the need to learn to trust one's own instincts, and the awareness that intelligence alone is not enough.

What qualities does Adam have besides intelligence? What qualities must he develop in order to play his role effectively? In what ways does he succeed in developing these qualities? In what ways does he fail?

Moser, Don. *A Heart to the Hawks.* (See Getting Along with Others for full description.)

What is your interpretation of the Robinson Jeffers quote on page 196? ("Give your heart to the hawks for a snack of meat, but not to men!") How does it apply to Mike's life? Can you apply it to your own? What do you think Mike will be doing in ten years? What steps must he take to get there from here?

See also Aloneness.

Paterson, Katherine. *Jacob Have I Loved.* (See Identity for full description.)

The story of gifted girls growing up with very different views of themselves shows by contrast how self-concept can affect a person's achievements.

What does Louise need besides giftedness in order to be happy? To be productive? What is the turning-point for her? Why is she able to make use of her intelligence? What would be other possible turning-points for someone like Louise? How might the book have ended so that Louise would take more command of her own future?

See also Getting Along with Others.

Peck, Richard. *Remembering the Good Times.* (See Identity for full description.)

Why did Trav kill himself? Whose "fault" was it? How might it have been prevented? What could Trav have done to prevent it? How do you answer the questions he raised about "deteriorating conditions" and the lack of challenge in school?

Peyton, K. M. *The Beethoven Medal.* (See Identity for full description.)

What must Pat do to stop the cycle of behavior in which he appears to be caught? What evidence do you see that he will be able to do so? What evidence to the contrary?

Rand, Ayn. *Anthem.* (See Identity for full description.)

How can you explain why Equality so strongly wants to study and to experiment? What personal qualities make him able to do so, while others cannot although they may wish to do so?

See also Getting Along with Others.

Rhue, Morton. *The Wave.* (See Aloneness for full description.)

What characteristics does Laurie have that make it logical for her to fight The Wave? Why is it important for her to use those characteristics? What would have happened to The Wave and to her if she had not?

See also Identity.

Rimm, Sylvia B. "It's Dumb to Be Smart." (See Aloneness for full description.)

Discuss Jennie's list of "don'ts." Do you have such a list? What are the consequences for gifted people of following each item on the list?

Tolan, Stephanie S. *No Safe Harbors.* (See Identity for full description.)

For both Doug and Joe, it is very important to be able to make the best possible use of their intelligence. What are the advantages to people who are able to do that? What are the disadvantages to those who cannot? In your own life, what steps must you take to become one who can make maximum use of intelligence or talent? How well are you doing at it right now?

Drive to Understand

Anno, Mitsumasa. *Anno's Medieval World.* Illustrated by the author. New York: Philomel, 1979.

The full annotation for this book is listed under Drive to Understand for grades four to six. The book is mentioned again for junior high readers because the ideas it elicits can be examined in greater depth by older students.

Questions for this age might include: What cherished beliefs of ours are being called into question by new developments, not necessarily scientific? Are ideas still dangerous? Who are present-day Brunos and Galileos?

Cummings, Betty Sue. *Hew Against the Grain.* New York: Atheneum, 1977.

Mattilda Repass is 12 when the Civil War begins, the youngest in her family. Her father has freed his slaves and the Virginia family is as divided as the nation, some fighting for the North and some for the South. Mattilda loses a brother-in-law and two brothers in the war and watches her father retreat into premature senility. One surviving brother loses a leg and one a hand, and finally Mattilda, too, is wounded, raped by a mean neighbor turned vicious. Through all the "dwindling" (as her grandfather calls it) of family and spirit, Mattilda has kept faith until this last event. The return of an estranged sister and her grandfather's love eventually restore her.

This story is not told from the point of view of North or South. It is a story of war from the human point of view, and each side suffers as it inflicts suffering. A subtheme is Mattilda's friendship with Docia, a freed slave girl of her age. The book is sobering, offering material for thought and discussion on a variety of themes.

In adversity, such as war, why do some people give up and others maintain hope? What do you think keeps Mattilda's grandfather going? What qualities are you building into your own character that would help you in a situation like this?

Dickinson, Emily. *Poems of Emily Dickinson.* Selected by Helen Plotz. Illustrated by Robert Kipniss. New York: Crowell, 1964.

Planned for young people, this collection of Emily Dickinson's poetry includes poems that illuminate nature, contemplate death, assess human nature, speak intensely of love, and express the poet's religious sensitivity in universal terms.

Dickinson's perceptive vision is incisive and her use of words, especially as she arranges syllables in her short-lined rhyme schemes, is astonishing. Further, she stands forth as an individual spirit voicing her thoughts, however unusual, with quiet confidence.

Dixon, Paige. *May I Cross Your Golden River?* New York: Atheneum, 1979.

When he is 18, Jordan Phillips learns that the uncharacteristic weakness in his wrist and knee signal the onset of amyotrophic lateral sclerosis, the fatal muscular degeneration known as Lou Gehrig's disease. Jordan and his large and loving family must face his death within a matter of months. They do so with sensitivity, humor, and a heartwarming support for one another and for Jordan that never becomes sentimental or maudlin.

Dixon has created a remarkable family unit in which each member actively pursues his or her own talents while contributing uniquely to Jordan's care. The humor in the book, intelligent and original, is especially fine. Jordan and his family use a variety of elements of life to come to terms with death. For Jordan, the natural beauty of his Colorado home plays a significant part. The birth of his nephew, Jordan's godson, implies what Jordan calls the going-on-ness of life.

The book provides an opportunity to consider the acceptance of death and the value of life, and the warm family life provides both emotional depth and a safe environment for pondering these themes — so difficult to grasp, especially for teenagers. Far from depressing, this is rather an uplifting and triumphant book.

How has the book helped you to think about death? To develop new values in life? Who is your favorite character, and why? What has the book added to your thinking about the importance of caring for other people?

Garfield, Leon. *Smith.* Illustrated by Antony Maitland. New York: Pantheon, 1967.

A street urchin and pickpocket in 18th century London, Smith steals a document from a man who is murdered immediately afterward by men seeking the document Smith has pilfered, but which he cannot read. The murderers pursue Smith. In his flight, he meets and guides home a blind magistrate who takes Smith into his home. The suitor of the judge's daughter accuses Smith of the murder, and Smith goes to Newgate Prison. With the suitor's help, Smith escapes, but he has been led into a trap. As Smith tries to protect his friend the judge, he discovers that he is being betrayed by a highwayman he has always admired.

Eventually the tangle of shifting friends and enemies is straightened out, the suspense lasting until the very end.

This exciting murder mystery, like all of Garfield's work, is well-written, challenging fare for gifted readers. Garfield provides a far better picture of the dangerous realities of the streets and highways in 18th century England than any nonfiction description could. Most of the characters are rascals or worse, presented sympathetically but with no excuses offered for their behavior — good background for discussion of the social implications of poverty and the diversity of human character.

Richter, Hans Peter. *Friedrich.* Translated from the German by Edite Kroll. New York: Holt, Rinehart and Winston, 1970.

The story is told through a series of vignettes of the friendship between the narrator, a Christian boy, and Friedrich, a Jewish boy in Germany from 1925 to 1942. Friedrich's family lives in the apartment upstairs, and the two families are distant friends. As pressure against Jews builds, the landlord arranges an attack on Friedrich's family, and his mother dies as a result. Eventually his father is arrested, and Friedrich finds a hideout elsewhere. Seeking a picture of his parents, he returns to the narrator's family just as the air raid siren sounds, but the landlord will not allow Friedrich into the shelter. When they return to the house they find Friedrich sitting on the stoop. He has been shot and killed.

From the early picture of joy and spontaneous fun between Friedrich and his mother as they play in the snow, the book moves relentlessly to the final scene, bringing the enormity of the Holocaust down to one family and one boy. This is an excellent example of the growing body of literature written to acquaint young people with the events of World War II in Germany, different from many others (thus more representative of the reality) in that Friedrich is not a survivor. The value of this literature for gifted students lies in the importance of educating a new generation of leaders about these events and, insofar as can be understood, the structures that allowed them to occur.

This story in itself will not provide enough information for a full discussion. Rather it provides the emotional impact that prepares students to look at the situation from both sides. Discuss the growing reluctance of the narrator's family to help Friedrich's family. Include discussion of similar hostilities elsewhere in the world, and why the results were not as catastrophic as in Germany. Aim for some understanding of circumstances that might cause, or prevent, a recurrence in any country.

Steele, Mary Q. *Journey Outside.* Illustrated by Rocco Negri. New York: Viking, 1969.

Dilar and his family live on one of the rafts that float on an underground river as the raft people seek an unknown goal they have almost forgotten. Watching the rock walls they pass, Dilar becomes convinced that they are traveling in a circle. When they pass a familiar rock ledge, he swims to it and scrambles up into the world above for the first time in his life. Traveling alone, Dilar meets several groups of people, each representing different attitudes and living patterns. As the book ends, the reader does not know whether Dilar will return to the raft people, and if he does, whether they will believe in the sunlit world he has found.

This is an unusual book which may require discussion before students can form their response to it. The different kinds of societies Dilar finds and the ambiguous ending make it a rich source for discussion with gifted students.

What kinds of thought and living patterns are represented by the raft people, the tiger people, Wingo, the desert people, and Vigan? Why does the author have Dilar meet all of them? (Compare this book to the *Odyssey* or *Watership Down,* all journeys from one form of government to another.) If the author is using Dilar's story to symbolize an inner journey, what would it mean? Why does Dilar not stay with any group (both literally and symbolically)? Add an ending: Will Dilar find the raft people? Will they follow him? What will happen then? If they will not, what should Dilar do?

Sutcliff, Rosemary. *Beowulf.* Illustrated by Charles Keeping. New York: Dutton, 1961.

In all of her books about prehistoric England, Sutcliff displays an uncanny ability to evoke the spirit of the age. The reader feels complete confidence in the validity of the atmosphere she creates; it is as if Sutcliff had lived among the people of whom she writes. Her translation on the Anglo-Saxon epic poem "Beowulf" is no exception.

College-bound students will probably read some of Beowulf in a high school English class. Junior high students, however, will relish it as sheer adventure and will enter into it with more abandon than senior high students, whose approach will be more intellectual. It will not be ruined for later reading; it is a haunting story that stands retellings well.

Senior High: Grades 10-12

Identity

American Association for Gifted Children. *On Being Gifted.* New York: Walker, 1978.

Written by gifted students from 15 to 18 who were participants in the National Student Symposium on the Education of the Gifted and Talented, this book is a collection of candid and thoughtful comments. It includes remarks about inner pressures and peer pressures, about relationships with parents and teachers, and about school programs for the gifted with suggested changes.

This book should be read by older gifted teenagers to whom the more informal Galbraith book *(Gifted Kids Survival Guide for Ages 11–18)* may seem too young. These twenty students do not claim to have all the answers, but they certainly have recognized, analyzed, and articulated the problems.

Discussion will arise quite naturally from student responses to various comments in the book. One predictable response will be "I'm not that gifted," and a discussion leader may need to point out that the discussants can relate to the problems mentioned in the book even if they are not as outstanding as the students chosen for the symposium.

Since the entire book is about one's identity as a gifted person, discussion can be based on almost any page. Some general questions: What are the advantages of being gifted? The disadvantages? What can you learn from these students?

See also Aloneness, Getting Along with Others, Using Abilities.

Auel, Jean. *The Clan of the Cave Bear.* New York: Crown, 1980.

This popular novel features several characters who stand out in their prehistoric clan because of their special abilities. The medicine woman of the Clan of the Cave Bear cares for a five-year-old girl from an unknown clan who was orphaned when an earthquake swallowed her home. As she grows, the differences between the Cro-Magnon Ayla and the Neanderthal Clan people become apparent. The Clan is deeply traditional, relying on a mixture of instinct and knowledge from past ages. Ayla displays flexibility, intelligent curiosity, a drive toward individuality, and a willingness to take risks that put her at odds with the Clan people.

These differences between Ayla and the people who surround her are analogous to the differences a gifted student may sense between himself and many of the people around him. Understanding how Ayla feels and seeing her responses to the situation should help him understand and respond constructively to his own situation.

How does Ayla come to recognize her differences? How does she feel about them? What is her self-concept, and how does it affect her behavior? How does it change as she learns more about herself?

See also Getting Along with Others.

Buck, Pearl S. *The Exile.* New York: Reynal and Hitchcock, 1936.

Based on the life of the author's mother, this book is more a character study than a novel. The story spans the adult life of Carie, a missionary to China from 1880 to about 1920. There are several strong threads in the book: Carie's concern for the role of women, America as the golden land, China in its pre-Revolutionary period, Carie's search for meaning in life and her inability to find it in the 19th-century version of God, and her turning to action rather than preaching as a result. Carie is bright, and she struggles against her "faults" of impetuosity, warmth, exuberance, humor, and love of beauty. She is a practical idealist, rearing her children with a fierce energy and determination to teach them the best that is American as she sees it, in her memory and from afar.

The book is recommended especially for gifted girls trying to define the roles they want to play, and for gifted teenagers who are questioning traditional religion.

How does Carie reconcile her idealism with the realities of her world? How is she able to question the idea she has been taught of God and be a missionary at the same time? What similar paradoxes have you encountered or are you likely to encounter in your own life? How can they be reconciled?

See also Using Abilities.

Galbraith, Judy. *The Gifted Kids Survival Guide for Ages 11–18.* Minneapolis: Free Spirit, 1983.

Written for gifted students from ages 11 to 18, this book speaks directly to gifted junior and senior high students about problems of growing up gifted, with practical suggestions for coping.

Adults may feel that the extensive use of graphics detracts from the seriousness of the book, but will find the content valid and important. For discussion, locate a relevant section and ask for the students' interpretation and what they have found useful. Senior high students may prefer to study this book and respond to it independently, rather than engaging in discussion which they may regard too personal.

The first five sections deal with questions of identity for a gifted student.

See also Getting Along with Others, Using Abilities.

Hanff, Helene. *84, Charing Cross Road.* New York: Avon, 1974 [c1970].

In 1949, New York writer Helene Hanff wrote a letter to an English bookshop inquiring about purchasing used books, beginning a 20-year correspondence that is recorded in this book. The pert, irreverent humor of Hanff contrasts with the proper but gradually warming responses from members of the bookshop staff and their friends, and the reader follows the growing and deepening friendship between Hanff and a group of people she never meets.

This book should be read for sheer pleasure — pleasure in the comraderie and love that grows among people who share a love of books. It evokes a very personal response from the reader; to attempt discussion, other than a general leading question like "What did you think of it?" may well place too much weight on the book.

Recommend it for senior high students to reassure them that there is room in the adult world for booklovers, and that reading does not have to isolate them; it can form bonds.

See also Getting Along with Others.

Hentoff, Nat. *Jazz Country.* New York: Harper & Row, 1965.

Tom Curtis is 16, the son of a prominent New York corporation lawyer. He wants to be a jazz musician, perhaps more than he wants to go to college, but when he attempts to get into the real world of jazz he is told that he has not paid his dues, that his life has been too easy, too white. Nevertheless, the black musicians see promise in Tom and he is able to learn from them, not only about music but about the realities of life as a jazzman. Tom finally faces the question of college versus jazz when he is invited to join a band.

Although the book is full of references to the mid-60s, these can be seen as enhancing rather than dating the book. The issues surrounding racial prejudice are well presented. This is a good choice for young musicians who are drawn to music as a career. It clearly raises questions about how one should use talents without finally answering them.

What personal traits make it possible for Tom to be accepted by Godfrey and the others? How does prejudice affect Tom? Mary? Fred Godfrey? Dudley? In what different ways does each respond to it? How are their identities shaped by prejudice? By their response to it?

See also Using Abilities.

Kerr, Barbara. *Smart Girls, Gifted Women.* (See Using Abilities for full description.)

Gifted teenaged girls should read this book as part of their task of recognizing how their intelligence affects their choices over the next few critical years. It may make them uneasy about choices they have already made that could limit their futures, and it will be quite natural for them to set the book aside unless they talk with women who are old enough to give living examples of what Kerr is describing.

Where in the book do you see yourself? Your friends? Your mother or other older relatives? What changes would you like to see in the pattern? What obstacles do you see? What suggestions would you have for young women who want to overcome the obstacles?

Thomas, Joyce Carol. *Marked by Fire.* New York: Avon, 1982.

Growing up in the black community of an Oklahoma town, Abby Jackson learns wisdom and strength from her mother, from Mother Barker, from the rural rhythm of nature and the sudden devastation of a tornado, and from the cruelty of some of her neighbors. After an assault, she stops using her lovely singing voice. Mother Barker and her mother help her gradually to regain her sense of self, and she reaches adulthood with a deep, sure sense of her own uniqueness, and a commitment to use her healing abilities, as well as her voice, for others.

The style moves imperceptibly between prose and poetry. Evocations of the rhythms of speech in the singing and story-telling of the women of the community are especially powerful. There is a haunting quality in the writing style and in the person of Abby herself that makes this a beautiful book to read.

What examples are there in the book of acceptance of human failings? Is it a strength or a weakness to be so accepting? Why? How is it related to Abby's acceptance of herself as gifted?

See also Using Abilities.

Webb, James T., Elizabeth A. Meckstroth, and Stephanie S. Tolan. *Guiding the Gifted Child.* Columbus: Ohio Psychology Publishing Co., 1982.

Although this book is subtitled *A Practical Source for Parents and Teachers,* it is such a clear explanation of the major emotional difficulties a gifted child faces that teenagers are able to gain much self-understanding from it. Stephanie Tolan's "Open Letter to Parents, Teachers and Others: from Parents of an Exceptionally Gifted Child" is especially recommended for highly gifted young adults. If they identify with RJ, they may begin to understand why they felt as they did in elementary school. This acceptance of their younger selves can be a wonderfully freeing catharsis.

Teenagers and adults can read this book separately, each noting page and paragraph numbers they would like to consider further, and then meet for discussion. The first three chapters will help young people develop a better understanding of their identities as gifted persons.

See also Aloneness, Getting Along with Others, Using Abilities.

Yevtushenko, Yevgeny. *The Poetry of Yevgeny Yevtushenko, 1953 to 1965.* Translated from the Russian by George Reavey. Bilingual edition. New York: M. Boyers, 1981.

A leader of the rebirth of Russian poetry after Stalin, Yevtushenko writes with a forceful, fresh honesty. His work is imbued with youthful idealism combined with maturity — perfect characteristics for poetry to be recommended to gifted young adults.

In addition, his subject matter is both informative and moving, including the effects of the Russian Revolution on ordinary people, his home town in Siberia, his longing to travel, his love of the Russian people, and his eagerness to overcome bureaucratic restrictions. Throughout the book is a boundless enthusiasm for living tempered with an awareness of the poet's responsibility to speak the truth.

Poems especially recommended for gifted young adults dealing with issues of identity include "Prologue," "Irreconcilable," and "The Angry Young Men."

See also Aloneness, Using Abilities, and Drive to Understand.

Aloneness

American Association for Gifted Children. *On Being Gifted.* (See Identity for full description.)

On pages 18 and 19 is a comment about the existential experience of not wanting to be human anymore, wanting to transcend the human condition, but wondering where one could go from there. What is the value of raising this question in a book on what it is to be gifted? What are other ways of raising the same question? What are some potential answers?

See also Getting Along with Others, Using Ability.

Bridgers, Sue Ellen. *Sara Will.* (See Getting Along with Others for full description.)

What is your reaction to the life Sara Will has been leading? What enables her to change? What generalizations or guidelines can you draw from this book concerning aloneness?

Hesse, Hermann. *Steppenwolf.* Translated from the German by Basil Creighton, updated by Joseph Mileck. New York: Bantam, 1963 [c1927].

Harry Heller, a lonely intellectual of 47, calls himself the Steppenwolf — wolf of the Steppes — in acknowledgment of the animal, uncivilized part of his nature. Loneliness and existential suffering have become the dominant forces in his life, bringing him to the point of suicide. Then he meets Hermine, a beautiful young woman who takes him in hand, teaches him to dance, and introduces him to the life of the dance halls in the Germany of the 1920s. The story culminates in a masked ball, reminiscent of a Faustian revelry, which becomes mystical and symbolic. Harry emerges with a resolve to re-enter the game of life, this time to learn to laugh.

Even at 47, Harry still struggles to balance his intellectual interests — writing, classical music, and political theory — with more common concerns such as dancing, jazz, people, and laughter. The two parts of the story represent extremes: too sober and depressing until he meets Hermine, then happy and wild to the point of unreality. Suicide, loneliness, and Harry's inability to fit in are themes throughout the book, yet the overall impact is not depressing because Harry learns that neither intellectualism nor socializing is sufficient in itself. There must be a balance, and he will continue to try to find it.

Steppenwolf is not easy reading and should be recommended for older, mature gifted students, who are likely to be dealing with similar issues. Ask students to identify themes they would like to discuss as they read the book.

Consider with students the implication that Harry takes himself too seriously, that he needs to laugh at himself. If they have seen the film, "Amadeus," compare and contrast Harry and his idol, Mozart, concerning laughter and taking oneself and one's work too seriously.

See also Drive to Understand.

Mann, Thomas. "Tonio Kroger" in *Death in Venice and Seven Other Stories.* Translated from the German by H. T. Lowe-Porter. New York: Vintage, 1960 [c1930].

Tonio is a writer who grew up feeling both an attraction to and estrangement from the blue-eyed people (Hans Hansen and Ingeborg Holm) whom, unlike himself, he regards as normal. He has the mark of the artist on his brow: he is different. As an adult, he talks to his artist friend, Lisabeta Ivanovna, about his sense of estrangement. It is a discussion which becomes the philosophical heart of the story. When Tonio sees Hans and Inge again, he does not speak to them, but loves them from afar, without resentment but with a strong sense of being an outsider. In a letter to Lisabeta, he reaffirms his love of the "blond and blue-eyed, the fair and loving, the happy, lovely, and commonplace."

This fine short story by one of the century's great writers is best understood if studied as literature. Although Tonio is an artist, the story is not about artists alone, but about any person who feels intellectually out of place with the norm.

Comment on Tonio's adjustment to feeling different. Could you improve on it? Should he try to change, or should he stay as he is? That is, should an artist or an intellectual try to minimize the differences between himself and the rest of society, or should he emphasize being himself? Can you name others in history who seemed to be driven or damned by a gift? Are their achievements worth their struggles? Why or why not? To what extent do they achieve *because* they are different?

Webb, James T., Elizabeth A. Meckstroth, and Stephanie S. Tolan. *Guiding the Gifted Child.* (See Identity for full description.)

The chapter on depression should interest people who are concerned about aloneness in the life of a gifted child.

See also Getting Along with Others, Using Abilities.

Wolitzer, Meg. *Sleepwalking.* New York: Random, 1982.

Claire is one of three Swarthmore freshmen who are so interested in the poetry of women who have committed suicide (Sylvia Plath, Anne Sexton, and in Claire's case, "Lucy Ascher") that they become known as "the death girls." Julian, an upperclassman, is intrigued by Claire, but her relationship with him is weakened by her involvement with Lucy Ascher and the death girls. Finally, Claire decides that she wants to be closer to Lucy than she can be simply by reading her poetry, so she goes to Lucy's parents' home and asks for work as a housekeeper. There, Claire gradually begins to comprehend the impact on her and her parents of the death of her brother several years earlier. At the same time, her presence helps Lucy's parents to resolve their own grief. In the end, it is one of the other death girls and Julian who help Claire make the decision to return to Swarthmore and her own life.

Flashbacks tell the stories of Claire's and Lucy's childhoods, so we can piece together the similarities and differences. Several themes invite discussion: relationships between parents and daughters, the importance of friends, handling aloneness, coping with death and grief, and, of course, suicide. This discussion should be planned with sensitivity to the needs of the group.

Why was Lucy so alone? Why did she kill herself? Why is Claire so interested in Lucy? What difference between them explains why Lucy committed suicide and Claire does not? Were Lucy's parents at all responsible? How did Claire's childhood and her parents affect who she is now?

See also Using Abilities.

Yevtushenko, Yevgeny. *The Poetry of Yevgeny Yevtushenko, 1953 to 1965.* (See Identity for full description.)

Poems relating to aloneness include "There's Something I Often Notice," "I Don't Understand," and "People Were Laughing Behind a Wall."

Getting Along with Others

American Association for Gifted Children. *On Being Gifted.* (See Identity for full description.)

An example of difficult relations with others is on page 25 and 26. Are there similar stories among the students in your group? How were the situations handled? Can you see them in a better perspective now? There is also a section on "People Who Helped." How have parents and teachers helped you? What kind of help do you need *because* you are gifted? How can you take the steps necessary to get it?

See also Aloneness, Using Abilities.

Auel, Jean. *The Clan of the Cave Bear.* (See Identity for full description.)

How does Ayla compromise her abilities in order to fit in with the Clan, and how does she decide when not to compromise? What mistakes does she make? Can you go on from this to draw a set of criteria to determine when compromise is adaptive, and when it is nonproductive? What would be Ayla's definition of personal integrity? What is yours?

Bridgers, Sue Ellen. *Sara Will.* New York: Harper & Row, 1985.

Sara Will Burney had lived a life of undisturbed solitude for more than 50 years when her widowed sister, Swanee Hope, came home to live with her some time ago. Sara continues to live in the past, her main preoccupation the care of the family graves. Suddenly three visitors — their dead sister's brother-in-law, Fate Jessop; his teenaged niece, Eva; and her baby — arrive and the chaotic, unpredictable real world invades Sara's home. Gradually she must expand her expectations to accept the needs of others, and even her own.

This book tells two love stories: that of Sara and Fate, and of Eva and Michael. Each person seems to face impossible obstacles to love, not merely in life events but also in personality difficulties, and yet gradually they shift, change, and open up to make room for each other's needs.

Why are Sara and Eva unwilling to be loved at first? Why are Fate and Michael able to love? What traits help Fate get along with others? What strengths does Swanee Hope have? For each character (Fate, Sara, Swanee, Eva, Michael) consider strengths and weaknesses in coping with life situations, and in getting along with others. What does Sara mean: she is more damaged than Fate? What generalizations and guidelines can you draw from this book concerning getting along with others?

See also Aloneness.

Galbraith, Judy. *The Gifted Kids Survival Guide for Ages 11–18.* (See Identity for full description.)

This book includes one section on getting along with parents, two on getting along with friends, and one on coping with teasing.

See also Using Abilities.

Hanff, Helene. *84, Charing Cross Road.* (See Identity for full description.)

For gifted students, especially those in small schools with little opportunity to meet other gifted people, this story of friendships carried on entirely by mail can be an encouraging reminder that kindred spirits do exist and are worth seeking — but one must reach out.

Hipp, Earl. *Fighting Invisible Tigers: a Student Guide to Life in "The Jungle".* (See Using Abilities in the Junior High section for full description.)

The section of this book about weaving one's own "safety net" of supportive friends will add to gifted students' understanding of getting along with others.

See also Using Abilities.

Moliere, Jean Baptiste Poquelin. *The Misanthrope.* Woodbury, N.Y.: Barron's Educational Series, 1959. (Written in 1666).

Set in Moliere's contemporary and fashionable 17th century Paris, this drama is one of the masterpieces of the great French comedian. Alceste values sincerity in communication with others so highly that he is uncomfortable with the flattery that is considered good manners in courtly drawing rooms. He becomes quite fanatical about it, ignoring and hurting well-meaning friends and finally resolving to withdraw from society altogether because in his eyes it is so dishonest.

Moliere's genius is to draw the comedic and the serious very close together, so this comedy offers material for thoughtful discussion. However, high school students may need some background to understand the excesses of the French court at that time. If the play is only read, the comedy will not come through nearly as poignantly as it does on the stage.

How far does it make sense to go in order to stand up for one's values? How much is Alceste losing? How might he have avoided the way the play ends? What standards do you feel very strongly about? In what ways do you compromise? Should you? Is Alceste justified in hurting others for his beliefs? How do we know whether and when to sacrifice honesty for politeness? What role does, or should, tolerance for human weakness play?

Webb, James T., Elizabeth A. Meckstroth and Stephanie S. Tolan. *Guiding the Gifted Child.* (See Identity for full description.)

The chapters on communication of feelings, peer relationships, sibling relationships, and parent relationships all offer information that will promote discussion of getting along with others.

See also Aloneness, Using Abilities.

Using Abilities

Adderholdt-Elliott, Miriam. *Perfectionism: What's Bad about Being Too Good?* (See Using Abilities in the Junior High section for full description.)

Like Galbraith's *Gifted Kids Survival Guide, Perfectionism* offers information which would ideally be presented to students in junior high. For senior high students who are not acquainted with the concept of perfectionism, this book can be used as an introduction.

American Association for Gifted Children. *On Being Gifted.* (See Identity for full description.)

How do you feel about the responsibilities that are part of being gifted (pages 7 and 8)? Are they a burden? Does the incident described on page 24 ever happen to you? How do you cope with it? What comments do you have about the "How to Cope" section, beginning on page 32? On page 75 is a story of a gifted student who took charge of his own education to a significant degree. Have you ever done this? What would be the difficulties? The advantages? How might you do so in the future?

See also Aloneness, Getting Along with Others.

Buck, Pearl S. *The Exile.* (See Identity for full description.)

Even though Carie lived at a time when there were more restrictions on women than there are now, her story still has relevance. What universals are there in the restrictions placed on her by her role in that society? To what extent did she surpass the roles most women played at the time? What attitudes and actions enabled her to make the use she did of the talents and interests she had?

Curie, Eve. *Madame Curie.* Translated from the French by Vincent Sheean. Garden City, N.Y.: Doubleday, Doran, 1937.

Gathering letters, family stories, and her own memories, Marie Curie's daughter wrote this biography shortly after her mother's death. She tells of Marie's childhood in Russian-occupied Poland and of her intellectual isolation while she worked as a governess to send her sister to medical school in Paris. When she was 24, Marie was finally able to go to Paris for her own studies. The book tells of her marriage to Pierre Curie, of their partnership in the discovery of radium, of the lonely years of dedicated work after his death, and of the honors she at last endured, having no talent for the life of the celebrity.

The book is a rich source for gifted high school students. It presents the different worlds of gifted children growing up in Poland, and the life of scientists in Paris at the turn of the century. Most stimulating for gifted readers is the glimpse of the excitement of intellectual life in Europe at that time; it made demands on Marie and Pierre which they gladly met. Marie's life is a ringing statement of the connection between hard work and accomplishment, as well as of the passionate absorption of a gifted adult in her work. Both she and Pierre were happiest in their laboratory, but they also had warm relationships with family and colleagues.

How did Marie's childhood and youth prepare her for her life work? How did specific incidents lead her to her career choice? How important was the influence of her family?

See also Drive to Understand.

Galbraith, Judy. *The Gifted Kids Survival Guide for Ages 11–18.* (See Identity for full description.)

Sections on stress, perfectionism, how to make school challenging, and goal setting are helpful in discussing how to use one's abilities.

See also Getting Along with Others.

Haensly, Patricia A. and William R. Nash. *Mountains to Climb: A Handbook of Resources for the Gifted and Talented.* St. Paul, Minn.: National Association of Gifted Children, 1983.

Behind this handbook is the well-founded assumption that gifted young people can (and in some cases must) take responsibility for their own educational enrichment and acceleration. The booklet provides general suggestions and specific information regarding advanced placement, early college entrance, and enrichment opportunities available to those living in cities, towns, and rural areas. It also lists summer programs and institutes for gifted students.

Although much information about national programs is given, many of the specific programs listed are offered only in Texas. Students living elsewhere can generalize from the suggestions offered, but they may need the help of adults to find their states' corresponding agencies and programs.

The appropriate response to this book is action, not discussion. The secondary school years can be rich in opportunities for growth and personal development, but using these opportunities requires knowing that they are there and where to start. *Mountains to Climb* offers a wealth of first steps.

Hentoff, Nat. *Jazz Country.* (See Identity for full description.)

How does racial prejudice (their own and others') affect the ways in which the various people in this book (black and white) are able to use their talents? What prejudices do you have, not only toward other races, but toward occupations, regions of the country or the world, social classes, colleges? In what ways are you limited by your prejudices? How are you working to overcome them?

Hipp, Earl. *Fighting Invisible Tigers: a Student Guide to Life in "The Jungle."* (See Using Abilities in the Junior High section for full description.)

Sections of the book on perfectionism, stress, taking charge of one's life, and time management are especially helpful in talking with gifted students about making full use of their abilities.

See also Getting Along with Others.

Kerr, Barbara. *Smart Girls, Gifted Women.* Columbus: Ohio Psychology Publishing Co., 1985.

This is nonfiction, a report of a research study done by Kerr as the result of a high school reunion. The gifted women in her class asked her to find out why they were pursuing typical careers or homemaking, instead of being the world leaders they had been told they would be.

In a readable style, Kerr discusses the developmental history of most gifted girls, the barriers to intellectual achievement, the family-career conflict, and ways in which gifted girls can be helped to aim higher. She includes several short biographical sketches of eminent women that illustrate her findings.

For parents and counselors of gifted girls, this book is invaluable. Gifted women will recognize themselves and wish they had read it earlier. Ideally, gifted girls in their late teens will read it and find a trusted gifted woman with whom to discuss whatever they find in the book that seems to apply to their own lives.

What critical decisions will you be making in the next few years that determine whether you can make maximum use of your abilities? What planning can you do to keep your options open as long as possible? What are the patterns of decision-making by gifted women that you should be aware of in yourself?

See also Identity.

Rimm, Sylvia B. *Underachievement Syndrome: Causes and Cures.* Watertown, Wis.: Apple, 1986.

Thousands of children in our schools, many of them gifted, are not performing up to their capabilities. *Underachievement Syndrome* discusses family patterns and educational practices that lead to underachievement. It then presents ways in which parents, teachers, and students can work together to reverse learning patterns that prevent children from achieving as much as they can.

Although this book was written for parents and teachers, Rimm has found that teenage underachievers who glance through it find themselves in it. Reading it carefully and discussing the relevant concepts with an adult may help older gifted underachievers to see themselves objectively and to think analytically about their learning patterns and ways of changing them.

Few teenagers would want to read the entire book. It will be most useful if parents and teachers read it thoroughly and then select excerpts and concepts to discuss with students.

Steinbeck, John. *The Winter of Our Discontent.* New York: Viking, 1961.

Ethan Hawley is a clerk in the grocery store once owned by his father, in the New England town where his merchant forebears had owned sailing vessels. He is reasonably happy with his lot, but when the perfect opportunity to become wealthy again comes to him, Ethan takes it, arguing the morality of it with himself as he does so. Ethan is gifted, interested in literature; his talents are clearly underused. He loves his wife, Mary, but does not confide in her; she is not his intellectual equal. Indeed, he has no intellectual equal in the town, except perhaps his boyhood friend Danny, now a drunkard, whom Ethan betrays (with Danny's knowledge) as he brilliantly works out his plan.

As a story of the underuse and then the misuse of high intelligence, this book can provide material for discussion of appropriate use of abilities. It is quite deliberately set in the spring of 1961, and contemporary high school readers will need some reminder of that to follow references to the time.

Margie Young-Hunt thinks about Ethan: "This was a superior man." What does she mean by this? How does Ethan deal with being gifted and underused? How had Ethan's giftedness contributed to the situation at the beginning of the book? How did it affect the way he responds to being a clerk? If you could be Ethan at twenty, what decisions would you make for a more satisfying life? What did Ethan learn from Aunt Deborah? Are there any Aunt Deborahs in your life? Was Ethan's intelligence wasted?

Thomas, Joyce Carol. *Marked by Fire.* (See Identity for full description.)

Abby's parents are Patience and Strong. How does Abby learn and use these qualities? Why are they especially useful for a gifted person like Abby? Are you aware of using or developing them in your own life? How do you know when to use which? Will Abby become a doctor? Should she? Why or why not?

Webb, James T., Elizabeth A. Meckstroth, and Stephanie S. Tolan. *Guiding the Gifted Child.* (See Identity for full description.)

Chapters that relate to making maximum use of potential are those on motivation, stress management, and discipline.

See also Aloneness, Getting Along with Others.

Wolitzer, Meg. *Sleepwalking.* (See Aloneness for full description.)

Lucy Ascher was obviously a gifted poet. Did she commit suicide because of this? How could her suicide have been prevented by her? By others? How do you feel about Claire's leaving school to pursue her obsession with Lucy Ascher?

Yevtushenko, Yevgeny. *The Poetry of Yevgeny Yevtushenko, 1953 to 1965.* (See Identity for full description.)

Poems in this collection relating to using one's full abilities include "Others May Judge You," "The Concert," "A Career," and "Let Us Be Great!"

Drive to Understand

Curie, Eve. *Madame Curie.* (See Using Abilities for full description.)

This title is listed with books recommended to meet the need of gifted students for a wide range of information because of the picture it provides of intellectual life in both Eastern and Western Europe before and after World War I. For gifted students whose only experience with meeting intellectual needs and interests has been the American high school of the 1980's, this view of Europe can be both stimulating and inspiring.

Douglass, Frederick. *Narrative of the Life of Frederick Douglass, an American Slave.* New York: New American Library, 1968. (Written in 1845).

Born a slave in Maryland in 1818, Frederick Douglass escaped to the north 20 years later. He had taught himself to read and write but was otherwise uneducated. Nevertheless, leaders of the abolitionist movement recognized his intelligence and eloquence, and by 1841 he was a public speaker for their cause. Later he became Recorder of Deeds for the District of Columbia and United States Minister to Haiti. This narrative is the story of his years in slavery, telling how he was passed from one owner to another, how and why he was beaten, what happened to his family and friends, and how a kind mistress taught him the alphabet and a few words before her husband forbade her to continue, saying that reading would make him unfit to be a slave — thereby firing in Frederick the determination to learn to read. The fact that he gives no details of his escape, fearing that the information would close the route to freedom for fellow slaves, creates for the modern reader a startling sense of immediacy and authenticity.

The contrast between the appalling descriptions of slavery and the clear evidence of Frederick's sensitivity, intellect, and ability to articulate experiences and feelings is deeply moving. The book is valuable both for understanding slavery and as the autobiography of a gifted person who fought against overwhelming odds to rise to his capacities.

Frankl, Viktor E. *Man's Search for Meaning: An Introduction to Logotherapy.* Translated from the German by Isle Lasch. Boston: Beacon, 1962.

The first part of this book tells of Frankl's experience in Auschwitz and other concentration camps, where he spent three years as a slave laborer. A psychiatrist, he focuses on the psychological reactions he observed in himself and fellow prisoners. From his experiences came logotherapy, sometimes called the Third School of Viennese Psychiatry, after Freud and Adler. (Frankl speaks of the will to meaning, in contrast to Freud's will to pleasure and Adler's will to power.) The final third of the book gives a brief explanation of logotherapy.

This will be a useful book for gifted young adults concerned with developing a philosophy of life, and may be especially helpful for those who experience existentialist depression. A few ideas which may be particularly intriguing to gifted young adults: While existentialist philosopher Jean-Paul Sartre says that we invent ourselves, Frankl asserts that we do not invent the meaning of our existence, we detect it. He speaks of the existential vacuum which often manifests itself in boredom. And he speaks of the need for each person not to ask the meaning of life but to ask the meaning of his or her own life: "to life [we] can only respond by being responsible." In contrast to Maslow, Frankl believes that human existence is self-transcendence rather than self-actualization. (There is some evidence that Maslow would have added self-transcendence to his pyramid had he lived longer.)

There is much material here for thought and discussion; the book can be read again years later for more depth. Adolescents will respond to those ideas for which they are ready. Leaders may do well to let them pose the questions for discussion.

Fuller, Iola. *The Loon Feather.* San Diego: Harcourt Brace Jovanovich, 1968 [1940].

Oneta, daughter of Tecumseh, grows up on Michigan's Mackinac Island in the early years of the 19th century, when Mackinac was a fur-trading center where French and Indian cultures met. Her French stepfather sends her to school in Quebec, and when Oneta returns to Mackinac at 24 she has learned to see the best in each culture and to understand reasons for conflict between them. Eventually she chooses her Indian heritage, but she does so by serving as a bridge for her people from the old ways to the new.

In the person of Oneta, this unusual book gently compels the reader to look at two conflicting cultures with respect and understanding for each. Fuller masterfully evokes the natural beauty and atmosphere of a specific place, and the story is set in an accurately depicted historical period. Nevertheless, the theme of accepting the differences of others is a universal human challenge which Oneta and others meet with dignity and a sustaining sense of self. The book is recommended for gifted readers because it will exercise their capacity to hold two conflicting views at once, stretching their minds and sympathies.

What qualities do you admire in Oneta? In Martin Reynolds? What knowledge of Native Americans have you gained from this book? What attitudes have changed as a result of reading *The Loon Feather*? What new understanding have you gained of other historical clashes of cultures? What applications are here for your own life?

Hersey, John. *Too Far to Walk.* New York: Knopf, 1966.

John Fist is a sophomore in a prestigious New England men's college when he loses a sense of direction for his life. Promised "experience" by fellow student Chum Breed, John makes a Faustian pact. He stops going to class and experiments with sex and LSD. In the end he concludes that he cannot find experience and intensity by artificial means and he does not renew the pact.

John's problem is one faced by many gifted young adults, that of wanting to know and experience more than is possible in one ordinary mortal lifetime. He attempts to do this by extraordinary means, focusing on experience per se, but finds that ultimately empty. His conclusion is one gifted people must adapt for themselves, chastening as it is: "I've come to see that there can't be any shortcuts to those breakthroughs I yearn for."

If no shortcuts, what are some of the slower, surer ways to the breakthroughs John wants? If we can't do everything at once, how do we establish priorities? What priorities have you established already, and what are your plans for achieving your goals?

Hesse, Hermann. *Steppenwolf.* (See Aloneness for full description.)

Themes for challenging discussion include the concept that some people are "the suicides," "those who see death and not life as the releaser"; Harry's dream of his interview with Goethe; his view of the bourgeoisie and of the immortals; Pablo's opinions on music versus Harry's; and Hermine's last talk with Harry, summarizing the views of both of them.

Smith, Huston. *The Religions of Man.* New York: Harper & Row, 1958.

The son of missionaries to China and a professor of philosophy at Massachusetts Institute of Technology, Huston Smith has written descriptions of seven great religions: Hinduism, Buddhism, Confucianism, Taoism, Islam, Judaism, and Christianity. His aim is to convey "the meaning these religions carry for the lives of their adherents." Accordingly, he writes little of doctrine and less of history (both of which are to be found in a good adult encyclopedia), but reveals for each "why and how they guide and motivate the lives of those who live by them." In the final chapter he presents a sound argument for accepting the validity of each faith for the people who follow it.

Gifted senior high students respond well to this book. It provides excellent background material for a discussion series. They appreciate Smith's objectivity, which frees them to reach their own conclusions. However, the objectivity is balanced by a respect for each religion and its people. This human perspective prevents the material from ever becoming intellectualized or dry.

Gifted young people seeking meaning for their lives will find here seven different broad approaches to the question of meaning which have stood the test of time. Moreover, while acknowledging the triviality and violence to which religion can descend, Smith describes each religion in its highest, most intellectually and spiritually challenging form. Readers will find stimulus for thought in each religion, and will gain a greater understanding for its followers.

Tillich, Paul. *The Dynamics of Faith.* New York: Harper & Row, 1957.

Tillich examines the phenomenon of faith objectively, analytically, and apart from specific doctrinal content, so that although he is one of this century's great Christian theologians, followers of other religions, too, can read this book for greater understanding of their experience of their own faith. Defining faith as "ultimate concern," he considers what faith is and is not, the symbols of faith, and types of faith. Sections on mythology and humanism as they relate to faith may be of particular interest to gifted high school students.

This book is suggested as an introduction for gifted young people to religious thinking at its highest and most challenging — therefore potentially most interesting — level. Whether they are among those who take religion seriously or those who question whether religion has any value at all, or those who read simply for exposure to a new field, gifted high school students would do well to meet Tillich. This book is a good introduction to his thought.

Yevtushenko, Yevgeny. *The Poetry of Yevgeny Yevtushenko, 1953 to 1965.* (See Identity for full description.)

Poems that will lead to a greater understanding of the Russian Revolution include "Weddings," "Babii Yar," "Moscow Freight Station," and "Honey."

SUBJECT INDEX

AUTHOR INDEX

(Chapter 8)

TITLE INDEX

(Chapter 8)